T0373568

The Psychology Student's Career Survival Guide

The Psychology Student's Career Survival Guide is designed to aid students in identifying their ideal career pathway and imbue them with the right tools and skills to not only achieve their desired job but to progress and thrive within the workplace.

The first half of the book focuses on how to find and get a suitable job. The remaining chapters explore gaining success in the workplace in terms of personal growth, navigating criticism, workplace relations and the critical job assignments that every graduate should pursue. Forsythe, an experienced organisational psychologist, helps students recognise and apply the acquired psychological skill set to develop a personal brand, increase personal visibility and develop professional networks. This smooths the transition from university into the world of work by developing effective working practices that will support personal performance and that of the workplace. This book can also serve as a practical guide for academics looking to bridge the gap between the developing student at university and demands of their future employers. It explicitly calls for vocational elements such as communication, team-working, goal setting and planning within the curriculum.

This engaging book comes with an abundance of resources to support students' individual development and to help academics run workshops. These resources include tool kits which include self-diagnostic tools and strength finders, networking skill development, job search strategies, difficult interview questions, personal branding and so on. This is an essential text for psychology students at all levels looking for employability guidance and for psychology academics who are seeking supportive resources and guidance on helping students achieve their career ambitions.

Alex Forsythe is Professor of Applied Psychology at the University of Wolverhampton, UK; Chartered Psychologist and Chair of Europe's largest governing body for business psychologists, the Association for Business Psychology. Alex specialises in improving outcomes for high-stakes graduates in the fields of medicine, dentistry and psychology and has been awarded two national awards for outstanding impact on student outcomes and the teaching profession: the National Teaching Fellowship and Principal Fellow of the Higher Education Academy.

"An invaluable, brilliantly written book full of insight and original ideas for young people hoping to start their first job or already in business life. *The Psychology Student's Career Survival Guide* gives outstanding advice, tips and actions on how to advance your career in the modern workplace. There is a great deal to think about here. I cannot recommend the book more highly".
— **Peter Saville**, *Fellow of the British Psychological Society, UK, and Founder and Chairman of the Saville Consulting Group and 10x Consulting, UK*

"The most fun I have had reading an academic text. An honest, entertaining and original resource that will help students with diverse career interests".
— **Debbie Stevens-Gill**, *CPsych, SFHEA, University of Wolverhampton, UK*

"This book made the endless list of careers available to a psychology graduate less overwhelming; it offers a simple, less academic guide of how to tackle not only the usual obstacles one is faced with when job hunting, but the extra hoops you may have to jump through after the year 2020. It made me feel less alone in the idea that I have absolutely no idea what I want to do with my life".
— **Ruby Allgood**, *Student, University of Liverpool, UK*

"This is the book we all need – a practical, research-based guide for psychology students to help develop and market your skills and get that dream graduate job, written in a light-hearted and accessible way".
— **Julie Hulme**, *Keele University, UK*

The Psychology Student's Career Survival Guide

Here Be Dragons

Alex Forsythe with Francesca Forsythe

Routledge
Taylor & Francis Group

LONDON AND NEW YORK

First published 2021
by Routledge
2 Park Square, Milton Park, Abingdon, Oxon OX14 4RN

and by Routledge
605 Third Avenue, New York, NY 10158

Routledge is an imprint of the Taylor & Francis Group, an informa business

British Library Cataloguing-in-Publication Data
A catalogue record for this book is available from the British Library

Library of Congress Cataloging-in-Publication Data
Names: Forsythe, Alex, author.
Title: The psychology student's career survival guide : here be dragons / Alex Forsythe ; with Francesca Forsythe.
Description: Abingdon, Oxon ; New York, NY : Routledge, 2021. | Includes bibliographical references and index.
Identifiers: LCCN 2020050045 (print) | LCCN 2020050046 (ebook) | ISBN 9780367424763 (pbk) | ISBN 9780367424800 (hbk) | ISBN 9780367824372 (ebk)
Subjects: LCSH: Psychology—Vocational guidance.
Classification: LCC BF76 .F67 2021 (print) | LCC BF76 (ebook) | DDC 150.23—dc23
LC record available at https://lccn.loc.gov/2020050045
LC ebook record available at https://lccn.loc.gov/2020050046

ISBN: 978-0-367-42480-0 (hbk)
ISBN: 978-0-367-42476-3 (pbk)
ISBN: 978-0-367-82437-2 (ebk)

Typeset in Adobe Garamond Pro
by Apex CoVantage, LLC

For Craig
for teaching me to laugh again

Contents

Introduction

I once went for a job interview for a TV psychologist. They wanted some photographs (sigh). I would never describe myself as a stunning beauty capable of immediately capturing the imagination of a producer with my doe eyes and apple-esque cheekbones; after all, this was back before filters could help you achieve that chipmunk look we all crave. So this was really challenging to pull off: I am more than a little camera shy and, not having managed to shift some postbaby pounds [Francesca: *pretty sure I was about 5 by then mum, but OK*], I was just not ready for my close-up, Mr DeMille. After 30 or so minutes of pouting and posing with books and specs trying to pull off the stunningly beautiful and intelligent psychologist look (with and without glasses, because we all love a good sexy secretary trope), I knew I needed another approach. I had an awesome pair of sky-blue Karen Millen sandals bedecked with blue and white crystal droplets. I really loved those sandals. I met my second husband in those sandals, and, unlike my second husband, I still have those sandals.

So, I painted my toenails and popped on the shoes. I watched an episode of *Sex and the City* to bolster my confidence, and then I emailed them a photo of my feet. I kid you not, the phone rang 20 minutes later, and I was asked to an interview the next week. I didn't get the job in the end, but I learned the value of thinking out of the box. Apparently Instafeet is now monetisable, and while I like to think I started the trend, I think I missed a trick.

My life and my career have been a series of misadventures. Having discovered boys (a recurring pattern throughout my life), I pretty much failed all my exams and wasted 2 years managing to get two A-levels, one in English and the other in guilt (I am Irish, after all; it is a cultural speciality). After rubbish A-levels and yet another bad boyfriend, my wise parents persuaded me that perhaps I might try to get a job. So, fresh with yet another broken heart, I managed to secure a job at Ratners the Jewellers. I loved my job polishing diamonds and dreaming of another Prince Charming. I worked hard, and the training and camaraderie were game changing. I was quickly promoted to assistant manager. All that ended thanks to Gerald Ratner's decision to speak at the Institute of Directors on April 23, 1991. *Thanks, Gerald, nice one* (google 'doing a Ratner')! However, I quickly found my new 'feet' in clothing retail management (and got me a husband, *yeah!*), but god, I was awful in that job. I was so awful that I gave permission to the then-Northern Ireland Royal Ulster Constabulary to raid the homes of my sales staff (true story). Perhaps not surprisingly to you, Dear Reader, it seems having the homes of your staff ransacked makes you about as popular as Jimmy Saville with Mumsnet. Not to worry, I quickly regrouped and managed to land a job at another retail clothing company, which promptly burned to the ground after a firebomb attack (*Northern Ireland eh?*). Then there was the job with the computer company that ended in a sexual harassment case (I was not the one doing the harassment #MeToo), the waitress job where I realised that it was not a good idea to use my fingers to put ice cubes into people's drinks (thankfully pre-Corona) and the job in the civil service processing DLA claims (zzzzz).

If Baz Luhrmann is to be believed, our choices are only half chance, and apparently so are everyone else's. But if you are making those choices on faulty, stupid, fake news to begin with, then no, Baz, your choices are not half chance. Your choices are dumb-ass mistakes that will play over and over in your brain. They will creep into your bedroom like Peter Spector (a.k.a. Jamie Dornan, and yes, some people might enjoy that). They will grab you, tie you up and proceed to strangle you whilst chattering and chattering to each other in your head until you make a larger, more dumb-ass mistake that blocks out the previous noise of the last mistake, which suddenly doesn't really seem all that bad anymore.

Professors are often thought to have some exalted life experience that creates the pathway to career success. There might be a few 'chosen ones' out there, but most of us got here through a combination of hard work, luck and fortunate misfortune. Fortunate misfortune is something that feels really awful at the time, but it sends you in a new direction. You just cannot really see what that direction is at the time. Fortunate misfortune usually needs a point of learning to be most effective. Yes, a lesson learned, an 'I told you so', a little 'whoops a daisy', a bit of 'why on earth did I do that?' or a really big "WT actual F". Otherwise known as that cognitive place that we have to find, deep, deep down where nobody else can see. When we find that place, it will act as vehicle towards self-awareness, enlightenment or just 'I am never f***ing doing that again, not ever'. Wherever and however you find your learning space, when you *do* find it, it will help you perceive, realise and then pursue your passions.

I definitely learned something from each of those jobs. At Ratners, I learned what really good management training looked like but also what truly awful publicity management looked like. In the civil service, I learned that people at work could get very territorial over minutiae but that the problems they were trying to tackle were much bigger than the size of someone's desk space or filing cabinet. In the computer company, I learned that sometimes people are just arseholes, and in retail management, I learned that sometimes I could also be a complete arsehole. However, armed with all that life experience, I still never really reached a point of deep personal learning that was going to move me forward.

Stagnated and directionless, I visited the Careers Service. People often think that careers advice is just for school-aged kids, especially dishing out bad advice. Like the time my petite, hair extension– and acrylic nail–embellished eldest daughter was told she should become a farmer. Or when the career aptitude test of my youngest daughter (who had just set up her own freelancing company to fund her studies) came back with 'Wife supporting husband in own business'. Really good careers services (they are everywhere) give brilliant all-age careers information, advice and guidance. They do not always advise a career in livestock management, trophy 'wife-ing' or serial killing, for that matter. Working for the Careers Service is possibly the most important job in the whole wide world, and if governments and universities placed value on career advice and spent time hiring and paying properly for brilliant careers advisors, then perhaps getting a great graduate job would be a much more certain outcome.

My awesome careers advisor pointed out that it takes some of us a few attempts to get things right (turns out this is very good advice not just for careers but also for husbands). My advisor also, with ninja-like purpose, was able to forensically track patterns in my values, my passions and my dislikes. She found inside of me things that I was only half aware of, creative thinking, a natural curiosity and a tendency to challenge the status quo or the commonly accepted. Most importantly, she persuaded me to stop thinking about the here and now and create a long-term vision for myself, and then she then suggested I study psychology. My world was quite literally rocked, and my greatest love affair (with the exception of husband #3) began.

The psychology of getting an actual job

Husband number 3 (sometimes I call him the middle husband just to keep him on his toes) always criticises me for peppering every sentence with the word 'actually'. Apparently, I sound like a perennially surprised Liam Neeson. 'This is actually delicious!', 'That was actually a great movie!', 'You actually look very handsome in that new shirt!', 'That was actually funny', when delivered with the harsh brutality of a Northern Ireland accent, makes everyone sit up and listen, be complimented for a nano-second, then feel insulted for the remainder of the evening.

[*husband: There is no compliment in the word 'actually'. You just make everyone sit up and be insulted.*]

I digress. The point of getting an *actual* job in this context, instead of a fictitious, non-existent, fake, fraudulent, Leonardo DiCaprio 'catch me if you can' kind of a job is that your actual job should define your best version of yourself. Never sure why that phrase has caught on in the way it has. Seriously, who *actually* goes out and tries to be the worst version of themselves? I blame lifestyle coaches, those pesky neurolinguistic programmers and people who make personality tests that assign you as some random colour for the rest of your life. Lady with floaty scarf: 'You are thistle'. '*WHAT?*' 'Yes, your colour is thistle. It is the colour that sank beneath your skin when your bruises surfaced to tell stories of the experiences you adventured through as a young and fearless child'. '*My god, it all makes sense now. I always thought I was heliotrope. But I am a thistle! I am an actual thistle! Now I can finally be the best version of myself. Thank you, floaty lady, Thank you*'. 'You're welcome. That'll be £500 please'.

Anyway, back to the *actual* point. Higher education should make us employable – we all want graduate jobs, to earn a decent living, to be socially successful, to find something meaningful to do. When we are satisfied with the work that we do, we lose ourselves in it. We are compelled forward; we feel in charge and in control; we challenge and stretch ourselves, gaining new expertise, developing mastery and autonomy over the work that we do. Work is synonymous with fulfilment; it is an opportunity for social engagement and a way to feel encouraged and valued. Work makes our lives and the lives of others better; it offers financial stability and structure to our day. Work makes us, and to be without work is very damaging both to our mental health and our physical well-being.

Hardly surprising, then, that psychology is right at the centre of the world of work and remains one of the most popular degree choices both in the United Kingdom and across the globe. Studying the mind and how it dictates and influences our behaviour, from communication and memory to thought and emotion, is right at the centre of both the pleasures and the stressors of work. Psychology helps us understand people and human behaviour and to use that understanding to systematically address personal and societal issues. Psychology students thrive in people-related jobs such as marketing, human resources, health and well-being but also in roles that require data handling and research expertise, for example, the legal professions, data science and ethics. For those reasons, psychology training is largely focused on areas that are knowledge intense.

Scotland is the only country in the United Kingdom that is explicitly required to support its higher education students in their transition to work. Universities in the rest of the United Kingdom are 'encouraged' (*read 'useless'*). This means that institutions are mostly free to decide how, and if, they should include structured work experience in their programmes.[1] However, most UK universities focus on developing employability strategies that centre on improving employer engagement for the identification of desirable student attributes for the future UK workforce. University partnerships with employers are the key to graduate employability, because the employers will provide more opportunities for students through the provision of opportunities to meet and network with prospective employers, graduate schemes, by promoting their vacancies through the university and by encouraging promising graduates to apply. Employers do not, however, have endless resources to partner with every university. It takes time and money to recruit good graduates, so employers will focus their efforts on a few select universities they believe will deliver the best candidates to them. Naturally, some universities are just better at attracting employers to their table (*read 'not useless'*), so the popularity of your university (or otherwise) means that significant diversity exists in the initiatives being employed.

During 2017, the student review forum Student Crowd asked students to evaluate their careers services. In times when it is almost impossible to engage students to complete surveys, the fact that 7,348 students gave up their time to comment on the quality of career support at their university speaks volumes about the value that they give to vocational guidance (Student Crowd, 2017). Universities that provided opportunities for students to gain first-hand experience in the world of work through initiatives such as internships, work experience, academic credits for meaningful work experience, job hunting and career coaching were rated as substantially better (*read 'useful'*). The message was clear: work experience matters, and good university career services play a pivotal role in developing entrepreneurial skills and commercial and business acumen, not only helping students on the road to their chosen career but also helping them to secure the part-time work that will provide them with financial stability throughout their programme of study.

These results are hardly a revelation. Students are not well resourced to know what options are open to them; even if they have an understanding of several options, they are not equipped to make meaningful evaluations between the many different career paths that are available to them. News flash: neither are the psychologists who have been teaching them. Presuming that every

psychology academic loves their career, then we can reasonably assume that they made at least some good choices based on the information that was available to them at the time. Having spent over 6 years at university studying for a degree and then a PhD, they understand the academic career path, but few understand very much else.

We don't know you

Even if your academic advisor could turn themselves into the psychology careers oracle, they do not know you. They do not know what you are like the way that you know what you are like. They cannot understand what your values are, what motivates you or, in the words of Marie Kondo, 'what sparks joy in you'. In other words, unless a degree has a specific vocational pathway, identifying the opportunities are not that obvious. This is all made even more complex by that fact that jobs just come, and they go. With the quantum leap that computers provided in the late eighties to early nineties, jobs came and went even faster. The job that you would love right now that seems perfect for you might not even be thought of, and the one that you have had your eye on may become obsolete.

It is hardly surprising that there has been considerable dissatisfaction within the academic community about the push towards 'employability-in-the-curriculum' which has forced disciplines to redevelop their programmes to include credit-bearing employability education. The advantages would seem obvious. Imbedding employability within the curriculum would have greater impact because students would be required to engage in future planning directly with very intelligent people. Except that academics know little, in fact possibly nothing, about how to give useful careers advice. The end result is that students who are known to be strategic and instrumental in what they study for (and they tend to study for exactly what they believe they will be assessed on) would suddenly become engaged in planning for their future. Not because their approach to career planning would contribute in a meaningful way to their graduate outcomes but because they were going to be assessed by academics who were by now frantically 'googling' how to grade a résumé, CV or supporting letter and design an employability module.

One widely shared grading rubric awards points for 'balanced', 'white space', and 'includes name, address, email'. Think about that for a minute? Students, you came to university to study psychology so that you can understand yourself and others, to grow and develop and refine your critical thinking. You can be awarded grade points just for putting your name and address on a 'balanced' piece of 'white space'. When researchers at University College London discovered that the secret to happiness was low expectations,[2] I wonder if they meant that low.

That is not to say that there are not any number of dynamic and innovative initiatives in psychology departments. For example, in psychology, the shift towards authentic assessment has seen a reduction in standardised tests such as multiple-choice examination and an increase in assessments that communicate real-life tasks, for example, portfolios of activity whereby students are able to place all of their training, volunteering or learning experiences in an online repository; writing a position piece that develops the capacity to argue in one direction with the purpose of winning a debate; creating a blog analysing significant news events through the lens of psychology; designing a building (or even a town) based on psychological principles to support well-being or working with organisations on their real problems.

This book

This book will help you explore some practical ways in which to find a career that works for you. Key to success is flexibility, learning how to trust and follow your curiosity, find new opportunities for a happy job life and make a plan that supports good decisions. To help you on that journey, we have packed this book with research, practical advice, exercises, top tips, careers stories and advice from all of the psychology graduates whom I have had the honour of working with over the past 20 years. Thanks to the collective efforts of my family, this book is written with a substantial amount of Northern Irish tombstone humour, storytelling, straight talking and some light profanity (I like that; you might not). Thanks to Francesca 'Rinder' Forsythe's efforts, we have toned down Professor Liam Neeson, given this book a student voice and spoken directly to you, dear reader (*read 'easy to read'*) [*not only was I not allowed to write third person, she even made me remove the APA referencing style!*], but most importantly, very little time has been spent dwelling on how to be a forensic, clinical, occupational, counselling, super-duper psychologist. There are plenty of those books and resources available from the British Psychological Society, your university library and every psychology open day and careers fair around the country. Knowing your own tribe is one employ-ability thing that psychology departments do fairly well. However, it is a flat fact that most psychology students do not go on to practice in the super-duper fields ($P < .05$). Rather they become superheroes in other cosmoses.

Chapter 1: what choice do you have?

There are something like 120,000 hours to fill across the course of our careers, and if we can find a job that we love, we are far more likely to make a success of it. There can be few things worse than spending that time in a job that we hate or, for that matter, working with someone who hates what they do. Of course, many people end up demotivated in their jobs, perhaps even hating them, but they stay in those jobs nonetheless. Most graduates are not burdened by the commitments of families and mortgages to keep them chained to jobs that they hate; rather, what keeps them in those jobs is that they still have not figured out what they want to do. Staying in a job you hate while you try to figure out your ideal career is, however, flawed thinking, because it stifles career discovery. The first part of this chapter explores the extent to which you are able to cope with ambiguity. Managing ambiguity is a key skill for career development; without tolerance for ambiguity, you will be unable to act without having the total picture, to handle risk, uncertainty and change. Tolerating ambiguity means being comfortable with not being totally sure where you are going.

The events of 2020 have made us all unwitting participants in the greatest ambiguity experiment of all time. We need graduates who can help us put our lives, communities, societies and countries back together, and the second part of this chapter is aimed to help you ground yourself to help make all that happen and more. Recognising what your values are and how they shape what makes you happy is a critical step in revealing to you how to make decisions, build relationships, decide on which company to work for and understand when you are not happy in your job. Values help us understand what we want to do rather than what we want to 'be'. It is not surprising, then, that some of the most successful organisations in the world have shaped the direction of their companies by discovering their core values, then centralising those values as key to their strategic policy. Here we help students unpick the foundations of their value system and to understand why some values matter more than others, to consolidate those values within the narrative of who you want to become and then to start to develop a strategy to use those values to guide relationships, decision-making and choices about the kinds of organisations that you would ultimately like to work with.

Chapter 2: my psychology DNA

Students develop a host of skills in psychology: IT skills, critical thinking, ethical practices, research skills and analysis, for example. They also develop a corpus of knowledge around different theories in psychology and the epistemology of the values, methods and scope of those positions. Isolating nuanced skill sets from such higher-level knowledge, even expertise, and presenting it in a simplified format that maps onto the skills that employers are seeking, then framing this skill set as evidence to support the pursuit of a desired employment opportunity is an employability skill in and of itself.

This chapter will support students in identifying the skills and expertise that they have developed from their time in higher education and then applying this knowledge to a range of occupational settings outside of the core BPS practising areas. We delve into core psychological content and diagnosing how and where university learning experiences can be used to differentiate yourself from the other candidates to increase the probability that you will be selected. Employability, however, cannot just be about getting skills that someone wants to pay us for; it must also be about how we grow as human beings and how we care for each other and our world. It's ironic, of course, that sometimes these are the very things some people might not want to pay us to do, but they are central to our professional success because they provide us with a clear sense of where we want to be in life and the values we wish to stand for. These values are your 'brand', and a well-developed brand will distinguish you from the graduate 'sea of sameness'. In this chapter, we help students develop a framework for developing self-understanding that will help self-improvement, give clarity and a sense of purpose and yield pride from the work that they do.

Chapter 3: tell me what you want, what you really, really want?

Your personal brand is a way of marketing yourself to others, both online and offline, and can be a critical factor in convincing potential employers to choose you over the next person. We all know that your reputation speaks volumes before you enter the room, but it's almost impossible to overestimate how impactful it can be to make sure that your digital brand is both cohesive and professional, because, as the old saying goes, *you never get a second chance at a first impression*. Your personal branding mission is also more than finding a job: it's about portability. Having a great brand means you can move from university into employment, from job to job and across organisations, because it makes it easier for you to develop relationships, peer networks and customer bases who trust you. This chapter identifies branding pitfalls and best practices – how to manage yourself safely and effectively but also how to leverage your digital presence to the greatest effect for your career.

Chapter 4: your personal brand

Only around 20% of applicants are accepted onto the traditional psychological pathways. Even if you have chosen this difficult route, the odds are stacked against you. If you do not broaden your horizons, you could miss out on valuable opportunities, and the earlier you broaden your horizons, the more of the horizon you will see. Exploration is key: developing an employability strategy and then a plan of action as soon as you leave your degree, if not, in fact, sooner. Serendipity is not a strategy. The best results are achieved on and with purpose.

Following on from the mapping of student skill sets and the creation of a personal brand, this chapter examines the search for employment, the tools and techniques for finding career opportunities and how to develop the social and cognitive skills that help identify opportunities and improve the ability to interact effectively with others. Personal interactions and social capital are explored. Social capital is the access to resources which are embedded in social relationships. Being able to extract the information that comes from social capital brings trust, status and opportunities which help both secure a position in the first instance and then help students continue to navigate and harness those networks for the value they bring to successful career progression. Building social capital is interdependent with building a career: the larger the network, the greater the probability of success. Some students are better able, however, to mobilise social capital resources than others, and this chapter explores the strategies that students can use to develop and maintain such strategically significant relationships.

Chapter 5: from applications to interviews that win

A well-crafted CV makes it easier for recruitment teams to identify how you meet job specifications and role criteria. However, the increased use of applicant tracking systems, or 'résumé bots', can mean that students suffer regular rejection without ever knowing why. It is important to take the time to examine the skills that you have and how they qualify you for the position you are applying for. Students often underestimate how time consuming this process can be, because to be successful, each CV and application letter need to be tailored to the position at hand. This chapter examines how to leverage your CV for job applications but also how to use technology such as personal webpages, blogs and social media to assist you in both the application process and the promotion of your personal brand.

Getting to an interview is a huge endorsement that you have met the advertised criteria for the position, and the interview is your opportunity to shine. The most successful graduates will have been thinking about and developing their interview personal narrative for many months before they even know they have a job interview. In other words, how they can give richness to any answer by using particular examples of their experience to answer different questions. Just as in formulating an answer to an undergraduate essay, the worst interview questions are general and descriptive, and the best answers are rich, explorative and evaluative. This chapter will provide a foundation for the student's personal narrative: how to effectively draw on and apply their experience at the interview and how to use that narrative to harness self-confidence.

Finally, rejection is part of the interview process. We need to learn from rejection and move on. Some rejection is actually very good for you, and we will examine how it is possible to harness rejection in the correct way and avoid personal depletion.

Chapter 6: starting work: measure up and make a difference

Career progress also means going beyond the nuts and bolts of a job, its salary limitations and the daily grind of 9 to 5. Making a difference requires going beyond your job description, the routine of work or the immediate task. Making a difference means expanding physical and emotional energy towards the people you work with and the customers and clients you come into contact with. Part of this process is dealing with criticism; the more you do, the greater your reach, the more exposed you become to criticism. When you are doing things that others are not doing, then you are taking risks that others are not taking. If you do a lot of big things, then there is room for big criticisms. This chapter will help you develop strategies to traverse the murky waters of feedback, its negative connotations and the emotions that it brings. If you want to be successful, you need to learn how to deal with criticism and feedback. We will explore why we often reject feedback and how it is possible to better improve our management by recognising that feedback can be complicated. The anxiety and fear that come with feedback may override our normal behaviours and, in order to improve, we need to understand what our personal triggers are.

Chapter 7: good relationships at work

What does it mean to have good relationships at work? Does it mean everyone gets along? Does it mean there is never any conflict? Or is outstanding performance the hallmark of good working relationships? This chapter explores current thinking on work relationships, in particular the development of mutuality and equilibrium, which leads to mutual trust, respect and support. It aims to develop insights that will support effective interpersonal interactions, establish trust and develop personal credibility in peer, supervisory and management contexts.

This chapter also explores the ways in which poor communication can impact work efficiency, effectiveness and staff well-being. Poor communication is a significant block to personal development, effective leadership and our overall effectiveness at work. Good communication skills are critical in strengthening our relationships with others, motivating individuals and teams and avoiding costly and time-consuming misunderstandings and disagreements. The factors that influence communication are examined, including how to generate a positive impression of yourself as well as understanding the potential significance of generational differences that may present unintended barriers to communication.

Finally, knowing what your boss, your team and your peers need from you is essential for good working relationships. Clarity about what results are expected from you reduces misunderstandings, blind alleys and poor decision-making, even accidents and sickness at work. Without understanding what results are expected, there can be no capacity for empowerment. Chapter 7 will help support the development of effective skills that are central to gathering the right information at the right time and then applying that knowledge to support both personal performance and the performance aims of organisations.

Chapter 8: influence and persuasion

This chapter examines how you can build on your knowledge and skills, your sense of yourself and your values to build your influence at work. We review the factors that influence people at work, exploring how to manage people who are influenced by evidence or those who are influenced by inspiring ideas, as well as identifying and removing barriers which protect your personal comfort zone. Building influence also means being understood effectively, using language that others will listen to, being respectful to our own needs and the needs of others, striving first to understand and then to be understood and recognising that communication begins some time before any personal interaction with others. However, influence in the digital age has changed how these principles are applied in everyday situations. Therefore, how to expand your reach of influence, how to communicate effectively to influence and how to share knowledge in a digital age are examined. Some individuals are influential because of the positions they hold, the ideas they share or their inspiring actions. Influence at work involves trust and reputation, personal leadership, resilience, being inclusive and being prepared to be wrong.

Chapter 9: chart your own course and set sail

This chapter examines why we should never rely on the skills and knowledge that we already have. The rate of change in the professional working environment places the employee under considerable pressure to keep up to date with advances in technology, developments in knowledge and new ways of working. The ultimate consequence of not keeping up to date with occupational knowledge is professional obsolescence. Careers are no longer a series of sequential activities, roles or experiences. Either by choice or necessity, individuals may have one, two or three careers in their life span; they may move across organisational boundaries or between departments, hierarchical levels and skills. By continuing to develop expertise and new skills, knowledge and experience across your working life, you increase your personal currency. This currency will insulate your career from the forces of change so that it becomes possible to move with change rather than simply reacting to it. Key to charting your own course is to know well in advance where you are going, so we provide you with a list of the job assignments critical to landing that top CEO job.

So, without further ado, let us begin to learn about how to get a job and succeed at your career, and hopefully we can have a few laughs along the way.

Notes

1 European Commission. (2018). EACEA/Eurydice, 6.2.3, p. 236.
2 Rutledge, R. B., Skandali, N., Dayan, P., & Dolan, R. J. (2014). A computational and neural model of momentary subjective well-being. *Proceedings of the National Academy of Sciences.* doi:10.1073/pnas.1407535111

Chapter 1

Here be dragons

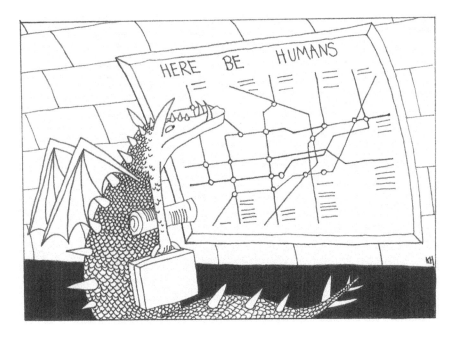

Millions of years ago (circa 1500) in a land far away (England and Europe), fear was just a part of life. The things feared the most included (but are not limited to):

- Purgatory
- Witches

- Plague
- The big bad wolf
- The living
- The dead
- The undead
- Fairies and elves
- Little girls with blond hair and a penchant for porridge
- Black cats
- Broken mirrors
- Horseshoes the wrong way up
- Horseshoes the right way up
- The colour black
- The colour orange
- The colour orange masquerading as 'the new black'
- Sea monsters
- Mermaids

But the most ferocious fear was the fear of dragons. Dragons were the most particularly scary thing about life and without proper management had a bad habit of creating a human barbecue. Since humans don't like to be barbecued, they went about adding warnings to maps so as to discourage sailors and travellers away from anything other than official trade routes. Areas they felt dragons were particularly hungry were marked *here be dragons*. It worked, yet much to the disappointment of many die-hard *Game of Thrones* fans, winter came, winter went, and the only wall that everyone spent time worrying about was the one being built by Donald Trump.

There are few things that people fear more than the unknown. There are no dragons or sea monsters that lie beyond the margins of our maps, but people will do just about anything to control the unknown, if not, in fact, avoid going there in the first place. As for yourself, do you want to be *better*, or do you want to be *safer*? Having ability means you have all the necessary raw resources to make things happen, but you also need to develop the will to make things happen for yourself, to put yourself out there, to commit in the face of obstacles and resistance. Call it ambition, grit, perseverance or resilience, you need the energy to propel yourself forward in the right direction. This chapter is designed to help students explore the numerous possibilities waiting to be discovered, because success is actually quite predictable (well, you can at least give yourself a better than random chance). Here we prepare students for the journey by helping them challenge what they may have accepted, to stay the course, to dig deep and think about what really matters.

"Psychology is the best degree you can study. I am slightly biased of course, but I genuinely believe you can craft a way of making it relevant to any job. What makes a good doctor? A: Bedside manner (how they relate to patients). What makes a good lawyer? A: One who gains their clients' trust (how they relate to clients). What makes a good film director? A: One who creates a compelling film (they understand how to anticipate and engage their audience). There are a number of specialised masters degrees: sports psychology. Fine. Go work in the sports arena. Criminal psychology – OK – go work in prisons or with the police. Even my field (occupational) is over obsessed with psychometrics, recruitment and coaching – when the potential is far wider. What is taught is merely the tip of the iceberg. Will you be the next expert in creative psychology? Bitcoin psychology? Cinema psychology? Cyberpsychology? Robot psychology? In short, the potential is endless, but you need to have the sort of proactive mindset you'll need to carve and create the jobs that I'd like to see being developed. Do not restrict yourself to the specialisms that already exist. Be bold, be brave and help create and develop the field".

Lucy Standing, Vice-Chair for the Association of Business Psychology and Head of Strategies and Partnerships at Bravestarts.com

Knowing what we want is a rare psychological achievement

You don't need a psychology degree to know that subtle and seemingly insignificant details influence the decisions you make. You'd have to be living under a rock not to have realised that social media and Hollywood culture have changed the way Western cultures view beauty and what a normal human should look like. Or that fake news has changed the course of global governance, reduced vaccination uptake and given legs to the flat earth debate. Whether you know it or not, we each have our own cognitive bias which feeds into the opinions we hold and the decisions we make, which in turn influences the subtleties of how we live our lives. Along with external pressures, these internal biases influence every aspect of our person. Call me a conspiracy theorist, but this potent combination can change the activities we pursue, our confidence about the grades we can achieve, the value we place on wealth or job titles, what we eat, what we drink, how much we *really* drink, our weight, relationships, where we go on holiday and of course the careers that we choose.

We live under the impression that we can do anything we want, have anything we want, *be* anything we want and all we have to do is do the right things and make the right choices and the rest will follow. Free will is of such great importance that it's peppered across charters, treaties and declarations the world over, but what really is free choice? How do we find it? And what the hell do we do with it when we get it?

Freedom to choose, or rather the lack of it, set Emma Rosen[1] on a mission. Unimpressed with the limited choices on offer by her careers service and feeling as if she were being nudged down a few narrow paths, Emma wanted more because settling on your first career choice is rather like marrying your first boyfriend: romantic but stupid. Limiting prevents the exploration of diverse career experiences. Students need more time to properly explore all their options without being pushed into narrow career choices. In 2015, having completed her degree, Emma propelled herself into what she called 'a radical sabbatical': a mission to try 25 jobs before she reached the age of 25. Emma then proceeded to write a book about her misadventures, then became a journalist, writer and public speaker. Freud might dryly speculate that deep down, Emma always wanted to be a journalist and those 25 jobs were simply an outstanding propellant into the self-help book market.

Emma's vision taps into what we psychologists call the 'sunk cost' fallacy, and students of psychology are particularly prone to this fallacy of thinking. Having kept their career pathways largely open, our students often find it difficult to settle on 'what next'. We are so poor at predicting what will make us happy, the more choice we have, the more likely we are to become paralyzed by our choices. Keeping options open can seem like the safest choice; no decision = no embarrassment, no ridicule, no reduction in self-worth and, most importantly, no failure. But then there are those nagging worries about all that debt. Pressure builds action, any action; even a bad action seems like a good idea.[2]

If free choice is something of a barrier to finding meaningful work, so is too narrow a focus. Humans have a unique propensity to keep doing an activity that is failing to meet their needs: staying until the end of an abysmal movie; finishing a terrible meal; keeping hold of clothes that don't fit or clothes that have never been worn or, worse still, continuing to invest time, emotions and money in something that should have been abandoned a long time ago (like bad relationships, and no, it will not get any better no matter what you do). From the outside looking in, we can see the mistakes of others 'the definition of insanity is doing the same thing over and over and expecting a different outcome' (said Albert Einstein *never*), but don't we all have our own pair of ambition jeans tucked away somewhere for the day we magically drop two dress sizes?

Making a career decision is complex and can cause much anxiety and mental distress,[3] so finding a 'good' reason to procrastinate is a useful coping strategy. The challenge then becomes that, when a choice is finally made, we may end up feeling dissatisfied with that choice. That choice requires us to give up on other things that also had very attractive features, which, maybe in that alternate universe out there, are making us very happy with stars, unicorns and mermaids. In other words, lots of choice brings lots of expectations, which produces lower levels of satisfaction; even if the results of those choices are good, people still feel dissatisfied because the grass always seems greener when you can't cross the fence. To overcome this mental spaghetti, we need to develop more self-understanding and awareness, better self-talk and self-control. One way to develop these skills is to embrace ambiguity as a window for learning, self-development and career exploration.

Managing ambiguity

Managing ambiguity is critical both for enjoying the legend that is Dr Seuss and for career progression, but some of us have a natural tendency to be better at this than others. Some people thrive when they are expected to make decisions based on incomplete information, cope with uncertainty or risk and adapt to change. Others find ambiguity intolerable. Ambiguity increases anxiety, rumination and even depression, and those who have a low tolerance for it will continually seek out certainty.[4] Having low tolerance for ambiguity means that you are far more likely to perceive situations as threatening and anxiety provoking rather than as promising opportunities. As anxiety increases, we are more likely to seek out additional information which might give more certainty in a problem. In the short term, certainty-seeking behaviour is rewarding; your brain detects a problem, something that is to be avoided, and it steers you away from the threat. However, the downside is that our tolerance for uncertainty decreases and we develop habits and routines built on predictability, see patterns that do not exist, blame others for not providing the necessary information to complete tasks and compartmentalise or silo tasks that should be synergistic. We are then less likely to explore a spectrum of possibilities that would forge new paths and solutions for people.

Self in focus

Think of a time when you had an assignment to complete. Have you ever felt that your lecturer did not give you all the information you needed to perform the task? How did that make you feel? What certainty-seeking behaviours did those thought processes trigger? And how helpful were they?

Test the 'null hypothesis'. Look for independent information that sufficient information *was* supplied. For example, was this an assignment which had been used to test previous cohorts of students? If it was used in the past, then it would be unusual for the lecturer not to have provided all the information that would be critical. Talk to other students in your tutorials about how they found the assignment.

Calm your inner chatter

- ■ The need for certainty will almost certainly change depending on the situation. Learn to know when you need more certainty in your life and monitor your certainty-seeking behaviour by keeping a record of your mood and behaviours. Note when you are craving more certainty in your life and the behaviours triggered. What were the responses to those behaviours?

■ Apps such as Headspace (www.headspace.com/) can help you manage 'inner chatter', relax and engage more with the uncertainties of life.

Remove the stick from your bum

■ Do not always choose news that fits your views. There is profound value in reading information that you disagree with, because it develops your perspective by providing new knowledge and understanding. For example, join a network social media group that you fundamentally disagree with (political parties you would never vote for, lifestyles you would never want to live – the flat earth society is one of my favourites – pro-life, pro-choice, gun ownership). Thanks to social media and the internet, you can comfortably and safely walk a mile in someone else's shoes (or jackboots). It's not necessary to shave your head, don the aforementioned boots and have a swastika tattooed on your forehead – and it's a lot safer not to – but you can listen to or read viewpoints from that side of the road which you would normally never venture to.

Engaging with ambiguity helps us make better decisions and become more creative. People who are able to tolerate ambiguity are much more likely to cooperate with and trust other people; they foster high levels of prosocial behaviour, including the prioritisation of the welfare of others.[5] This makes people who can tolerate ambiguity better employees than those who avoid risk and continually seek certainty.[6] Tolerant individuals cope with organisational change and are more creative; they are content to work with unconventional people, are self-starters and avoid at all costs what is known as satisficing.[7] Rather than holding back, gathering information and postponing decision-making until a range of options are in place, individuals who are prone to satisficing will look to satisfy the minimum requirements to achieve their desired goal, which means they are prone to accepting the first solution that appears credible.

Exercise: test yourself: how tolerant are you of ambiguity?

You can test yourself with Budner's tolerance for ambiguity scale. Budner determined three primary sources that triggered intolerance for ambiguity: novelty, complexity and insolubility. Novelty is the extent to which people are tolerant of novel or unfamiliar situations, complexity is the extent to which people are able to effectively manage multiple sources of information which may be distinct and unrelated from one another (in other words, being able to hold two conflicting ideas in your mind at the same time and not go insane) and insolubility relates to the degree to which people persist when a problem presents itself as particularly challenging to solve. These facets impact not only how we cope with our studies at university and how we approach tasks and responsibilities at work but also how we view and interact with those who are different from us. In other words, black-and-white thinking leads to bad decisions.

Respond to the following statements by indicating the extent to which you agree or disagree with them. Circle the number that best represents your evaluation of the item. 1 = Strongly Disagree; 2 = Moderately Disagree; 3= Slightly Disagree; 4= Neither Agree nor Disagree; 5 = Slightly Agree; 6 = Moderately Agree; 7 = Strongly Agree.

1 An expert who doesn't come up with a definite answer probably doesn't know too much;
2 I would like to live in a foreign country for a while;
3 There is really no such thing as a problem that cannot be solved;
4 People who fit their lives into a schedule probably miss most of the joy of living;
5 A good job is one where what is to be done and how it is to be done are always clear;
6 It is more fun to tackle a complicated problem than to solve a simple one;
7 In the long run, it is possible to get more done by tackling small, simple problems rather than large, complicated ones;
8 Often the most interesting and stimulating people are those who don't mind being different and original;
9 What we are used to is always preferable to what is unfamiliar;
10 People who insist on a yes or no answer just don't know how complicated things really are;
11 A person who leads an even, regular life in which few surprises or unexpected happenings arise really has a lot to be grateful for;
12 Many of our most important decisions are based on insufficient information;
13 I like parties where I know most of the people more than ones where I do not know many people;
14 Teachers who hand out vague assignments are giving one a chance to show initiative and originality;
15 The sooner we acquire similar values and ideals, the better;

16 A good lecturer is one who makes you wonder about your way of looking at things.

High scores indicate a greater intolerance for ambiguity. To score the instrument, the even-numbered items must be reverse-scored. That is 7 = 1; 6 = 2; 5 = 3; 4 = 4; 3 = 5; 2 = 6; 1 = 7. After reversing the even-numbered items, sum the scores for all 16 items to get your total score. Three subscales can also be computed to reveal the major source of intolerance of ambiguity: Novelty score (2, 9, 11, 13), Complexity score (4, 5, 6, 7, 8, 10, 14, 15, 16), Insolubility score (1, 3, 12).

Adapted from; Budner, S. (1962). Intolerance of ambiguity as a personality variable. *Journal of Personality, 30*(1), 29–50. Printed with permission of John Wiley and Sons.

The good news is that you can slowly grow your tolerance. In the first instance, be tolerant of your own uncertainty. Absolute knowing (at least in science) doesn't exist, and openness to experience (despite what the personality specialists would have you think) is a life-long endeavour. It is unlikely that you are intolerant of uncertainty in every situation; for example, most people enjoy the experience of a television drama, a thrilling movie or a good book without being consumed with the need to know the ending, unless you are one of those weirdos who read the last chapter first. ☺ It is also worth recognising that you have in fact experienced. . .

The greatest ambiguity experiment of all time

We are all just a little bit bewildered at the moment. *Social distancing; furlough; second, third wave; support bubbles; travel bubbles; covidiot; infodemic; elbow bump; coronacation; R rate; zoombombing; quarantinis* and my favourite, *Hamsterkaufing* (panic buying). As I write this book, the world of human experience as we know it has been rewritten, perhaps forever.

The lives of over 970,000 people have been taken by a global pandemic (an increase of 20,000 since I originally crafted this chapter two days ago), and projections suggest the worst recession for 300 years (when the Georgians were fighting wars, famine and a great freeze). Whilst the individual, social and economic costs are widespread, the full impact of the pandemic to our young people remains unfathomable. However, necessity being the mother of reinvention, humans have always been incredible at shaping and reshaping themselves.

COVID-19 has shaped us, but we have shaped ourselves, our families, the people we work with, the organisations that employ us and the governments that regulate us. In the absence of a vaccine, the people of the world found that solidarity, common purpose, creativity and humour could inoculate them against fear and helplessness. Isolated and yet under each other's feet, we reached into each other's worlds through the internet and social media. We replaced international travel with staycations, swapped shopping with making and doing and in the process created space for new hobbies and interests we never knew we had. We worked and cooked, cleaned and gardened, zoomed and binge watched Tiger King, all whilst working hard for our employers and educating our now-home-schooled children.

Organisations who rallied against homeworking policies suddenly found that their staff continued to be just as or more productive away from the office. It was easy to see why. The release from long and expensive commutes, the reduction in air pollution, the unnecessary expense of prime office premises, the unaffordable mortgage on an inner-city shoebox bedsit and the flexibility and freedom that came with this great homeworking experiment have significant value. Good homeworking improves productivity, well-being and staff retention, but whilst we know that happy staff are productive staff, in an economy facing recession, the new normal has to be financially viable. Pre-pandemic estimates suggested that homeworking would save UK employers £3 billion a year and over 3 million tons of carbon a year.[8] The aim must now be to reset and to build what we do better and for the longer term. As a country, we need graduates with the capacity to create something new. Dreamers who can turn an idea into a profitable reality by discovering new ways of combining resources, changing the function of a department, building a new team, creating new services or products. The remainder of this chapter is aimed to help you lay the foundations to achieve all that and more, because one thing is certain: post-pandemic, there will be a sharp focus on the idea of purpose. To define purpose, you first have to understand what it is that you stand for.

My emergent values

Your scores for ambiguity tolerance may in part be explained by your value system. Are you the kind of person who values self-control, certainty, resolution and closure? Do you seek concrete explanations to complex questions? Is needing to know and knowing as quickly as possible something of personal significance to you?

The most potentially powerful thing that any student can do when setting out on their career journey is to spend time discovering what is important and valuable to them. We each hold a range of different values in varying degrees, and those values differ in number and in degree between individuals. Values are important because they are the foundation of our lives. They represent what is important to us, our moral and cultural foundations, our family and heritage, how we feel about freedom, exploration and the thirst for knowledge. These foundations are ours, but they also shape the relationships that we have with the people we love and the organisations we choose to work with and stay with. When we understand our values, we understand ourselves and develop a better understanding of others.

Many of our values are formed and consolidated through the educational curriculum and during professional training. Governing bodies often set down for students the core values that they expect them to adhere to. These often speak to levels of professionalism, prosocial and ethical behaviour, moral practice, nurturing and protecting personal and mental well-being and establishing a mature professional identity within the field. However, at this point in your fledgling career, it is more appropriate to think about 'emergent values' because, really, we need some significant past experiences to start building a foundation for values. While many 20somethings will talk about loyalty, autonomy, the environment and saving the planet, as you grow and your roles and expectations change, you may find there is significant value in family, self-interest and prudence. Figure 1.1 provides a representation of over 100 of some of the most common values that tend to resonate with people. This list is not exhaustive, so once you have spent some time studying it, you might find additional values that resonate with you.

Whilst we differ as individuals, the nature of values has some common features.

1 **Arousal**: Values are intrinsically linked with arousal and physiological responses. When our values are challenged, for example, we may become angry, whereas experiences that are compatible with our values will trigger feelings of satisfaction and pleasure.
2 **Motivation**: We are motivated by our values to achieve our goals. For example, someone who values social justice may be motivated to work with organisations that pursue equality goals.
3 **Evaluative**: Values act as ideals by which to evaluate actions, policies, people and events. These evaluations are often unconscious, but they operate as important standards by which to make decisions about the consequences of our actions (and the actions of others); whether something is worth doing; whether it is a good, bad or valued activity.
4 **Transcendent**: Our values are transcendent. In other words, they are greater than any specific action or situation. For example, students learn the importance of ethics in psychological research, but those principles also transfer outside of the research environment into everyday life, relationships at home and work, business and politics. As described by Abraham Maslow[9]

Transcendence refers to the very highest and most inclusive or holistic levels of human consciousness, behaving and relating, as ends rather than means, to oneself, to significant others, to human beings in general, to other species, to nature, and to the cosmos.

(p. 269)

When individuals transcend, they often talk about seeing things from a higher perspective, feeling at peace and having a heightened sense of awareness.

5 **Hierarchical**: Values are also hierarchical in nature. We attribute more importance to some values over others. So important is this hierarchical structure thought to be in our decision-making that it has been developed into a prominent US legal analysis which focuses on the ordering of social values and how those values influence judicial decision-making. For example, it has been demonstrated that in the United States (in contrast to

Figure 1.1   Common values

Europe), commercial interests have now taken precedence over values such as data privacy and freedom of expression.[10]

6 **Synergistic**: Behaviours are typically grounded in more than one value. Valuing freedom of expression is linked to valuing democracy and holding governments to account but linked to de-valuing the right to privacy.

Table 1.1 provides an opportunity to reflect on the common features of values by considering times of arousal, motivation and evaluation or when you have transcended information or operated personally outside your usual limits and to write some details about those experiences. Can you identify any common themes from your values or times when some of those values were more important to you than others? Knowing what is important and what you really want to do next is powerful because it enables you to identify and pursue positions with organisations whose values are compatible with yours. A compatible match between your values and an organisations' values is known as a good person-organisational fit, and a good fit is related to work-force well-being. Employees will report lower levels of stress, higher levels of work-related motivation, higher job satisfaction and increased work engagement.[11] In other words, engaged staff employ and express themselves at work on multiple levels: physically, cognitively, emotionally and mentally. Working becomes a positive and fulfilling state of mind which is characterised by dedication to and absorption in the tasks at hand. Engaged staff are more energetic; they feel in control over events in their work lives; they seek out opportunities to create positive feedback and appreciation for themselves

Table 1.1 The nature of my values

Arousal: reflect on a moment of anger or joy. What triggered that experience; what values were being met or challenged?
Motivation: reflect on a time when you felt driven to complete a task. What values would be met by success? What values would be challenged by failure?
Evaluative: reflect on a time when you judged an action, person or event. What values and standards were you applying to make your assessment? What does this tell you about the values you apply to yourself and others?
Transcendent: reflect on a time of peak experience or when you were able to move past your own personal concerns for something of greater importance. What was unique about that experience? What emotions did you feel?
Hierarchical: are there any prominent themes that suggest that you have some very important core values?
Synergistic: in what way do other values that you hold build onto those important core values?

and tiredness becomes a satisfying state associated with productivity and achievement. For organisations, this work-related enthusiasm and enjoyment improve key performance indicators such as client satisfaction and financial turnover.[12]

Given how important values are in managing your motivation and commitment, the first step towards success should be understanding yourself and how those factors can play a critical role in shaping your job search. Taking time at this point to conduct a self-assessment will greatly increase the chances of you finding a position where you will feel that your contributions are valued and rewarded and your skills are usefully used. Conducting an assessment of your values and interests can be a useful activity to help you develop a good understanding of what your career preferences might be. Such personal profiles can be useful in helping you determine what you might offer employers because they empower you to have more meaningful conversations about yourself and what interests you.

Exercise: practicing values with others

1   Help your peers stay motivated: talk to your peers and ask them what is important about their final-year project or dissertation: what matters to them and why they are motivated to study it. See if you can spot what their values are in how they respond. Support them by getting them to talk about how they use those values to stay on course.

2   Get to know your supervisor or employer: Talk to your employer or dissertation tutor. See if you can find out what is important to them about a project they are currently working on. Can you identify any critical values? Do you share their values?

3   Get a project back on track: When something is not going well, instigate a meeting to talk about why the project is of importance. Design a values exercise for your team and use the results of that exercise to help everyone set targets and get back on track.

Career advisory services are also an excellent source of support in helping you identify your values, interests, skills and personal preferences, then using that information to identify the kinds of career pathways where those skills are known to be a suitable match. However, as any psychology student knows, assessment and inventory-style tests produce predefined results. You can only produce tests that measure the specific, and career measurement devices also measure states, not traits. They capture how you are feeling and thinking at the moment you take the test. Since you cannot know what you do not know, the skills and knowledge you have not yet acquired are in no way captured in these tests. Equally, if you are in anyway entrepreneurial, creative, openminded, prepared for adventure or ahead of your time, the test will reduce your profile to the best match, and that match is often a fairly pedestrian career prescription.

Value measurement devices (which are often simply checklists) are also highly problematic because they are typically an exercise in extracting positive constructs, which means it can be a challenge to find any differentiation between values (known as end-piling). Tests that ask respondents to choose least and most valued descriptors tend to provide somewhat better differentiation, but they still suffer in their inability to determine the reasons people find those values personally important. For example, people often wax lyrical about valuing people or time over money. However, valuing money may for that individual be linked to financial security. Financial security enables the creation of free

---

Career story in focus: behavioural therapist and career counsellor

"Before I started my master's in applied psychology degree, I was working in higher education in faculty support roles. One of my goals in completing my master's degree was to start working in student support and development, ideally in higher education. After I completed my master's degree, I arranged an internship at a mental health clinic in Oman where we had just moved. This was one thing that was lacking in the online applied psychology degree – work exposure. While my passion is to work in higher education, there were no available positions for expats to work in colleges and universities there. In addition to this, there was a huge demand in Oman for mental health services for children, particularly at the elementary school level. My supervisor at the clinic suggested I consider working with this demographic and after several months of training, I became licensed as a behavioural therapist. I had always been interested in behaviourism. I began working as a behavioural therapist and saw clients privately, helping shape their behaviour through applied behavioural analysis techniques. I also started working part time as a learning and behavioural support teacher at an elementary school. The school I worked with began referring clients with behavioural issues to me and I became quite busy. We have recently moved back to Doha and I am happy with this development as there are many universities and colleges here. I am currently working through my Academic Advising and Career Counselling certificate from the University of Calgary and I plan to work as an advisor in one of the universities here once schools open up again".

Emer Cogan, Academic Advisor, Oman

time and the capacity to look after the people we care about. For that reason, the activity in Table 1.1 empowers a more qualitative perspective of your personal value system, enabling you to generate your own framework, shaped by what is significant for you.

What do I stand for?

"Contrary to popular wisdom, the proper first response to a changing world is not to ask, 'How should we change?' but rather to ask, what do we stand for and why do we exist? This should never change. And then feel free to change everything else"

Collins and Poras, xiv–xv

This may sound enormously complicated, but it is necessary if you want to find the right career path. But it is very simple, really: once you have the value framework that you have arrived upon (Table 1.1), apply it to as many positions as are best matches. Try to ignore any preconceptions or pressure from outside and apply for any job which matches up. However, it is important to point out this isn't a one-time deal; your personal circumstances will inevitably change throughout the course of your life. Marriage, children, loss and extra responsibilities are all things that life throws at you which may change what you want from your career. So, you may have to go through this process a number of times.

Getting a job cannot just be about getting skills that someone wants to pay us for; it must also be about how we grow as human beings and how we care for each other and our world. It's ironic, of course, that sometimes these are the very things some people might not want to pay us to do, but they are central to our professional success because they provide us with a clear sense of where we want to be in life and the values we wish to stand for. These values are your 'brand', and a well-developed brand will distinguish you from the graduate 'sea of sameness' (more about this in Chapter 4). The following exercises (Who will I become and Table 1.1) are designed to help students develop a framework for developing self-understanding that will help self-improvement, give clarity and a sense of purpose and yield pride from the work that they do.

Remember, there are no right or wrong values, so do not let self-judgement (or the judgement of others) creep in. Someone who values money and achievement is not better or worse than someone who values caring for others and giving back to the community. What is key is that you can start to become aware of how those values shape your thinking and decision-making and how sometimes those values might actually inadvertently do damage to others. Values always have a flip side. If you value honesty, you might use this as an excuse to be overly direct and hurtful to people. You could cause sadness, anxiety, frustration, anger or worse simply because you felt you were being honest.

Jobs in focus: copywriting

Copywriting subsidises your studies and enables you to work at home. Not only is it a great source of income, but it will also help you improve your writing.

Freelancing webpages such as iwriter, FlexiJobs, Freelancer.com and Upwork hire content writers at different skill levels to write everything that there is to write about!

Each company operates slightly differently, but generally students can bid for work or agree to a tariff. As your skill level improves, so does your rate of pay. Most students find they can comfortably earn around £200 per week without affecting their studies.

Further reading

Furnham, A., & Ribchester, T. (1995). Tolerance of ambiguity: A review of the concept, its measurement and applications. *Current Psychology: A Journal for Diverse Perspectives on Diverse Psychological Issues*, 14(3), 179–199.

Holmes, J. (2015). *Nonsense. The power of not knowing*, New York: Crown Publishers/Penguin Random House.

Exercise: who will I become?

Someone once said that if you find a job you love, you will never work a day in your life – a great soundbite that explains nothing much at all. You can get your heart broken when you have fallen in love, but does that mean you stop trying and give up on relationships altogether? As careers go, you can't really afford literally and figuratively to be Miss Havisham (great expectations; shame about the cobwebs) when it comes to the job marathon. This exercise is to help you find your inner Pip and avoid handing your heart over to Estella.

Create a vision of yourself and where you would like to work three to five years from now. In answering this question, however, most people will use what is called the availability heuristic. Human beings have severe cognitive limits which cause biases, so setting out some plans for your future may well feel limited depending on what career examples readily come to mind. A narrow strategy can feel like a certain option; there are a perplexing number of options available and no systematic or simple way of comparing them. At the end of the day, it is important to start with a framework which gives some structure to what your options are. But that list should not be so narrowly framed that the search for alternatives is continually anchored to the most available examples in the psychology profession.

The following activities are designed to help you stimulate your career planning. The objective is to create not just one five-year plan but three. These plans should be very different from one another and not three versions of the same plan. Students who are sure of their career paths often find that Plan 3 is the most difficult to develop but stay with it and work out a third plan.

Plan 3 is the plan that exists in the outer ring of the ideas and expectations that you will have formulated for yourself (including 'I do not know'). It is therefore worth investing additional time and effort in this part of the exercise in an attempt to overcome any rigidity in thinking that you may have developed. The exercise is designed to direct your focus away from the obvious, the concrete or the predetermined towards an exploration of intangible categories such as 'ideas', 'influencers', 'attitudes', 'values' and 'beliefs'. Such reflection can increase levels of self-awareness which trigger new career pathways for inquiry and consideration.

Steps:

Choose a title for your first plan. Jot down the life categories that are important to you.

Journal, using as much detail as possible, how you see each of those categories changing over the next three years. It is important to ignore the nagging inner chatter and self-judgement. If you cannot ignore it, then write it down as well. *How will that inner chatter change over the next five years? What will you do to change it? What kind of job do you have? How valued do you feel? What does that look like? What is your health like? Why is your health like that? How is your relationship with your family? What has contributed to the quality of those relationships? Where do you live? What is that like?*

Psychology as a science requires you to write in the 'third person'. The next step is to take all reflections that you just noted down and turn them into a first person 'I' story. Written as if you already have achieved in the areas that are critical to you. 'I am . . . "

Repeat again for Plan 2 and again for Plan 3.

Plan 3. "The ideas that influence me are . . . " "I get my understanding from . . . " "I read [what media, books] to develop my thinking . . . " "People who influence me are . . . because . . . " "Five years from now, my thinking in this area will have . . . "

Notes

1 Rosen, E. (2015, March 3). Careers guidance is pushing students down a narrow path before they have chance to explore their options. *The Telegraph*. Retrieved from www.telegraph.co.uk/education/2017/03/03/careers-guidance-pushing-students-narrow-path-have-chance-explore/
Rosen, E. (2019). *The radical sabbatical, the millennial handbook to the quarter-life crisis*. London: John Catt.
2 University of Virginia. (2014, July 3). Doing something is better than doing nothing for most people, study shows. *ScienceDaily*. Retrieved from www.sciencedaily.com/releases/2014/07/140703142154.htm
De Gayardon, A., Callender, C., & Green, F. (2019). The determinants of student loan take-up in England. *Higher Education*. doi:10.1007/s10734-019-00381-9
3 Page, L. (2014, May 19). How to deal with employability anxiety. *The Guardian*. Retrieved from www.theguardian.com/education/2014/may/19/employment-anxiety-students-job-worry
Okay-Somerville, B., & Scholarios, D. (2017). *Emotional barriers to job search success: Job search anxiety during university-to-work transitions*. Academy of Management Meeting, Atlanta, GA, August 4–18, pp. 15–23. doi:10.5465/ambpp.2017.12805symposium
Kwok, C. Y. N. (2018). Managing uncertainty in the career development of emerging adults: Implications for undergraduate students. *Australian Journal of Career Development (Sage Publications Ltd.)*, *27*(3), 137–149.
4 Andersen, S. M., & Schwartz, A. H. (1992). Intolerance of ambiguity and depression: A cognitive vulnerability factor linked to hopelessness. *Social Cognition*, *10*(3), 271–298.
5 Vives, M-L., & FeldmanHall, O. (2018). Tolerance to ambiguous uncertainty predicts prosocial behavior. *Nature Communications*, *9*(1). doi:10.1038/s41467-018-04631-9
6 O'Connor, P., Becker, K., & Fewster, K. (2018). *Tolerance of ambiguity at work predicts leadership, job performance, and creativity*. Creating Uncertainty Conference, 2018-07-01-2018-07-05.
7 Runco, M. A. (2014). Personality and motivation. In *Creativity, theories and themes: Research, development, and practice edition* (2nd ed., pp. 265–302). doi:10.1016/b978-0-12-410512-6.00009-6
8 Carbon Trust. (2014). *Homeworking: Helping businesses cut costs and reduce their carbon footprint*. Retrieved from www.carbontrust.com/resources/homeworking-helping-businesses-cut-costs-and-reduce-their-carbon-footprint
9 Maslow, A. H. (1971). *The farther reaches of human nature*. New York: Arkana and Penguin Books.

10 Petkova, B. (2019). Privacy as Europe's first amendment. *European Law Journal.* doi:10.1111/eulj.12316

11 Christian, M. S., Garza, A. S., & Slaughter, J. E. (2011). Work engagement: A quantitative review and test of its relations with task and contextual performance. *Personnel Psychology*, *64*(1), 89–136.
Rayton, B., Yalabik, Z., & Rapti, A. (n.d.). Fit perceptions, work engagement, satisfaction and commitment. *Journal of Managerial Psychology*, *34*(6), 401–414.

12 Bakker, A. B., Albrecht, S. L., & Leiter, M. P. (2011). Key questions regarding work engagement. *European Journal of Work and Organizational Psychology, 20*(1), 4–28. doi:10.1080/1359432X.2010.485352

Chapter 2

My psychology DNA

Poor old Mickey Mouse. The argument goes that some degrees just exist to exploit the naïve. Golf studies, communication studies, clownology and circus studies, surf science, homeopathy, and every now and again, psychology pops onto the doom's day list, but then so does maths. Fiona Pok Wong received an out-of-court settlement in 2019 from Anglia Ruskin University for the false promises that she was given about the career that would follow her first-class degree in international business strategy. She argued that she had been sold a 'Mickey Mouse' degree.

International business strategy can hardly be described as a Mickey Mouse degree any more than psychology can. It's hard to imagine that if Disney were in any way interested in delivering international business strategy that the Harvards, Yales and Oxfords of the academic world would not be. What can, however, let students down is the delivery and teaching of their programme, and Wong argued persuasively that her education was not where it should have been. Wong did not let that get in her way. Be it grit, perseverance, resilience, fury or 'hellfire and brimstone', Wong was propelled forward. She went on to study the graduate diploma in law and the legal practice course, and in between times, she managed to squeeze in a paralegal course and sued Anglia Ruskin University. *Talk about a dish best served cold!*

A random story about scones

My son loves scones. He calls them "tummy cheerfulness". I mean if child marriages were legal in the United Kingdom, my little boy would marry a scone. During the coronavirus-scone-making crisis of 2020, there were a lot of scones in our house. I'm not ashamed to admit that my clothes feel a little tighter.

Scones are a pretty easy thing to make – *you would think*. There are only a few ingredients (about five ingredients, unless you're following a weird lemonade version from Facebook) and a stable, no-nonsense temperature of 'rack it up as high as you can for 12 minutes!' The perfect controlled environment. However, for every perfect batch of golden brown tummy cheerfulness I have managed to produce, I have undercooked, over-cooked, burned, dropped, left the sugar out, put the wrong flour in or added too much salt, and then there was the Facebook lemonade scones recipe (Muriel, if you are listening, was it five cups of flour sieved three times or three cups sieved five times?).

The point is that not one batch of misery came from my lack of effort or lack of trying new things. Most critically, my mistakes never came from a disregard for the scone-making process or my son's pleasure from eating them. Sometimes stuff goes wrong, so when things do not work out, be fair, be patient and be kind and make sure you say thank you and let people know when things go well, because next time it could be you putting diet lemonade into a scone mix.

But, "I paid nine grand for these scones", I hear you say. Your mind is more important than your money. Making a large payment for education does not mean that you will learn anything, and it also does not guarantee that you will have a commodity of any value to sell at the end of your journey. The point of university is that you will gain knowledge that will not only be useful but will shape your life. With that in mind, it is folly to treat a degree as a commodity. If it were, you may as well nip down to ASDA and pick up a packet. I have learned not to put lemonade (diet or otherwise) in scones, that doubling the scone recipe does not mean you have twice as much cheerfulness and that microwaving doesn't work as a method of cooking. Francesca, however, who has quietly observed my plight, has taken everything that I have learned from making scones, and not making scones, and learned to make Turkish poğaça' (like scones but with yeast and filled with feta), and they were jolly tasty. Demonstrating once again that Vygotsky was on the money with his theory of vicarious learning.

Becoming competent

Ability is how we affect our world. It is composed of our knowledge and wisdom, practical and technical skills, 'soft' social and emotional skills, attitude and outlook and the ways in which we pull all of those characteristics together to do something efficiently and effectively. Ability reflects our competence in the world, our standing with our friends, colleagues and family, and it is the basis on which expectations for future interaction with others are built and upon which individuals develop perceptions of their own behaviour. You *gotta* go get yourself some competence, and fortunately psychologists have had a thing or two to say about that.

Broadwell's (Figure 2.1) four stages of competence and later adaptations outline how we progress through the stages of skill awareness, development, practice and execution.

1 **Unconscious incompetence**

You're stuck in the mud (or any other brown substance you wish to substitute) and don't know why or even what this brown stuff is. This is about where most students are when they finish the first year of a three-year undergraduate course. Unconscious incompetence means that you might have learned something, but generally you are unaware of your own proficiency. You may or may not realise you are incompetent or more likely do not understand how to do something. You may even deny the usefulness of what it is that you are learning to do. Unconsciously incompetent students will need more scaffolding to support

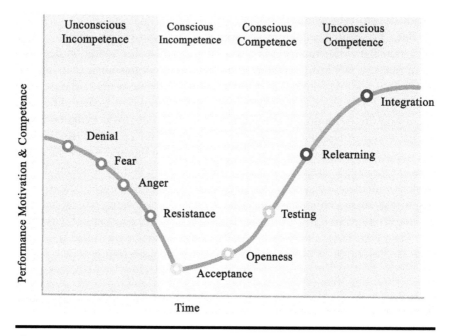

Figure 2.1   Competence
Source: Adapted from Broadwell (1969)

their learning; they will (and should) seek out more advice and support from their peers and from tutors. This is critical, to recognise and acknowledge your own incompetence quickly and find value in what you are learning and doing. If you do not, you will become frustrated and highly dependent, blame others for your incompetence and become trapped as an unconscious incompetent for a protracted period of time. Incompetence does not mean ineptitude; it just means traditional teaching methods won't be as effective.

2 **Conscious incompetence** You know you are stuck in mud, and you know what mud is. But the harder you fight and struggle and get frustrated, the faster you sink. It's a skill to learn not to panic, find that conveniently placed branch and slowly and deftly pull yourself out. This happens towards the middle or the end of the second year of your degree: you should be developing some conscious incompetence. You are aware of skill(s) and knowledge but are not yet proficient. You understand the value of the new skill and have internalised its importance but cannot quite get it together yet. At this stage, expect to make lots and lots of mistakes. If you do not get comfortable with making mistakes, you may revert back to unconscious

incompetence by devaluing the skill and giving up. Not surprisingly, this is also the stage when students are most likely to complain *a lot* about their undergraduate learning experience. Braking through a threshold hurts, and it is easier to externalise the challenges and barriers than focus on getting over that hurdle. Keep going, and be kind to your lecturers, please.

3 **Conscious competence** You know where the mud is and avoid it when possible, but even if you do go in, you know you have the skill set to find the branch and help yourself out. You are in your final year, and, not surprisingly, students are happy, less stressed and thriving. By now you know what you are doing, why you should do it and how it will be effective. You are happy with the odd mistake, but performance is still effortful. It takes focus, concerted effort and concentration. Those research questions eh? and those statistics? That final year dissertation to complete? *You can do it!* [(Oh no I can't)] *No, seriously, you can.*

4 **Unconscious competence** Here, learning ceases. You graduate and you are sent out in the world, and you start to wonder what the point of that psychology degree was. This is because your competence has become automatic and can be performed 'second nature' beyond conscious awareness, perhaps even while carrying out a second task. At this level, sometimes people talk about operating at a level of subconscious intuition, although more likely this is simply our brain's capacity to draw deep and retrieve information that it has carefully filed away.[1] You tend not to go anywhere near mud and now have the skill set such that it effectively is not there; even if you do fall in, you don't notice it or, better still, get someone else to go into the mud for you.

The purpose of models such as Broadwell is to help individuals understand better why an obstacle to development might exist, to overcome resistance by helping people understand the relevance of the skills they seek to develop, to stay the course and become expert in their chosen domain and ultimately go on and develop unconscious competence in others. The first stage of identifying where you are in the ladder of ability is to create awareness of the skills you are developing throughout your degree. Such efforts will help you develop a well-rounded self-concept and feel confident about your knowledge, skills and abilities in a meaningful and effective way – with the caveat that as soon as change comes (and it will), you will no longer be competent (see Chapter 9).

Becoming consciously competent

The Quality Assurance Agency (QAA) for Higher Education is the independent body that checks on standards and quality in UK higher education. It conducts quality assessment reviews, develops reference points and guidance for providers and conducts or commissions research on relevant issues and develops subject benchmark statements that describe the academic standards that students are expected to reach, the knowledge they might be expected to know and the skills they should develop. The QAA subject benchmark statement is an excellent place to start for students who are attempting to unpick the myriad of skills they have developed and then to apply those key words to convince potential employers that they are skilled for the job.

The concrete focus on knowledge development and critical thinking in a psychology degree means that students will thrive best when the jobs they eventually obtain are intellectually challenging. Unchallenging work can feel nice for a while, but longer-term students will also find themselves feeling understimulated, disaffected and frustrated at work.

The psychology student's skill set is often described as 'psychological literacy', and for those of you who don't know what that means and don't necessarily want to read the dry spiel that explains it, let's think of these as being analogous to the lessons we learn from *Pulp Fiction*. ⚠ (**SPOILER ALERT**) ⚠

1 **Presenting multiple perspectives in a way that fosters critical evaluation and reflection**. Can you pull together a grisly, non-linear, nonsensical storyline in a way that pulls on your heartstrings while at the same time telling a truth that makes you cringe so hard your toes curl? Congratulations, you have a skill. 🏅
It is also worth mentioning that later in your career when you are expected to have developed (or are seeking to develop) high-level strategic thinking skills, your psychology degree has already given you a head start. Challenging your own thinking and the thinking of others and reflecting through many lenses before taking decisive action is an essential competency of the adaptive strategic thinker.

2 **An understanding of the role of empirical evidence in the creation and constraint of theory and also in how theory guides the collection and interpretation of empirical data.** What if I told you the famous scene of driving the adrenaline needle into Uma Thurman's chest wasn't real? Well, sorry to break it to you, but Vincent Vega (John Travolta) is actually pulling the needle out of her chest. Tarantino reversed the footage (most likely to make sure Uma Thurman didn't actually get a needle driven into her eye as opposed to her chest). Look at it this way: you have a conclusion – something you believe fundamentally to be real. When you were a kid, you probably believed in Santa (sorry for those who still do), and every piece of evidence that fed into that belief was considered more evidence corroborating a true fact. Well, those were plane lights in the sky, and your mum and dad were the ones writing 'from Santa' on the tags. Sorry. Psychologists, good psychologists, anyway, always centre themselves on their training and seek out the evidence that

disproves their thinking. If the interpretation still stands after we've stabbed it in the chest with a needle, then it might (not must) be true for now. Congratulations, you have another skill. 🏅 🏅

3 **The scientific understanding of the mind, brain, behaviour and experience and how they interact with the complex environments in which they exist.** While we all have some pretty wild dreams sometimes, they don't always have a symbolic meaning, but a good psychologist knows that some things have certain symbolic power. Maybe it's your grandmother's pearls; maybe it's an old photo. For Butch, it was his great-grandfather's gold watch. Having the living daylights knocked out of him, he was shocked awake by the powerful story of how the gold watch came to be his. Now, the shock could have come from the fact said watch lived in not one, but three, orifices (that we know of) or that he realised he didn't know whether it had been cleaned by then; all we know is that he needed that watch back, even if it meant risking his life.

Understanding when the brain is actually trying to tell you something, and when your room is just a little too warm for comfort, that's skill #3. 🏅🏅🏅

4 **The acquisition of a range of research skills and methods for investigating experience and behaviour, culminating in an ability to conduct research independently.** Picture this. You're on a rescue mission to get your archnemesis out of a weird, gross, gimp dungeon and you don't know what weapon to pick. Your options are a claw hammer, a baseball bat or a chainsaw. Which one do you pick? Trick question. You go for the much more badass samurai sword. You might be wondering what I'm trying to say here. When you're faced with a conflict, you need to know which skills apply and how to use them correctly. You might consider yourself to be judging your weapon of choice, and you may have so many weapons (skills) that you can't figure out the right one. Don't be afraid to go for the secret third option, which is much cooler and means you get to slice through your enemy's chest like a hot knife through butter (read here: solve that psychology problem).

For knowing you have a hidden skill that applies perfectly to the situation, you have just collected skill #4. 🏅🏅🏅

5 **Developing knowledge, leading to an appreciation of theory and research findings, including relevant ethical and sociocultural issues.** Everyone has always wondered why America stuck so fervently to the imperial system whilst the rest of the world went with metric (except for the United Kingdom, since we just love a good fence to sit on). Well, now we know. It's because they'd rather have the Quarter Pounder than the Royale with cheese, even though they're the exact same thing (or so says John Travolta).

There comes a time when you realise that you might not see eye to eye with the next person and, when you're practicing, that culture and personal ethics play a serious role in personal behaviour (also highly useful if you ever want to get an executive position on a board – see Chapter 9).

For your excellent tolerance, you gain skill #5. 🏅🏅🏅🏅🏅

6 **An understanding of real-life applications of theory to the full range of experience and behaviour and the application of psychological understanding to real-world questions.** Everyone has had one of those flirty back-and-forth exchanges. You know, the ones that switch from declarations of love to an orgy of violence. However, before Honey Bunny and Pumpkin threaten to "execute every mother****ing last one of ya!" they debate the relative risks, merits and ethics of robbing bars and liquor stores. What would actually happen if you applied all that knowledge and understanding to how humans would behave in a restaurant robbery. Nobody expects to get robbed in a restaurant, but that doesn't mean there aren't plans in place in case it happens.

For having the ability to apply your knowledge accurately to the real world (and for not robbing restaurants), you have the full set of skills.

Pass Go, collect $200. 🏅🏅🏅🏅🏅

What does it all mean?

It's all well and good understanding that Freud thinks all women actually want to be men (when actually all we wanted was freedom, the right to vote and equal pay) but how do you move from 'this big psychologist man says X so that means you feel Y and we should fix you with Z'? You do it with the methods of empirical investigation and critical analysis that psychologists draw upon, enabling them to develop a body of knowledge inferring cause and effect. These systematic skills equip students to apply abstract knowledge to practical problems, to innovate and develop new knowledge for problems that we do not even know exist yet. The exciting news is that you can get paid for using this knowledge and expertise to solve problems in *Pulp Fiction*, the media, finance, criminal behaviour, mental health, politics, computer games, relationships, the world of work and the broader community.

Psychology is a thriving academic discipline and a vital area of professional practice. The diversity in practice that exists within psychology can be observed in the vast number of subfields within the discipline (Table 2.1). This makes psychology both an exciting and interesting subject to study and a subject that equips graduates with a broad knowledge base and a range of transferable skills for the workplace. Psychology students leave university with an impressive skill set which includes scientific analysis, critical thinking, problem-solving and reflectiveness about their own attitudes and behaviour and the attitudes and behaviours of others, which makes them particularly effective in areas related to ethical behaviour, dignity and respect. These skills are a huge advantage in all sorts of career fields, which means that psychology students are reported as being some of the most employable graduates, and students can end up working in a diverse range of professions. Which means that there is high demand for psychology graduates outside of what tends to be considered the core or typical professional routes (examples of these posts are documented in Table 2.2).

More subject-specific skills from the British Psychological Society (BPS), this time without *Pulp Fiction* ('cos as any academic knows, the QAA is a lot more *Pulp Fiction* than the BPS, and don't get me started on Gavin Williamson #lecturer joke). The trick is to pepper your CV with the language of skills and abilities. We cover much more of this in Chapter 5, but effectively, you want to try to pin these descriptors down throughout your career story. Working to develop conscious awareness of what you can do will help you learn how to tell a good, authentic story in an interview. This will help you see the path through your experience, open your eyes to future connections and pathways and connect you to the occupations you may like to connect with. So, the tedious but very important list is:

1 **Apply multiple perspectives** to psychological issues, recognising that psychology involves a range of research methods, theories, evidence and applications.

2 **Integrate ideas and findings** across the **multiple perspectives** in psychology and **recognise** distinctive psychological approaches to relevant issues.

3 **Identify and evaluate patterns** in behaviour, psychological functioning and experience.

4 **Generate and explore** hypotheses and research questions **drawing on** relevant theory and research.

5 **Carry out** empirical studies involving a **variety** of methods of data collection, including experiments, observation, questionnaires, interviews and focus groups.

6 **Analyse, present and evaluate** quantitative and qualitative data and evaluate research findings.

7 **Employ evidence-based reasoning** and **examine** practical, theoretical and ethical issues associated with the range of methodologies.

8 **Use a variety** of psychological tools, including specialist software, laboratory equipment and psychometric instruments.

9 **Apply** psychological knowledge ethically and safely to real-world problems;

10 **Critically evaluate** psychological theory and research.

11 **Carry out** an extensive piece of **empirical research** that requires them individually to demonstrate a range of research skills, including planning, considering and resolving ethical issues; analysis and dissemination of findings.

"It's important to note that achieving your degree, as in the actual qualification, is just a small piece of a much wider skillset. For me, going to university allowed me to develop skills in organisation and time management, working independently, drive and self-motivation. These aren't skills that you'll be 'taught' on a degree, you simply pick them up as you go along. However, it is these underappreciated skills that set you apart when the time comes to get a job and employers are certainly looking for evidence you have them".

Gary Stevens, Psychology Graduate and Learning Engagement
Co-Ordinator

Generic skills: Psychology students are able to:

1 **Communicate effectively**. Effective communication involves developing a coherent argument supported by relevant evidence and being sensitive to the needs and expectations of an audience. This is accomplished through essays and scientific reports and through experience in making oral presentations to groups.

"At first, I was in charge of the Student Care office, caring for the mental health of 2500 students, where the knowledge I developed during my psychology degree allowed me to review and enhance policies to support students with special education needs. The awareness of psychological processes and human behaviour has also developed my competencies in communication and negotiation and I now head up the Alumni Office at the Nanyang Academy of Fine Art".

Oscar Ng, Head of Alumni Relations, Nanyang Academy

2 **Demonstrate numerical reasoning.**

"The statistic and research method skills I acquired during my psychology degree have allowed me to approach evidence with a critical eye. These skills have allowed me to go on to study for a PhD and working on a range of external projects, working on systematic reviews to large epidemiological data sets. Having such skills has allowed me to build a network of connections and enabled me to be involved in multiple projects outside of my own work".

Sam Burton, PhD Student

3 Be **computer literate**; skills in the use of word processing, databases and analytic software packages and so on.

"The solutions to many of our problems require close interdisciplinary collaboration. My view is that knowledge of computing prepares you to build solutions to solve problems across business, scientific, and social contexts, conceptually through to software. More often than not these solutions are intended to serve people. The increased technical flexibility that you gain through study of computing – interpreting requirements, algorithms, data structures, etc. – coupled with the very important knowledge provided by psychology – of forming research questions, statistics and data analysis, ethics and data collection/ protection, and of competing theoretical perspectives – gives you a clear edge. It's difficult but it's really worth it. Not only does this give you the ability to recognise and unlock the ubiquitous and significant human aspects of the 'digital world', but also the unique ability to synergise and communicate the views held by both communities of practitioners, and more practically apply the respective contributions".

Emir Demirbag, Computing Science and Psychology Graduate, PhD Student

4 **Retrieve and organise** information effectively. Psychology graduates are familiar with collecting and organising stored information found in library books and journal collections and online, critically evaluating primary and secondary sources.

"I work as a researcher for a global legal directory, conducting market research on lawyers and law firms across a broad range of markets. The research elements of my Psychology degree have been a big help as we use methods that I had practice of during my time at university. The majority of data we collect is qualitative and comes from the likes of surveys and telephone/face to face interviews. The hands-on research experience I gained during my degree definitely helped when applying to the role and has enabled me to stay organised and keep on top of a sometimes very hectic schedule".

Ben Glover, Senior Research Analyst

---

5 **Recognise** what is **required for effective teamwork** and articulate their own strengths and weaknesses in this regard. The complexity of the factors that shape behaviour and social interaction will be familiar to psychology graduates and will make them more aware of the basis of successful and problematic interpersonal relationships.

"I have taken part in many group projects whilst studying at the University, with some of those groups being very good and others being very very bad. Having to work in a group is a big learning experience for a student because you will often discover that you need to find your own role within a group, such as being a leader or helping to keep a group organised and on track. You will be required to deal with people that may have very different personalities to you and also those who may not have a work ethic that is similar to your own. But despite this balancing act, working in a group can be rewarding and teach you valuable life skills for the future, particularly when it comes to learning how to communicate with other people and effectively convey your own thoughts and opinions so that other people can understand you. Working in a group can help you to figure out how best to motivate other people so that work can be completed in a timely manner and it can help to develop your social skills that you're able to make effective contributions to the team in a variety of ways. Through completing group projects at University, you can learn about how to resolve conflicts which may occur within a group and you will learn about how other people may have different skills or different ways of working and how to get the best out of their particular skill set."

Mark Hume, Postgraduate Student

---

6 **Take responsibility** for their own learning and skill development (this will include effective personal planning, self-reflection and project management skills, so they become more independent and pragmatic as learners).

"I have noticed that I have found solace in study, and that it is something that I now keep returning to. In a strange way I feel it gives me a purpose that is only for me, rather than for others. My confidence in myself is a strange beast, as it is clearly there and is what enables me to achieve in both work and play. Yet it is easily momentarily shaken as I have an overwhelming sense of not being good enough, or not quite 'making the grade'. I still feel I have a lot to prove to myself about what I can achieve in my future, which acts as a driving force that spurs me forward, but that I also find intimidating".

Anna Moore, *Psychology Graduate and Policy Consultant*

What does psychology not do just yet?

Just like you (and the rest of our country at the moment), psychology is a work in progress. The rapid transitions between the culture and the priorities we once knew and the pandemic world we find ourselves in has plunged our world into the most monumental changes we are ever likely to face for generations. Whilst most transitions bring with them creativity, hope, excitement and some discomfort (change is never easy) the coronavirus pandemic has exposed the fault lines in our society that we failed to confront: issues of inequality, co-operation, good governance, effective leadership and saving lives versus saving the economy. Psychology, along with every other discipline, will be unpicking for some time what it means to be a graduate and what skills, knowledge and abilities are needed for the future. Universities, even under COVID-19, move at a glacial pace, so you cannot afford to wait for the 'mental anchor' of benchmark statements and learning outcomes to present themselves. If you wait, you become obsolete, so it is time to ask yourself some tough questions. What skills and abilities will employers be looking for down the road? Chapter 9 offers both a more detailed route map of the critical work tasks you will need for your future career and a vision of what skills and specialisms are likely to be in demand. At this stage, the most critical area for you to explore are skill sets relating to information technology and all forms of digitalisation of communication and knowledge. For now, these are the ones you should turn your attention to. We give this area a more in-depth treatment in Chapter 9.

Coding: Technology is deeply affecting our everyday lives and the global economy. We are entering what is called the 4th Industrial Revolution, where the speed and complexity of how we do things will be unprecedented. For you, our 'Minecraft generation', coding is already second nature, and most of you probably also have an IT/Computing GCSE. Turn up the volume on your skill.

Flexibility with different software packages: Psychology degrees do not overtly develop coding skills, but it is still a fundamental component of how psychology does business. For example, the R environment and Python have radically changed the way in which psychologists handle and visualise their data but are still not widely taught in undergraduate programmes. Rather, universities are persisting with IBM SPSS, seemly not comprehending that most employers do not have an IBM-sized budget. The University of Amsterdam and Open Science project were, however, more forward thinking when they created JASP (and we now also have JAMOVI), which are both free open source statistics software packages. Both use the same SPSS steps you will have been taught in your courses (so you do not need to learn an entirely new package), but arguably they are both much less confusing than SPSS and frankly more fun to use.

Big data: Building your competence with big data and data amalgamation from different disciplines presents an opportunity for major breakthroughs and is most certainly the direction of future travel. Key to success in this area, however, is learning how to ask the right questions and learning how to extract knowledge from large data systems.

Social media: Rather than spending your time 'being' on social media, start turning your attention and psychological expertise to what makes social media effective. How do trends develop; how do people interact with one another; how do posts gain traction and impact people at an individual, community and society level? How is the larger social media landscape developing? What new technologies or legislation could be on the horizon that could shape that trajectory?

In the future, academic publications are also more likely to become 'wikified', with pre-proofs appearing for critical review by peers. This will greatly increase the accuracy and speed at which research papers are available. Build up your competence by blogging about a science paper of interest and encourage debate amongst your peers.

Leadership: Globally, the COVID-19 pandemic has exposed the deep divisions and inequalities in our society. Addressing these issues requires graduates who are not only ethically competent (something already well covered in psychology programmes everywhere) but who are articulate and trained in rhetoric. To meet this need, universities need to invest more time in training students in public speaking and debate. The odd group presentation will not do.

Becoming a **T-shaped** professional: In every possible work environment you will work in, you will be collaborating with professionals from different backgrounds. Whilst is essential that you focus on disciplinary training, this cannot be at the expense of developing interdisciplinary competencies. Two simple places to start are by building up your understanding of other professions' knowledge and scope of practice and finding work experience outside of your own 'tribe'. To do that well, it helps if you ask yourself the question . . .

What are your greatest strengths?

Knowing what skills you have and where you need to develop is pivotal to your career. However, without understanding yourself and how you function, you will never be able to narrow down the job search to things that you will be really good at. Call them gifts, talents or even quirks, strengths are what make us thrive at work. Strengths create work engagement, enhanced productivity and citizenship, and they contribute to a general all-round quality of life. How? Because they unlock potential, helping you to become resourceful during difficult moments in your life, garner support and stay centred.

Most interviewers will ask you about your strengths in some form or another, so it is well worth investing some time in developing your self-awareness. We all address problems in a different way, based on our strengths, personality and personal interests, so without awareness of what our strengths are, it is almost impossible to know what skill gaps we might need to plug to function effectively in a team, recover from setbacks and eventually lead and inspire our own teams.

Gallup[2] has demonstrated extensively that strengths really matter for:

1 **Productivity:** Teams that focus on strengths every day have 12.5% greater productivity.
2 **Profitability:** Teams that receive strengths feedback have 8.9% greater profitability.
3 **Turnover:** When employees received strengths feedback, turnover rates were 14.9% lower than for those who did not.
4 **Performance:** Employees who systematically apply their strengths at work are 6.2 times more likely to feel that they have the opportunity to do what they do best every day.
5 **Engagement:** People who use their strengths every day are as much as six times more likely to be engaged on the job. If a manager primarily focuses on an employee's strengths, the likelihood that employee will be actively disengaged is 1%; however, if a manager primarily focuses on an employee's weaknesses, the likelihood that employee will be actively disengaged is 22%.

Versatile
Resilient
Ambitious
Enthusiastic
Authentic ·Honest
Team player Flexible
Open minded
Optimistic Creative thinker Motivated
Interpersonal skills Leadership
Time Responsible
Persistent Relationships
Self controlled Detail oriented
Motivational Analytical
Dependable Writer
Listener Caring Communication
Dedicated Problem solverOrganised
Logical Trustworthy
Integrity
Negotiation Experience
Effective
Management
Technical

Figure 2.5   Find your strengths

What are your blind spots?

This is a bit of a daft question, because if you knew what your blind spots were, they would not be blind spots. However, that doesn't stop people from asking it. What they are really probing at is "Are you aware of the damage that your strengths can cause?" If, for example, you are a persistent, resilient individual who is able to cope with change and pull teams through complex tasks to completion, are you aware of the damage you leave as you take a wrecking ball to the hopes, dreams and plans of your peers? As you climb the ladder to task completion, do you notice their withering bodies rotting on the stairwell? A better question is . . .

What are your greatest weaknesses?

We all differ individually in a multiplicity of ways; we have natural strengths and areas where we do not get such a tremendous return on investment. But being a winner does not mean investing our time and resources into something that doesn't work. Despite your parents' efforts in pressuring you to improve that C in maths, putting more investment and energy into something that is perennially going to fail is a bad idea. If you are in any doubt, imagine investing your hard-earned cash with someone who was continually trying to fix his losing streak on the stock market.

Whilst we ought to be spending time thinking about investing in our strengths, it is still critical to be aware of our weaknesses. Not because not being good at something demonstrates some personal flaw but because this self-awareness is critical in putting together good teams. So rather than recoiling from this question, lean into it, because what is really being asked is "How self-aware are you?" or "How will you fit in our team?"

Avoid waxing lyrical about being a perfectionist or working too hard; those answers will not land well with an interview panel. Equally avoid being too honest by declaring yourself lousy with time management. What you want to do is provide balance. Are you a creative thinker or an ideas person? Great, but those characteristics also bring with them the tendency to be very poor at establishing ideas that are immediately workable. The constant firing out of ideas can give an impression of being unfocused. If you are one of these individuals, then a good answer is, "I am a creative thinker and I am aware that sometimes the way in which I can generate lots of ideas or think in an unstructured way can be a challenge for other team members. To make sure that my ideas are converted into something workable, I like to work closely with teammates who are great at taking my ideas and turning them into something practical". You can also use this in the reverse. Are you someone who is more organised and predictable? Then you can talk about struggling sometimes to find creative new ways of doing things. That you realise how important creative thinking is, so you like to surround yourself with creatives and work closely with them to help turn what can be abstract and unworkable ideas into something that can be executed within the organisation.

These answers are good, because they demonstrate that you are aware that everyone has a common goal. That organisations and teams succeed because of co-ordinated human action. In all cases, whether you are creative or organised, you should give a specific, concrete example. Answers to interview questions that are devoid of narrative are never as strong as those that are grounded in personal experiences. For one thing, without the back story, the interview panel will find you entirely forgettable; second, personal stories add authenticity and third, they are demonstrable evidence that you do in fact have the skills that you are describing.

Top tip: Plan what you want to say, and do not be tempted to try to cover too much ground. Make your message memorable through a story that connects you to them. Then,

1 Say what you are going to say
2 Say it
3 Say what you have just said

Interview question: what is your greatest strength?

In addition to some self-exploration, in preparation for this question in an interview, you should do your research on the organisation in question. If you are applying for a job in data management, you probably do not want to cite your greatest strength as multi-tasking. They will want candidates who are able to attend to detail for long periods of time. When answering, try to give a list of both hard and soft skills that would be strong attributes for the job. For example, outstanding data analysis skills in the handing of quantitative data work best if complemented by natural curiosity and a strong problem-solving mindset.

Always remember that you are a work in progress

Never be afraid to learn from the mistakes of others. Not only does it save you the pain of making the mistake in the first place, but it teaches you crisis management without having a stake in the crisis solution. Despite how awful and plentiful our personal cockups feel, we do not really make enough of them to maximise our learning potential. This is why many organisations use "action learning sets", because they enable professionals to address problems in new ways and learn from the screw-ups of others. There is a reason we pesky academics got you to learn from case studies. By exploring what went well and what went wrong and then developing new ideas and thinking about how to solve problems, everyone can learn from the mistakes of others with a full understanding of how they fell into the pit in the first place without having to fall into the pit themselves.

At university, the peer-mentoring network will be the most immediately productive way to learn from others, particularly if your mentor is a final-year student who has already navigated their way through the student journey and they can guide and advise on the bits you just 'don't get'. The challenge is that, left to their own devices, students have a bad habit of gravitating towards students similar to them. Birds of a feather don't just flock together, they stick together and are damn well afraid of any other flying animal, especially one that looks

bigger and stronger than they are (even though we're all a little bit afraid of bats right now).

In Chapter 3, we talk quite a bit about networking. Building strategic relationships might seem a little superficial to you, but if you really want to do better, you need to surround yourself with high-achieving friends. The quality of information that circulates within a peer group is directly related to the performance of the individuals in that group; high-achieving students make high-achieving friends.[3] So if you are not doing as well as you would like, find yourself a peer mentor, preferably someone who is doing very well and willing to spend time to bring you up to speed. If you are the student who is doing well, then helping or explaining to someone else is an important skill. This is the greater depth that employers will look for. It's not just good enough that you know; it's how you can share this knowledge and improve those around you.

Fun fact

Singapore maths, for example, is a widely used method of teaching primary school children, where top-level children are encouraged to teach peers who are less able. The Singapore system enabled its children to outperform their international peers.

Mentoring and invisible barriers

As if knowing exactly what skills you have and how to perform and advance in your career were not enough, there are silent barriers to be negotiated. The theory goes that as our self-concept develops throughout our career, we develop a clearer understanding of our goals, interests, motivations, skills and abilities. We are able to make increasingly informed decisions about our occupational interests, then use that information to make predictions about where we want to be in the future. Later, we make decisions about and cope with career development challenges. However, a major criticism of this model is that it fails to seriously consider the impact that opportunity has on career decision-making and the role that self-efficacy (our belief in ourselves) plays in shaping our expectations about our goals and career outcomes. In other words, while many white middle-class children are socialised and supported into having a clear sense of their likely career outcomes by adolescence, the inherent nature of the social and economic contexts and the opportunity structures that surround those contexts can be a major obstacle to overcome when making decisions about what interests us and what choices we really have.

Double discrimination (or even triple or quadruple) is a reoccurring theme whereby some forms of prejudice are connected. Intersectionality is the complex interplay of race, sexuality, gender, disability or religion that results in some individuals holding multiple stigmatised identities which interact to shape not only their workplace experiences[4] but also their health and well-being.[5] Simply put, if the stereotypical white middle-class male is the 'ideal', anything that deviates from that normal is less, in some way deficient. For every additional different characteristic, the individual shifts farther from the norm. If the ideal is the white man, a woman is one step away from that ideal, a woman of colour is two steps away, a woman with a head scarf that signals her religion is three steps away and so on. Each one of those different characteristics can result in an individual experiencing compounded discrimination or discrimination by a specific group of people. For example, an Islamic gay woman may experience discrimination from her community for her sexuality but not necessarily experience discrimination on the grounds of sexuality at work. She may, however, be overlooked for client-facing positions because her line management are quietly uncomfortable with her head scarf.

It is not all bad news. Over the past decade, successive governments have been pressuring organisations to do a better job of supporting Black Asian and minority ethic (BAME) people's success in the workforce. It has been estimated that if BAME people had the same opportunities as their white peers, if they were able to participate and progress in the same ways, the United Kingdom would see an £24bn boost each year to the economy.[6] Organisational underperformance, reduced productivity and competitiveness may finally act as a catalyst for enhancing access to employment, leadership and boardroom positions. While the majority of organisations have some way to go, there are a number of excellent examples of best practice in supporting people development, inclusive leadership and promotion practices, along with movements for the transparent publication of statistics.

This is why working with a mentor can help in the navigation of your career journey. Mentoring would appear to have the most substantial impact in giving fairer opportunities for promotion and senior roles. Pairing employees with senior partners, managers, directors and CEOs can open the door to women and black minority ethnics by opening their eyes to a world of possibilities and encouraging them to pursue their ambitions, not just the what and the why of

---

Find yourself a mentor

Before you begin asking people to mentor you, it is important to spend some time exploring why you need a mentor and why this person would be a good fit. Exploring your strengths and your values and thinking and planning for the next stage of your career is critical before preparing your mentoring request. This preparation should be formed from this evidence and then used to outline what you would hope to achieve from the mentoring relationship.

the journey but also the how. The employability benefits are enormous; not only will you come out the other side with improved communication skills, practicing active listening and increased confidence, you will also have the invaluable opportunity to reflect on not only what you have achieved but how you got there. All fodder for that dreaded interview question: *What are your strengths and weaknesses?*

Further reading

BPS, *Become a psychologist*, www.bps.org.uk/public/become-psychologist Any of the "How to become. . . " books on Amazon.

Roth, T. (2007) *Strengths Finder 2.0: A new and upgraded edition of the online test from Gallup's Now Discover Your Strengths*, New York: Gallup.

Table 2.1 Top psychology jobs

Subfields	Role profile	Qualifications and postgraduate training
Clinical psychologist	Clinical psychologists work towards the alleviation of psychological distress and improving well-being. Clinical psychologists work with cases of anxiety and depression but also with serious and enduring mental illness, neurological and developmental disorders, addictive behaviours, childhood behaviours and family relationships. Find out more here: https://careers.bps.org.uk/area/clinical	A BPS-accredited undergraduate degree and then further study on an accredited clinical doctoral programme.
Counselling psychologist	Counselling psychologists apply theory and research in helping clients resolve a range of life issues such as relationship difficulties, bereavement, sexual abuse and trauma. Counselling psychologists differ from clinical psychologists insofar as they have a stronger focus on healthy individuals who have fewer pathological mental health problems. Clinical psychologists often work with more difficult problems such as serious mental health problems and psychosis. Find out more here: https://careers.bps.org.uk/area/counselling	A BPS-accredited undergraduate degree and then an accredited postgraduate qualification in counselling psychology through an accredited doctorate programme or the BPS qualification in counselling psychology.

(Continued)

Table 2.1 Continued

Subfields	Role profile	Qualifications and postgraduate training
Neuro-psychologist	Neuropsychologists focus on how injuries and illness of the brain impact a person's cognitions and behaviours; how they think, feel and behave. Conditions include, for example, dementia, stroke, traumatic brain injury, Parkinson's disease. They often work as part of multidisciplinary teams in a range of health and social care settings, for example, the NHS, rehabilitation services, educational services or for court services. Find out more here: https://careers.bps.org.uk/area/neuro	Trainees will specialise in this area through the doctorate in clinical psychology and then complete the BPS qualification in clinical neuropsychology.
Develop-mental psychologist	Developmental psychologists help us better understand how people develop over the course of their lifespan. By understanding how people change and grow, we can help them live up to their full potential. Developmental psychologists focus not only on children but individuals at all stages of their life course. Developmental psychologists have extensive knowledge of the cognitive, social, intellectual, perceptual, personality and emotional milestones of infants, children and adolescents, but they also offer assistance in adult development issues such as marriage or divorce and aging in later life (for example, retirement and old age). Developmental psychologists are often employed by universities and research institutes, and they also find work in schools, children's homes, mental health facilities and retirement homes. Find out more here: www.apa.org/action/science/developmental/education-training	An undergraduate degree in psychology followed by a period of postgraduate study. For example, a master's focusing on developmental psychology or doctoral study.

Subfields	Role profile	Qualifications and postgraduate training
Educational psychologist	Often working with local education authorities, schools, special education units, colleges and nurseries, educational psychologists work with children who are experiencing social, emotional or learning difficulties by providing assessments, counselling and other interventions. They work one to one with children but also with teachers, families and other professionals so that children are able to reach their potential. They may also be used to consult on learning environments in mainstream education. Find out more here: www.aep.org.uk/	A BPS-accredited undergraduate degree and then an accredited doctorate in educational psychology. In Scotland, an accredited master's course, followed by the qualification in education psychology.
Health psychologist	Psychologists who are involved in the study of the role that psychological, behavioural and cultural factors play in our physical health and illness are often known as health psychologists. As many factors can directly impact our well-being, health psychologists use their knowledge and skills to further understand well-being and to promote healthier lifestyles. They achieve this through what is known as the biopsychosocial model, which is an approach that promotes understanding of health through a multifaceted lens. For example, there is the biological aspect (a tumour or virus), the social process (social group, ethnicity), behavioural facets (our preferences and habits) and also the psychological (our emotions and thoughts). Find out more here: https://careers.bps.org.uk/area/health	A BPS-accredited undergraduate degree and accredited master's degree in health psychology. Two years' structured supervised practice on Stage 2 of the BPS qualification in health psychology.

(Continued)

Table 2.1 Continued

Subfields	Role profile	Qualifications and postgraduate training
Forensic psychologist	Working in a wide range of settings, forensic psychologists typically work with law enforcement agencies, rehabilitation centres, law firms and other government agencies. They typically carry out psychological assessments of prisoners, explore evidence for psychological disorders and evaluate mental health of defendants. They will often provide psychotherapeutic support and counselling as well as carrying out their own research into the causes and impact of offending behaviour. Find out more here: https://nationalcareers.service.gov.uk/job-profiles/forensic-psychologist	A BPS-accredited undergraduate degree and accredited master's degree in forensic psychology. Two years' structured supervised practice on Stage 2 of the BPS qualification in forensic psychology.
Sport psychologist	Sports science is an interdisciplinary science that synthesises knowledge from a diverse range of fields, including biomechanics, physiology, kinesiology and psychology, with the aim of applying this knowledge to help athletes and non-athletes enhance their performance and achieve their goals. Sports psychologists examine how psychological factors influence performance, how engaging in sport can impact psychological and physical well-being. They might work one to one with athletes in helping them regulate their performance in the face of intense pressure or help athletes overcome injury, but also with non-athletes, perhaps helping them stick to an exercise routine. Find out more here: https://careers.bps.org.uk/area/sport-exercise	A BPS-accredited undergraduate degree and accredited master's degree in sport and exercise psychology. Two years' structured supervised practice on Stage 2 of the BPS qualification in sport and exercise psychology.

Subfields	Role profile	Qualifications and postgraduate training
Researcher	A substantive component of qualifying as a psychologist involves training and development in the scientific method. From the undergraduate level, students are immersed in experimental methods and statistics. They learn to formulate and test research questions, design and conduct experiments and collect and analyse data, as well as reporting those findings and drawing conclusions. Find out more here: https://careers. bps.org.uk/area/academia-research-teaching	Although research training can feel intensive, as undergraduates, most students will not graduate with the advanced understanding, skill development and experience necessary to work in a fully psychological research setting (although those skills may be suitable for work in other fields). Most students will require a further period of study. This will normally take the form of a master's degree in research methods and/or a doctoral degree (PhD) which is the product of 3–5 years of study, culminating in an original piece of research.
Occupa-tional/ business psychologist	Psychologists who focus on how people behave at work have a range of job titles, but most typically they are described in the United Kingdom as an occupational or business psychologist. They focus on human behaviour in the workplace (physical and virtual) in order to increase aspects such as productivity, job satisfaction and organisational effectiveness. Find out more here: https://theabp.org.uk/ and here: www.bps.org.uk/member-microsites/division-occupational-psychology/careers	A BPS-accredited undergraduate degree and accredited master's degree in occupational psychology. Two years' structured supervised practice on Stage 2 of the BPS qualification in occupational psychology. Industrial and business psychologists vary in their training. They may have completed an undergraduate

(Continued)

Table 2.1 Continued

Subfields	Role profile	Qualifications and postgraduate training
		or postgraduate qualification accredited by the Association for Business Psychology.
Engineering	Normally a branch of occupational psychology, engineering psychologists apply their expertise in the study of how humans interact with technology and machines. They apply that knowledge in the design of products and services, improving technology and consumer products as well as working in areas such as residential homes, medicine, health and safety, military and aviation, the government or for software and engineering firms. Find out more here: www.apa.org/gradpsych/2007/03/engineering and here: https://committedtoscience.org.uk/?gclid=EAIaIQobChMI0J zMosT86gIVB7LtCh3IEQqtEAAYAiA AEgJhrPD_BwE	Engineering psychologists do not normally hold postgraduate qualifications. Typical routes for postgraduate advancements include training as occupational psychologists and specialising in human factors or doctoral study (PhD) focusing on engineering psychology as a research topic.
Cyber-psychology	As our reliance on technology has increased, engineering psychology has become a significant growth area, as has the area of cyberpsychology. Cyberpsychology is the study of the human mind and behaviour in the internet and cyberspace, specifically how technology impacts the ways in which people think and behave. For example, they might be interested in examining how social media impacts our connectivity with others and how identity and self-concept are shaped. Other areas include how new skills and knowledge are developed in a virtual environment, how mobile phones have changed our behaviours, how virtual communication changes team behaviours and collaborative working.	A number of universities offer undergraduate programmes in cyberpsychology and postgraduate qualifications such as the master's in cyberpsychology. For an up-to-date list of accredited programmes, see the British Psychological Society.

Subfields	Role profile	Qualifications and postgraduate training
	Cyberpsychology is still a relatively new discipline, and as such, the majority of positions tend to be in areas related to consultation and research. With the increase in online learning and technology uptake in schools and colleges, the education sector is a growth area for the employment of cyberpsychologists. Find out more here: www.bps.org.uk/member-microsites/cyberpsychology-section	
Political psycho-logists	Political psychology is a specialist field within politics whereby psychologists use their training and experience to examine politics, politicians and political behaviour. It is not uncommon for political psychologists to be employed by governments to help understand issues such as voting behaviour, attitudes to policy making or the role of the media in political behaviour. Find out more here: www.ispp.org/	An MSc in political psychology may be beneficial. Such degrees also provide opportunities to combine with other subjects, such as international relations.

Table 2.2 Psychology-related careers

Other careers	Role profile	Qualifications and postgraduate training
Data scientist/ statistics specialist	Data creation, management, analysis and visualisation. Database management; working with 'big data'. Employers include industry, government and charities. Find out more here: www.ons.gov.uk/aboutus/careers	On the job, although many courses exist at postgraduate or 'bootcamp' level. Joining online communities is also an excellent way to stay up to date with major and emergent trends in data science.

(Continued)

Table 2.2 Continued

Other careers	*Role profile*	*Qualifications and postgraduate training*
Ethics and humanitarian work	Human rights work poses difficult, fundamental questions. It is a net which operates to provide safety and ensure that all of us, in particular the most vulnerable in our societies, are shielded from risk, injustice and incompetence. Find out more here: www.amnesty.org.uk/get-involved	None.
Politics	This role involves developing a good understanding of local and national issues and being up to date with current affairs. As an intern, you will likely be using your psychology degree working as a research caseworker for an MP, developing further into playing an integral part in political events that will shape the future of our nation. Find out more here: www.parliament.uk/about/working/jobs/ Graduate programmes are listed here: www.parliament.uk/about/working/faststream/	Become involved with your student union and engage in student-related issues, or perhaps become involved with a trade union. Postgraduate programmes are available nationally.
MI5, MI6, GCHQ	The security services offer a range of jobs and training programmes to graduates. Psychology graduates can find varied careers in areas such as cyberpsychology, data analysis and intelligence. Find out more here: www.mi5.gov.uk/careers/working-at-mi5	On the job.
Media psychologist	Social media and the media more broadly hold tremendous power to change the way people think and behave. The ways in which different genders, races and sexualities are portrayed and how issues of diversity and inclusion are addressed change how we think. If psychologists can change how people think, they can change how they behave.	Postgraduate study. Master's degrees are an option but not required.

Other careers	Role profile	Qualifications and postgraduate training
	Media psychologists apply their understanding of the ways in which people form and maintain attitudes, how bias is formed and how it is prevented. They apply their skills and knowledge in this area in a diverse range of professions. For example, designing advertising campaigns or projecting images or storylines in entertainment programmes, they work in the entertainment industry shaping our emotions through drama and humour and with politicians in the use of propaganda that shapes policies and ideological thinking. Find out more: https://careersinpsychology.org/becoming-a-media-psychologist/	
Careers advisor	Careers advisors provide advice, information and guidance to help individuals make decisions about career paths and different industries and sectors as well as giving direction and advice on additional training and education. The work is varied. You may be working to design digital and print literature, carrying out face-to-face consultations, running group sessions or giving public talks. The scope of the role is not limited to university students. Advisors also work with school children over the age of 13 or adults who are seeking a career change. There are also a number of specialist areas where careers advisors play a vital role in transforming people's lives by helping people overcome barriers to employment, such as working with adults with learning disabilities or with ex-offenders. Find out more: https://nationalcareers.service.gov.uk/	Postgraduate programmes do exist.

(Continued)

Table 2.2   Continued

Other careers	*Role profile*	*Qualifications and postgraduate training*
Police officer	The Police Now National Graduate Leadership Programme is a salaried two-year graduate training programme where you'll develop skills in leadership, negotiation, problem solving, decision-making and emotional intelligence. During the two-year programme, you will become a visible, reliable and proud leader in the community you serve. Find out more: www.policenow. org.uk/national-graduate-leadership-programme/	On-the-job training.
Business management	Management trainee posts vary from sector to sector, so it is important to think about why you are interested in this industry. Roles are varied and include positions such as HR management, public relations, market research, communications, consulting and business ethics or coaching. Find out more: https://targetcareers. co.uk/career-sectors/business/338-would-a-career-in-business-suit-me	Industry-specific postgraduate courses exist.
Play therapist	Working with children and young adolescents, making sense of difficult life experiences and complex psychological issues through play. Find out more: www.bapt.info/play-therapy/job-description/	Psychology degree and work experience. CPD opportunities exist nationally.
Art/creative therapist	Art, music and drama can be particularly helpful when there are things people cannot say in words. This could be because the emotions are too distressing. Art and creative therapists design activities to support people to explore and address their mental health issues. Find out more: www.healthcareers. nhs.uk/explore-roles/wider-healthcare-team/roles-wider-healthcare-team/clinical-support-staff/creative-therapy-support-roles	CPD opportunities exist nationally.

Notes

1 Kahneman, D. (2011). *Thinking, fast and slow*. Farrar, Straus and Giroux.
2 Asplund, J. (2012). *Seven reasons to lead with strengths*. Gallup. Retrieved from www.gallup.com/workplace/236930/seven-reasons-lead-with-strengths.aspx
3 Flashman, J. (2012). Academic achievement and its impact on friend dynamics. *Sociology of Education, 85*(1), 61–80. doi:10.1177/0038040711417014
   Vignery, K., & Laurier, W. (2020). Achievement in student peer networks: A study of the selection process, peer effects and student centrality. *International Journal of Educational Research, 99*. doi:10.1016/j.ijer.2019.101499
4 Lavaysse, L. M., Probst, T. M., & Arena, D. F., Jr. (2018). Is more always merrier? Intersectionality as an antecedent of job insecurity. *International Journal of Environmental Research and Public Health, 15*(11), 2559. doi:10.3390/ijerph15112559
5 Perry, B. L., Harp, K. L., & Oser, C. B. (2013). Racial and gender discrimination in the stress process: Implications for African American women's health and well-being. *Sociological Perspectives: SP: Official Publication of the Pacific Sociological Association, 56*(1), 25–48.
6 McGregor-Smith, R. (2017). *Race in the workplace report*. Retrieved from https://assets.publishing.service.gov.uk/government/uploads/system/uploads/attachment_data/file/594336/race-in-workplace-mcgregor-smith-review.pdf

Chapter 3

Tell me what you want, what you really, really want?

Legend has it that that Socrates once plunged his student's head (some say this was Plato) under water until he turned blue. Plato had come to Socrates to ask him for knowledge. Socrates walked the student to the sea, waited until the water was shoulder height and then plunged the boy underwater. The student kicked and fought until he turned blue, at which point Socrates grabbed him and pulled him up. "Why did you do that?" demanded the student. "What do you want?" responded Socrates. "Knowledge", Plato said. Then Socrates plunged him back under the water until Plato finally blacked out. This time, Socrates pulled him back up and dragged him out of the water and resuscitated him. "What do you want?" Socrates asked again. "Air", responded the student. "Good", said Socrates. "Now, when you desire knowledge as much as you desire air, come back and see me – then we will talk about knowledge".

Most vice chancellors now disapprove of lecturers who regularly waterboard their students, but most heads of department will turn a blind eye to a bit of light "ducking". The point is that there is a great difference between wanting something and truly needing it. When you need something, you will put the work in. You will spend time, quite literally, inside of that desire. Alexandre Dumas (*Three Musketeers, The Count of Monte Cristo* and other great works) wrote over 100,000 pages of literature by hand in his 40-year career. He also found time to campaign for the unification of Italy, was a royal scribe, ran a newspaper and much more. All of this whilst managing being mixed race in the 1840s. In fact, his father's nickname in the army was "the black devil". So, along with others such as Victor Hugo and countless other examples, those guys and girls, they certainly knew about drive, ambition and a go get 'em attitude.

What ever you do, use your full ass

My kids know not to say to me they 'did their best' or one of those half-arsed 'I tried' variants, because it is almost exclusively met with 'well, do better'. Best is only what you have done before. Which is negative and backward facing, not looking forward and trying to better. Sure, personal bests are looked to be bettered in sport all the time, but they are bests that are tangible. Like 10 seconds to run 100 meters or 2 meters 5 in the high jump. The coach or trainer doesn't have a

BESTOMETER 5000

'bestometer' because it doesn't exist. Economists, sales directors and businessmen and -women always want to improve all the time. Year-on-year growth, quarterly comparisons and ever-increasing sales targets. Why? Because maintaining something is really hard to do. Normally, when you reach a plateau and stay there for any length of time, the only way to go is down. So, don't be half-arsed about getting stuff done.

When we want to get something done, we set ourselves specific goals and deadlines in order to get where we want to be. We set ourselves these goals because we know what we need to achieve in order to progress. Whether it is in our careers, our lifestyle or our fitness, goals create a specific psychological reaction that makes us all the more motivated to accomplish the goals we have set ourselves. Goal setting works to promote our performance by directing our attention and effort, because even if you march a hundred steps a minute trying to get to Chester from Bath, it's going to take a really long time if you are facing York. Focus and direction help energise our behaviour so that we are able to perform persistently, commit prolonged effort and seek out and use strategies that help us succeed, and employers will want to know about your journey.

You are going to need that focus and energy to find that job, deal with the rejection from that job interview, pick yourself up again and try to get that job, pick yourself up again and then eventually get that job. Then you have to keep that job and get promoted in that job before you start the process all over again because you want a new job. The search for employment is for life, not just for graduates, and the journey starts the minute you start university and never really stops, even in retirement (see Bravestarts: www.bravestarts. com/).

In the words of Mahatma Gandhi, "Strength does not come from a physical capacity. It comes from indomitable will".[1] Indomitable will is the difference between failure and success, and it is the power to do whatever is needed to achieve what needs to be done. From Justin Gallegos, the first professional marathon runner with cerebral palsy to sign with Nike, to Chris Gardener, who raised his toddler whilst homeless before eventually founding his own brokerage firm (Gardener is played by Will Smith in *The Pursuit of Happyness*), indomitable will is the unquestionable drive to succeed that will spur us onwards to break records, to save our children from a life of poverty, to reach far beyond our comfort zones and to persevere in the face of adversity. If your indomitable superpowers are a bit low at the moment, do not worry, because willpower can be learned, developed and enhanced, and trust me, you are going to need some indomitability to cope with rejection and remain completely focused on the bigger picture.

In focus career story: clinical psychology

"Becoming a qualified psychologist is difficult; there is presently only one route in the UK to do so. Every year (around September time) thousands of hopeful applicants apply to up to four of their chosen universities via the clearing house system. There are a limited number of positions per course centre and competition is fierce. The first time I applied I got as far as two interviews with two universities; this was followed by two rejections. The second year I applied I had four interviews and was accepted onto one course (I was placed on the 'waiting list' for the other three – a kind of applicant purgatory which relies on other successful applicants rejecting offers; if a place does not become available then you are left having to wait a whole year to apply again)".

Tamsin Williams, Clinical Psychologist

Habits and happiness

From Gok Wan persuading us that we can 'look good naked', Khloé Kardashian teaching us how to get that revenge body and Trinny and Suzanna and their magic knickers – I mean, who doesn't love a good misery/transformation show? *Bibbidi bobbidi boo* – five gay men with killer outfits and one-liners pitch up and fix our insecurities, improve our outlook on life and make us look fabulous. We are no longer enslaved and shackled to our rag-ridden misery, hardship and suffering. At last, 'You are living your best life, queen' (that fecking phrase again!).

Imagine what psychology would be like if Freud had known about magic knickers. Not only do magic knickers flatten your bumps and pick your boobs up from the floor, magic knickers are able to channel positivity and fight toxic femininity, and they may even be able to reform your moral character. Let's get real. It doesn't matter how many uplifting and inspirational Makeover Guy® videos you watch or that post-breakup hair transformation, that new hair colour is not going to change your life. To know how to change, we have to understand the psychology of habits, and to do that, we have to start with self-control. Self-control, discipline and willpower all mean pretty much the same thing. They are our capacity to exert control to do something and to restrain impulses that get in the way of that action. The problem is that self-control is effortful: it takes self-control to be self-controlled. In fact, if you google "self-control doesn't work", you will find innumerable disgruntled Mac users trying to troubleshoot "SelfControl". If Apple cannot make self-control work, then how can we as mere mortals rely on it?

The reason self-control doesn't work is because of our habits. Habits both eliminate the need for self-control and create the conditions whereby we need self-control to conquer our habits. That glass of wine which was once a delicious treat at the end of the day slowly turns into a habitual bottle of wine. Scrolling through Facebook at bedtime looking at your friends' latest posts morphs into late night email checking and binge watching on Netflix. That one time sleeping in for an extra 15 minutes then just about making the train to work soon turns into a last-minute panicked morning commute. Habits make us become numb to our behaviours, and then we try to use self-control to fix the problem, and it doesn't work. In particular, when you are stressed and overworked, your self-control will go out of its way to persuade you that it is a prodigiously good idea to go out and get trolleyed with your mates. The only thing that works are more habits, habits that eventually replace the bad habits. People who have good habits are freed from self-control. They are free because their habits are already integrated into their lives and they can operate those behaviours on autopilot. They no longer need to spend energy making decisions choosing between the things they think they ought to be doing, they are less worried and anxious, they cope with stress and conflict better and, critically, they have more time.[2]

Good habits are hard to form because bad habits are so rewarding. It isn't just Sheryl Crow who loves a good beer buzz early in the morning; just look round you the next time you are catching an early morning flight to Ayia Napa. When a behaviour happens and the context is rewarding, the brain takes note. We might 'know' what we are doing is a bit less than ideal, but your brain is just coding the actions, the thoughts and the feel-good factor, and it is remarkably good at providing a compelling incentive to repeat the activity again. It does this because those pesky habits are actually very efficient.

Your brain uses more power than any other organ in the body, about 20% of the body's energy. There are some fearsome debates in neuropsychology around the metabolic cost of self-control,[3] and whilst the jury is still out on whether self-control uses more energy than any other cognitive function, in general, mental processes require energy, and the brain doesn't have an unlimited supply. This is why your brain loves habits. Habits become physically wired into the basal ganglia of your brain, and the brain can then use its resources to feed other cellular activities.

The good news is that it is possible to hardwire the good habits just as much as the bad ones. The more you do something or behave in a specific way, the more your brain adapts. The right thought processes and behaviours, when repeated in the right contexts, will create brain connections that develop us into better businesspeople and better athletes and make us better at speaking languages. This 'neuroplasticity' even explains why it is possible for some people to completely recover from neural injuries and strokes. If we simply accept that our brains are in control and there's nothing we can do about it, we are falling down the rabbit hole of failure. Neuroplasticity, however, helps us recognise that knowledge is always changing and so are our brains.

So, with enough work, we can develop our brains to work for us rather than assuming that they are in charge, and the secrets to that success are goals and their relationship with dopamine.

Goals!

There is quite a lot of very poor advice on goal setting which seems to have been largely written on the back of a fag packet. SMART goals, for example, make a regular appearance in university skills programmes and with self-help gurus and lifestyle coaches. Who doesn't love a good acronym that can dumb down a complex process and make us all feel like all we need to do is get ourselves a notepad and pen? For every complex problem, there is an answer that is clear, simple and completely wrong. Don't get me wrong, there is a reason that everyone is interested in goal setting; it works, but it takes more effort than most people think.

A goal is an idea of the future or desired result that a person envisions, plans for and commits to achieving. Goals mobilise our effort, direct our attention and encourage us to persist in the face of challenges. The hidden secret of goal setting lies in the fact that our brains cannot differentiate between what we want and what we have. Instead, the brain absorbs the information of what we want and projects it onto our self-image. When our reality doesn't match up to our self-image, we are all the more likely to motivate ourselves to change the reality of what we see in the mirror to the self-image we have in our brains.

We have a unique reward and punishment system in our brains to support this, and this system is stronger than anything that we can ever put in place for ourselves. It tops your endurance level playlist, your mother's 'positive encouragement' and Cosmo the yoga guru who 'tailors each session to each individual's abilities and gets the best out of everyone'. When we achieve a goal, our brains produce dopamine, creating a sense of pleasure in our achievements. When we fail at attaining a goal, this dopamine production cuts off, and this is not pleasant! The pain caused by the lack of dopamine makes us all the more motivated to keep working towards our goals and get that dopamine back into our systems.

There are six important guidelines to get your brain on board and keep you motivated (or in as much pain) as possible.

Step 1: write down life value goals

> In my back pocket in my wallet is a boarding pass with my goals for this year. I don't really want to share them with anyone else. They are just my little goals; I'll try and achieve those, and I'll take that boarding pass out at the end of the year and see how well I've done.
>
> Rory McIlroy[4]

Writing down what we want to achieve keeps us accountable for what we want to do. If we are constantly looking at reminders of our goals, then we are less likely to get demotivated and stop working towards them. Something special happens when we write down our goals. The brain's encoding processes are streamlined and improved. The same principles apply to studying. Copying out verbatim from a textbook doesn't improve your performance (no, it really doesn't, so pack it in) but generating the material yourself does, because the processes that are involved are more complex, and that means not only is recall generally improved but recall for really important things like goals is greatly improved. For that reason, revising your goals on a daily basis, looking at those goals and plans and articulating again what you want to achieve and how you are going to achieve it will make your goals vivid and improve the chances of success.

Step one is learning how to write down your goals properly so that your brain can easily encode them. To do this, you need to avoid the conditions of vagueness, confusion and fuzzy-mindedness.

Clarify what you want in life, then set goals to achieve what you want in life. Write down your goals and say why they are important to you. Explore how those goals relate to your values, as this will help you determine what it is that motivates you. Try to be specific. If you find yourself formulating broad, vague or ill-defined goals, then spend some time reviewing and revising the manifestation of those goals within context. 'I want to be a better writer' is a clear step in the writer direction, but it is also so broad that it can overwhelm. You need something more specific so you know where to start, why you are starting and what the rewards could be. For example,

Goal: I want to be a better writer.
Rationale: I want to be a better writer because I have things I want to say. Things I feel others would want to listen to, but the quality of my writing gets in the way of that message.
Subgoals: To become a better writer, I will:
1 Read more and study the writings of others. I want my writing to instruct and inspire, and to learn how to do that, I shall read and study the writings of others who instruct and inspire.
2 Write something every day and experiment with different styles that could work with different audiences.
3 Find a mentor who is willing to help me develop my voice by reviewing and critiquing my work.

Exercise one skill

Take a page and write down now the list of achievements that you can visualise for yourself in the next two years. Write in the present tense and use positive language so that your plans make immediate sense and can be processed by your neuroplastic brain.

What one skill, if I developed it and practiced it in an excellent fashion, would have the greatest impact on your career? This is a question that should guide your career for the rest of your life. Look to yourself for this answer; you probably already know what it is. Ask your friends, ask your family. Then, whatever the answer is, work each day to bring up your performance in this area.

Step 2: a commitment to action

Goals are not aspirations. I can aspire to be thinner, to be paid more money, to be happier but not actually set about doing very much about it other than ruminating or feeling annoyed. However, people who are committed to their goals will work unrelentingly in the face of setbacks and failures to achieve what they want. Commitment is most effectively leveraged when we consider how our goals are aligned with who we are. These are the goals that people will work longer and harder for, because alignment fosters ownership and ownership fosters value-driven committed action.

Goals that are not aligned with who you are (self-concordant) are not goals that are truly owned, and they will not elicit the correct behaviours. Therefore, your goals need to be grounded in what matters to you, not what wider society has persuaded you is key. Think about how your goals are aligned with the person you really are and what matters to you. What is your goal story? Why are you doing what it is you are doing.

Concordance: *Writing matters to me because I value clarity. Writing helps me exercise what I see, what I believe and what I care about and then share that message with others.*

Where does that value come from? *My father was a poet and a musician, but most of all, he was a compelling storyteller. When I was a child, he would take me for long walks through the countryside or along the beach, telling me stories of his childhood. My sister and I would ask him to repeat those stories over and over again. I wish I could create that experience for others.*

How will you feel if you cannot achieve your goal? *When I am not writing, I feel like something is wrong and I do not know how to put it right. I feel perpetually disappointed with myself. I want to stop feeling like that.*

What barriers/challenges/hurdles are in your way? Many people will have a confidence issue or time management or commitment problem that means they just keep getting in their own way. They pay too much attention to inner chatter of why I cannot or why I should not and will seek out information to confirm their worst fears about themselves. If you are one of those people, then ask yourself, 'What emotion am I seeking?' Rather than seeking proof that you are no good and feeding your brain with evidence that you are a one-star individual, start exploring the world as it really is. The writer Seth Godin has a great explanation when he says, "When I go and I read my one-star reviews, I know what emotion I just signed up to get. I have never met a signed author who said I am a much better author now because I read all their one-star reviews". Stop writing and reading your own one-star reviews.

What will you do to overcome these hurdles? *I need to build in other habits to support my writing. I need to think about what those habits will be. For example, I could get up earlier and start writing when there is nobody about at home. That would give me some protected time when I do not feel guilty about taking time out of other activities.* Time to go back to the start recrafting your subgoals, then . . .

Step 3: revisit step 1 and then step 2 again

Most people find that when they complete step 2, this is where the real goal setting begins. So, go right back to step 1 and start again. You may find you need to do this a few times to build up a detailed goal commitment plan.

Step 4: statement of intent

At this point, you should have a deeper sense of what you want to achieve and why you want to achieve it. This self-understanding creates the right environment for one of the most fundamental principles of goal achievement, that of goal commitment. This commitment is the extent to which you are galvanised towards achieving your desired outcome.

We can make those commitments to ourselves, but sometimes it can be helpful to draw on the strengths of others at this point to publicly affirm our commitment (a bit like marriage vows). However, for this social pressure to work, the timing and the audience have to be just right. There is a very common pitfall when we are setting our goals, and this is the social element of them. The more we talk about our goals, the more praise and encouragement we receive. This creates an almost pre-achievement dopamine reaction in our brains, which can mean that we get lazy and presume that we have already achieved the goal we have set. If, however, you spend more time crafting your goal story (steps 1–3) and then share this information with someone you perceive to be of high status, you are far more likely to stay the course, because your commitment to achieving that goal is enhanced.[5] When we tell someone of perceived higher status, that relationship triggers an evaluation apprehension. We worry about being judged favourably or otherwise by someone whose opinion really matters to us. This social context creates additional pressure which changes our behaviour, and our likelihood of achievement is enhanced. So tell your mentor!

Step 5: make it measurable

Real measurements are key to a good goal. The praise you get for setting the goal will be nice, but you won't feel a sense of achievement until you've hit that measurement.

Measurement: "This week I will write a 2000-word blog post on career goal setting for students" is better than "I want to write something every day and experiment with different styles that could work with different audiences". The more detailed you can make that measurement plan, the better the outcomes. For example, adding *one* career building activity to your résumé every six months (examples could include volunteering, blogging, joining a committee or professional organisation) is better than "building my résumé". You need measurement processes that enable you to be specific about the degree of your success, and they will ensure that you direct your resources towards the right activities. A goal of just getting interviewed could, for example, direct resources towards sending out multiple generic applications that will simply end up in the bin. The goal of two interviews per month focuses attention on a few high-quality and appropriate applications that match your interests, skills and knowledge. There are no shortcuts to finding a great job, so researching those organisations takes time and effort. This strategy is, however, far more likely to have a successful outcome than making blanket job applications. When you know you have to identify one career-building activity every six months, planning for that activity keeps you focused on your current strivings, helps you avoid career complacency and reduces the chances that you will take an unnecessary, unproductive detour and do things exceptionally well that never actually needed to be done in the first place.

It is probably also worth pointing out that competent measurement skills are valued by employers. Staff who know how and what to measure stop organisations from measuring the wrong things and going down blind alleys and avoid the availability heuristic and becoming organisationally complacent. So, the sooner you start thinking about tracking your performance, the better. Good habits and activities are habit forming. The old adage that the first year of university doesn't count doesn't stand any more. Employers offering that great job look at what you've done over a longer period (past behaviour being the greatest predictor of future behaviour and all that). The greatest of jobs require considerable investment from the employer, so they want to minimise the risk of placement failure. So, the more positive history you create, the higher your chance of gaining that "pot of gold at the end of the rainbow" job.

Step 6: become reward literate

What does success look like? What does success feel like? What is your gold star? Understanding your reward systems is something that is rarely attended to enough, which is unfortunate because understanding what the prizes are helps people stay goal oriented. The process is circular; individuals become engaged because they are experiencing rewards, and because they are experiencing rewards, they are engaged.

The response–consequence relationship can be positive, but it can also be negative. Therefore, understanding your rewards will also help you avoid derailment (more on that in a moment). The trick is also to try to identify what psychologists call the "coercive contingencies". In other words, rewards that either related to someone else's goals – *If I do not get a good degree, my parents will be disappointed in me* – or rewards that are more about punishment than reward – *If I do not get a good degree, I will be a failure, and nobody will ever want to employ me*. Achievement under these circumstances gives permission to stop. Such rewards and punishments produce escape and avoidance behaviours: low energy, lack of focus, lack of time and even sickness are used to explain lack of engagement and poor performance. Lack of ownership for both success (*I succeeded because of my parents' pressure*) and failure (*I failed because of my parents' pressure*) acts to insulate us from taking responsibility when things go wrong and enjoying our achievements when things go well.

Again, this problem comes down to lack of ownership. Lack of ownership can result in people just sticking to what is safe and then just stopping working all together. In other words, achievement under these circumstances gives us permission to stop, so rather than working to decrease the negatives, work to increase the positives. We are much more likely to work for something that we want and we enjoy rather than constantly criticising ourselves and feeling bad about our current achievements. Keep goals positively oriented and you will find yourself much more motivated to keep going when things go wrong.

An unshakable, shaken truth

"I volunteered to work in a mental health charity running drama clubs and cooking classes with people suffering from severe psychiatric conditions. Early on, there were days when I felt I was making a small and important difference, but very quickly I was overwhelmed with feelings of disgust, fear and anger. It was a horrendously chaotic, confounding and complicated experience. I would show and tell people 'how to do it' but they would end up acting like I was an intrusion and a disturbance to their lives. My compassion eventually took a holiday and I found myself on the verge of exploding with resentment at what I would describe as the overwhelming heaviness of mental illness. I was starting to blame the people I wanted to help. This realisation was like a side punch. It didn't matter how much I tired or what courses I studied: I knew that I would never, ever be 'qualified' for the job".

Anon Student

Step 4: good task management

Spending your time on low-value tasks or misdirected activities with no clear beginning or end is to be avoided at all costs. So, students, you must eat some

3imagine that you have to eat a live frog (sorry, vegetarians). You must eat it, and there is no escape. Write down your strategy for eating that frog. When will you eat that frog? How would you eat that frog? The tasks you don't want to do are the frogs you must eat. So figure out when you can best manage those frogs and eat them one by one.

How students approach this task can tell us a lot of their problem-solving style or lack thereof. Most will aim to eat the frog in one go first thing in the morning (which rather nicely reflects the caustic route of frog eating recommended by the French witticist Nicholas Chamfort: "We should swallow a toad every morning, in order to fortify ourselves against the disgust of the rest of the day"), but some will opt to torture themselves by carving the frog up and eating it in little bits over a longer period of time. If you are one of these students, take action. If you have to eat a live frog, it does you no good to stare at it all day. It is still going to be there; it is going to try to make friends with you, and then it will be even harder to eat.

Planning each day sounds pretty obvious, but there are many people who just wander through the week generating lots of activity but getting very little done. Largely this is because they spend their time reacting to whatever is taking place at that moment. It takes quite a lot of energy to be constantly responding to clutter, so think, plan and execute your day. The sense of accomplishment that comes with a successful day doesn't just increase productivity; it also lowers anxiety.

Source: DILBERT © 2013 Scott Adams, Inc. Used by permission of ANDREWS MCMEEL SYNDICATION. All rights reserved

Apparently, Mark Twain took the sport of frog eating to new heights by arguing that if you had two frogs to eat, you should always eat the ugliest one first. In other words, identify the biggest, hardest, most unpleasant task that you have to do and start with that. Discipline yourself to start it, and do not stop until it is completed. In particular, deadlines are deadly. They give people permission to wait. This is where the Eisenhower (Ike) Matrix can really help (Figure 3.1) by helping to indicate what you should work on and when you should be working on it.

Important activities have an outcome directly related to the achievement of our goals. For example, spending time researching the organisations we are interested in, crafting a great CV, meeting with the careers service. Urgent activities demand immediate attention and are often related to someone else's goals. For example, you may have a deadline to apply for a job or to prepare for an interview. These are the ones that you have to focus on, because the consequences of not dealing with them are immediate. The trick is to ensure the non-urgent is scheduled and managed before it makes it into the urgent section. You really do not want to be putting together your organisational research and PowerPoint presentation the night before an interview.

Exercise: Ike

Use Ike to manage your performance. Make a list of everything that you do this week.

1 Which one of those tasks contributes the most to your academic performance?
2 Which contributes the second most value?
3 Which contributes the third?
4 If there were one thing on that list that you would do all day long, what would it be?

Items 1, 2, and 3 are your productivity. Everything else is a support function. Keep them out of your peak performance time.

Good timekeeping empowers you not only to achieve what you need to do, but it also improves your motivation, lowers stress levels and reduces the chances of error. Timekeeping will be used as a measure of your performance and productivity in the workplace, so don't wait until you start work to figure out how you can improve your punctuality. Another very strong reason for you to start taking time seriously at this point in your career is that at an interview, you may be asked about time management. Good answers to interview questions are rich answers, peppered with timekeeping strategies and analogies of when good timekeeping saved the day. However, good time management is not being early. Being too early and inconveniencing your host, your lecturer or your employer can be demotivating and rather selfish. That's not to say that if your final essay

Eisenhower Matrix
Urgent-Important Matrix

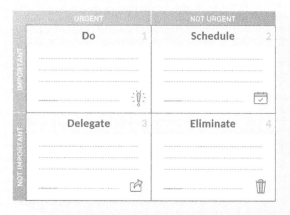

Figure 3.1   The Ike time management matrix

is submitted 10 days early that your lecturer will get annoyed, but don't expect them to grade it 10 days sooner.

Exercise hacks

Your phone as your coach

There are hundreds of apps available for your phone to help you achieve your goals, but how many of them really work? Goal setting can be complex, as no two goals are achieved the same way, but we've found and reviewed three glorious little apps to help you become the person you want to be.

Goals on Track allows you to track your goal, the purpose of your goal, the start date and the desired achievement date, then create a sort of action plan of smaller goals in order to achieve it. The app visually tracks the progress you have made towards your goal, so seeing how far you have come can help to motivate you further. www.goalsontrack.com/

Strides has a very pretty, very simple layout that looks almost like a dashboard. The app allows you to track in three different kinds of ways: targets, habits and average tracking. This allows the user to develop habits in order to achieve their goals, as well as tracking smaller goals in relation to their long-term goal. www.stridesapp.com/

Coach.Me is a great app for those who achieve goals better with plans. Users can create their plan and share it with the community and even join other users' plans. This social aspect of the app creates much more responsibility on the user, as others can see the progress they are making. However, if you prefer to be selective about with whom you share your goals, this app can be quite daunting. www.coach.me/

The circle of life

Goals are more of a cycle than a linear process. Each step takes exploration, reflection, further exploration, reflection and then planning, which may ultimately need to be replanned. The secret is to become not just more self aware but also more aware of what surrounds you. What surrounds you is your history, influences, values and strengths and how to draw on those to be able to stop, breathe and ask yourself, Where am I? What am I doing? To be present and in the moment, then mindfully choose what next and how. In the next chapter, we build on this skill set to help you understand and manage 'your brand'.

Further viewing

Dr. Lara Boyd describes how neuroplasticity gives you the power to shape the brain you want. Recorded at TEDxVancouver at Rogers Arena on November 14, 2015. "After watching this, your brain will not be the same" www.youtube.com/watch?v=LNHBMFCzznE

Merzeich, M. (2004) Growing evidence of brain plasticity, TED, TED Conferences, LLC. www.ted.com/talks/michael_merzenich_growing_evidence_of_brain_plasticity?language=en

Shawn Achor argues that, actually, happiness inspires us to be more productive. The happy secret to better work video. TEDxBloomington, May 2011 www.ted.com/talks/shawn_achor_the_happy_secret_to_better_work

Notes

1 Gandhi, M. (1920, July 1–November 14). *The collected works of Mahatma Gandhi* (Vol. 21, p. 134). Retrieved from www.gandhiashramsevagram.org/gandhi-literature/collected-works-of-mahatma-gandhi-volume-1-to-98.php

2 Gardner, B., Lally, P., & Wardle, J. (2012). Making health habitual: The psychology of 'habit-formation' and general practice. *The British Journal of General Practice: The Journal of the Royal College of General Practitioners, 62*(605), 664–666. doi:10.3399/bjgp12X659466

3 Ampel, B. C., Muraven, M., & McNay, E. C. (2018). Mental work requires physical energy: Self-control is neither exception nor exceptional. *Frontiers in Psychology.* doi:10.3389/fpsyg.2018.01005

4 Murray, E. (2015). *Rory McIlroy reveals that he writes his yearly goals on the back of a boarding pass.* Retrieved from www.theguardian.com/sport/2015/jan/13/rory-mcilroy-golf-goals-boarding-pass-abu-dhabi

5 Klein, H. J., Lount, R. B., Jr., Park, H. M., & Linford, B. J. (2020). When goals are known: The effects of audience relative status on goal commitment and performance. *Journal of Applied Psychology, 105*(4), 372–389. doi:10.1037/apl0000441

Chapter 4

Your personal brand

What is my brand?

Your brand is your story – or at least the story you tell other people. It signals your strengths and values; it is about who you are, what you have learned, what you have done and how you will use that knowledge. How will you apply your knowledge today, tomorrow and into the future? Your personal brand is a bit like a wardrobe choice. What items do you have in the bottom drawer that felt like a good idea at the time but have never seen the light of day? What pieces are still hanging up that don't quite fit anymore? What about your essentials? The pieces you know you cannot function without. The crisp white t-shirt, those faded jeans, that black rollneck or your little black dress with that fitted blazer. Then there are the bits that make you feel really great about yourself: the dark wash skinny jeans with the animal print jacket and those Kurt Geiger shoes. Your personal brand is more couture than prêt-à-porter. It is intended to be worn by you without significant alteration because it has been crafted by you, for you and so whilst a few people might fit into it, most people will not. To get your brand right, you need to spend quite a bit of time figuring out who you are, determining what you want to be known for and what you want to achieve. The first step to this is thinking about your values and strengths, who you are professionally, where you want to be and how you are going to achieve your goals (conveniently Chapters 1–3 of this book). The second step is to hide the old and poorly fitting clothes you've got at the back of your wardrobe.

There are plenty of books out there that focus on brand marketing, how to build a webpage and the like, but this is a psychology book, so naturally we're not so concerned with what your Instagram looks like and a bit more concerned with the human aspects of building and protecting your brand. So, this chapter focuses on the behavioural principles about how to promote yourself and, critically, how not to.

Build your tribe

Time consuming and sometimes just downright awkward, whom you network with and the channels you develop matter to your career – something not so easy to do when you are in a job you hate with a boss you hate. Love it or hate it, a mountain of research demonstrates that *networking* leads to more jobs, more business opportunities and faster advancement, and it improves work satisfaction as well.[1] Networking = social capital, and social capital is the relationships and networks that allow us to draw on resources from other members of those networks. That might take the form of useful information, personal relationships or the capacity to organise groups. Increased social capital has been linked with many positive outcomes, such as better public health, lower crime rates and more efficient financial markets.[2]

Fun Fact: The Chinese have a word for professional relationships, *guānxì*. It has its own symbols 关系 and is considered one of the cornerstones of commerce in Chinese culture.

Unfortunately, the marmite of networking leaves many people just feeling 'dirty' (Casciaro et al., 2016). Not a *Human Centipede* or xhamster.com kind of dirty, more just that some people really struggle with the difference between networking as a mechanism for nurturing relationships for friendship and personal support and networks that can increase exposure to career and business opportunities. When people have such an aversion to networking, they manage networking as an obligation, approaching the activity with lower levels of excitement and curiosity, and commit less effort and time, and their careers could flag. This failure is explained by the fact that everyone relies on others to succeed. Humans cannot help it; they just need each other, so trying to go it alone is rarely successful. Networking works because it gives you access to other people, their knowledge, their contacts and their jobs. Networking quickly helps you learn the unwritten rules of professions, what the individual and organisational values really are and what the industry hot topics and priorities are and will ground you in a community of like-minded people who want to succeed. The key is to focus less on the outcome (a job) and much more on the value of long-term relationships, because it is the relationship that is the real prize. Building that network and keeping it alive and healthy takes time and effort, so if you hate or really love networking, these are some tips that can help you build your tribe and stop you from feeling overwhelmed by what others are doing.

Ditch the business cards. People need to be able to find you, but business cards cost from £4.00 a pack. However, the problem with business cards is that they rely on two things. (i) that you stand out from the other business cards and (ii) that someone actually does something with that business card. Better to collect business cards or, better still, carry a notebook and pen. Not only do you get to capture the contact details of the person you want to connect with, but you also get to spend a few less awkward moments like a BBC reporter writing down something meaningful about what they do or what they are interested in. You then have a much better chance of meaningfully connecting with them outside of the networking event. The responsibility also then shifts to you to take the initiative with your collection of cards or notes by following up with an email and connecting on sites such as LinkedIn.

Develop an open mindset. Carol Dweck's theory of mindset has taken a bit of a battering in recent years.[3] Her theory of mindset has been embraced and rejected in equal proportions by the psychological community. Whatever your opinion on the robustness of mindset, it still offers a very useful model to explore the different ways that people approach the world and why some attitudes are more likely to foster success. Individuals with a 'fixed mindset' believe that human intelligence and abilities are fixed and there is nothing that can be done to change these fundamental traits. Individuals with a 'growth mindset' believe that intelligence and abilities are malleable and can be adjusted through learning and adapting.[4] There are a few places you can test your mindset online for free. If you find you identify as a fixed mindset, the goal-setting activities will help you shift your focus and improve your thinking. Surrounding yourself with people who seem to have a more open mindset can also help you adapt and change by shifting you out of your comfort zone.

 Foster some interests. People at networking events have lives outside of their jobs, so working the room focusing on what you can learn about them and identifying common interests makes for more meaningful conversations where people are more likely to remember and bond with you. Talking about interests is both an enriching and relaxing experience and a great way to remove direct focus (and pressure) of the purpose of the networking event. Remember that many of the people that you are networking with may be reluctant networkers themselves. They may also be feeling the discomfort of engaging with people in an instrumental way. By taking the focus off the purpose of the event, you send a clear and authentic message that is congruent with who you are at heart, before you start to focus on what you do in your job. Having interests is also (sadly) important to levelling the career playing field:

> When you're looking about how people network and forge relationships, there is a huge problem because most of these activities are aligned with typical male interests – golfing, cigar bars. But it is in those settings that trust is established. It's having a bigger impact than people think.
>
> (Female, CEO, cited in Oliver Wyman, 2019, p. 8)[5]

> The problem is the sense of not having anything in common. I get around this by striking up a conversation on topics that men have something to say about, such as sport – something they are interested in. It may not be something you want to talk about, but you need to do it in order to move on the conversation. With men you have to think harder and be prepared.
>
> (Senior manager, FTSE 100 company, cited in Wichert, 2011, p. 179)[6]

 Stay informed because current events are everything. As a graduate going into a professional field, you cannot afford to spend your days just on TikTok, Instagram or Netflix. You need to connect with something bigger – the rest of the world. Staying informed of world events and changes in industry helps you craft your pitch and pique the interest of people you wish to influence. You cannot stay effectively informed by just looking at your Facebook news feed. People will always want to talk about the latest major scandals, sports and politics, so having an informed opinion (informed by more than one source) is critical. The worst thing you can do is start discussing something you consider common knowledge only to have someone else in the room tell you it's not true. There are also some not insignificant issues with biased media reporting and fake news, and selecting sources from reputable organisations is not that straightforward. Pulitzer provides a list of prize-winning news organisations for the United States which include the Associated Press and Reuters. The "i" and the Guardian tend to be rated as the most trusted newspaper organisations in the United Kingdom, with the BBC, ITV and Channel 4 all being ranked for impartiality and trust.

Continually educating yourself on industry developments ensures that you are not only informed but also relevant. The rate of change in knowledge-based working environments places employees and employers under considerable pressure to keep up to date with advances in technology, developments in knowledge and new ways of working. The ultimate consequence of not keeping up to date with occupational knowledge is professional obsolescence. Good employers are making regular efforts to arm their employees with the skills and resources to expand their knowledge and skill sets. Therefore, demonstrating that you are already curious and informed puts you at a significant advantage. You are never done learning, so do not let it end with your degree.

 If you dress and look like that, you can't be suitable for this. The United Kingdom was aghast in 2015 when Nicola Thorpe arrived to work as an agency receptionist for PwC in London wearing flat shoes. She was promptly sent home (without pay) for failing to comply with the company dress code. Women were required to wear shoes with heels of between 2 and 4 inches. The widespread media coverage resulted in an online petition to make it illegal to require women to wear high heels. The petition failed and the UK government (after some considerable confusion) rejected any moves towards legislative change, arguing that the laws in existence already provided sufficient protection. It was 2018 by the time that the Government Equality Office finally published new guidelines to the effect that dress codes can be a legitimate part of an employee's terms and conditions of service but confirmed that any less favourable treatment because of sex could be direct discrimination. Dress codes do not have to be identical for men and women, but they should be comparable, and thus, high heels, makeup and painted nails could be required at work, but employers would have to have a clear rationale for why.

Fashion, or lack of it, has always been fascinating in its capacity to make a powerful and silent statement. Be it the reflection of protest, a symbol of social class and status or a shield both from the elements and from other people, it can be empowering and aspirational (dress for the job you want, not the one you have), but it can also discriminate not just against women who do not want to dress like Lee Holloway in *The Secretary* but also against people who may be ethically, religiously and cognitively diverse.

The clothes that we wear are superficial, socially engaged, political and cynical. It is not surprising, then, that how people dress at work has a direct impact on both morale and productivity and normality (although high heels as a receptionist is highly suspect). So, if you are in pursuit of a client-facing, front-of-house role that reflects the brand of the organisation you are going to work with, then the expectation is that you will step up and dress up. Organisations that are disruptors of the dress code do exist everywhere, but by and large, humans are visual creatures and a conservative bunch at work, so your appearance is critical.

 Make a game plan. Networking requires effort, so have a plan. If you want to develop meaningful and valuable relationships, you need to plan for them in advance, spend time figuring out who or what organisations are likely to be there and learn a bit about their industry. You only have a finite amount of time, so spend it well and choose your events wisely by taking advice from the university career services about where you are most likely to find graduate events that are a good match for your interests and ambitions. It is also worth speaking to your academic advisor or dissertation supervisor about attending research conferences. Student conferences in particular are low-stakes environments where you can practice your networking skills, but this only works if you are prepared to push yourself out of your comfort zone and network with students who are not just your mates. So, make a concerted effort to work the room and not just hang out with people you already know, because one of the first steps to networking is to meet new contacts, and you never know where your fellow students will end up in the future.

It sounds obvious, but get to the event on time, if not, in fact, a little bit earlier. You would be surprised how many people show up early to events, and it immediately gives you a chance to relax into socialising by connecting to a few people and having a chat with the organisers before the event begins. However, if you do arrive and see some people in conversation, do not interrupt; they may be annoyed. The same principle applies throughout the networking event. It is best to join a group of more than two people, start by speaking to the person who is silent and do not spend too long speaking to one person. Remember, the object is to work the room, so keep the longer conversations for the next time you meet. Make sure you get some decent sleep the night before so you are not tired. You need to spend quite a bit of time concentrating and actively listening, and a misplaced yawn will not curry much favour.

Nurture your network. Back to networking again! Finding the right people to help you garner work knowledge and opportunities is easier than you think, but persuading them to give over their time is hard. If you want people to help you, then you need to be the kind of person people want to help. In particular, if you go into tribe building with the intent of getting a job, you will be disappointed. So do not expect to show up to a graduate or industry networking event or connect to someone on LinkedIn and believe that a job offer will materialise. There is no instant gratification. Networking takes time, discipline, commitment, energy and a marathon mindset to nurture those relationships.

People who think of networking as a collaborative endeavour behave and think very differently from those who see it as a short-term means to an end of getting a job or breaking into an industry. Those differences in behaviour convey enhanced messages of the success characteristics of commitment, trustworthiness, adaptability, selflessness and being forward looking. True networks create a mutual dependency, and those are the ones that will have the most lasting significance to your career. Investment in 'the relationship' also enables all parties to identify any potential lack of alignment, difference in values or lack of esprit de corps and to either work out those differences, learn from each other's mistakes or dissolve the relationship entirely.

Professional networks on an international level are also critical for landing and making a success of international assignments (more on this in Chapter 9). Whilst this may not be something on your radar right now, it is worth noting that people who really get to the top of their game almost exclusively have an international assignment at some point in their career. They do not just miraculously land such assignments; they spend many years nurturing such relationships. LinkedIn is a good place to start, but there are also many different international psychology networks that you can connect with that may relate directly to your areas of interest or practice. These groups may not meet your long-term needs in being directly relevant to the direction that your career ultimately takes, but they are a great place to start building the 'international' section of your CV.

Finally, do not solely focus on networking vertically; network for your life, your friendships and your health and well-being. Those relationships are just as important for your future; they bring a great source of support and encouragement (and mentoring; see Chapter 4), and they also bring with them their own networks. This means that the first stop in your networking strategy should be to develop a solid peer network whilst at university. Friendship and peer networks are the first lesson in networking; *give, give, give*. Healthy friendship and peer networks create mutual benefit and support. The same principles apply when seeking to nurture the networks that will help you in your professional career. Networking is about long-life evolution; pay it forward and remember your network wants to benefit in the long term from you.

Industry know-how . . .

Volunteering to help in an unpaid capacity can be a critical key to a long-term partnership, because it creates the conditions for forward-looking mutual intent, intent to directly and substantively complement and support each other's purpose, values and goals.

Stay in touch regularly; do not just appear and disappear (like someone with a new boyfriend). Do not send 'holding' emails. Remember that networks need mutual interest, so be sure to make time to compose emails that are sincerely written and interesting, perhaps by providing some new piece of information or an article that you have read.

Participating in discussion boards and blogs demonstrates you are able to contribute to the international dialogue on your subject matter. If you are able to provide evidence and subject matter expertise from your psychological training, you will quickly establish yourself as trustworthy and a reliable source of information.

Psychology networks, national and international

The British Psychological Society member networks: www.bps.org.uk/members/networks

Association for Business Psychology: https://theabp.org.uk/about/the-abp/

The Psychology Professionals Network: www.nwppn.nhs.uk/

The International Association of Applied Psychology: https://iaapsy.org/

The International Positive Psychology Network: www.ippanetwork.org/

Exercise: industry know-how . . .

The Fast Company publishes an online magazine that focuses on developments in technology, business, design and the environment. www.fastcompany.com/

If you can suffer the endless adverts and tedious lists and rankings, *Forbes* features articles on industry, investing and finance. It tends to have useful analysis on global events, politics and society, as well as useful feature content on areas related to careers and leadership. www.forbes.com/

The *Harvard Business Review* is generally a management review which covers hot topics in areas such as management, negotiation, strategy, marketing and finance. It also provides focused podcasts and webinars on the most pressing issues facing organisations and prints accessible airport-fodder books through it subscription and storefront services. https://hbr.org/

Links for women

Woman Who is a community for working women sharing inspiring stories and celebrating success. Through panel discussions, blogs, newsletters, podcasts and networking events, Woman Who provides resources and support to help support better working and network building. www.woman-who.co.uk/

Women on Boards supports its members to make the connections and career choices to take on board roles as non-executive directors, trustees or governors. They provide resources, training and master classes to help craft and build a board-level CV as well as access to board-level vacancies across the United Kingdom. www.womenonboards.net/en-gb/home

Where Women Work is an organisation that showcases the work and achievements of women whilst shining a spotlight on the organisations that support them. Its philosophy is that by showcasing organisations were women thrive, it will motivate more women to apply to those organisations. If you are interested in researching or applying to a prime employer for women, you can search its pages learn about organisations, apply for jobs and join their careers community. www.wherewomenwork.com/Employers

Links for minorities

UK-BAME represents the diverse collective interests of the UK's Black and Minority Ethnic communities who have expressed interest or require assistance in developing small businesses, community groups and career and family opportunities. www.uk-bame.com/

LGBT+: The British LGBT awards honour organisations and networks each year that promote and support the needs of LGBT+ people. It is an excellent source of the most up-to-date organisations to connect with or join and perhaps work with.

How not to brand yourself

As the social media way of life integrates itself further into our everyday routines, online personal branding has been of growing importance and has been receiving a lot of attention as recruiters and employees look more and more into social media to vet the competition for particular roles. The steady pace of this practice was recently rushed to the finish line. As I write this book, the global work culture has been changed, and it's likely permanent. The COVID-19 (coronavirus) pandemic forced even the industry dinosaurs to dust off their Gavilan SCs (a very old computer) and make the move to online and remote working. Although there are both positive and negative consequences from this shift to remote, online working environments, the impact on employability is significant. If we thought we were under a microscope before, coronavirus changed the magnification.

At no time in our history has the dichotomy between online and offline been more blurred. The internet is no longer a distinct space; it is embedded in our lives. In particular, the COVID-19 pandemic has necessitated an enormous adjustment in a very short space of time, with people putting in longer and more irregular hours. Virtual interactions are both highly complex and very fatiguing. The challenges compounded for many who are also juggling family commitments means that being efficient and productive during lockdown is irreconcilable. From the manager's perspective, how do you even begin to support or watch over someone you cannot see? Stress levels are high and tolerance low. There are always times when we need a more fluid approach to our personal boundaries (but less COVID-laced fluid), but in order to be able to modify our boundaries, we need to be clear where those boundaries are to begin with.

Careers in focus: the ergonomics/human factors specialist

Several key studies have demonstrated over the past decade that home working and mobile working are related to higher levels of job satisfaction and employee engagement. The relationship is in part explained by the increased levels of autonomy and control that flexible working (work/life balance) and agile working (using technology to support effective patterns of working) afford. Advances in cloud storage, lightweight laptops, 4G (soon 5G) networks and public and private Wi-Fi mean that, for most, the internet has become a basic necessity.

The human factors specialist applies psychological principles to how people behave physically and psychologically in response to environments, products or services. They examine issues such as the impact of communication, stress, teamwork and norms, resources (and the lack thereof) and assertiveness on performance, in particular in areas such as safety and hazard management.

During the COVID-19 crisis, human factors specialists have been applying their collective knowledge to guide not only manufacturers and designers in changing their production towards key medical equipment such as ventilators and personal protective equipment but also on advising organisations on creating workplaces that will minimise the transmission of the virus. Find out more: www.ergonomics.org.uk

---

Boundaries are how we communicate the expectations of our relationships. Historically, work relationships tended towards a formal contract that indicated when employees were available and what they were available for. In the new digital world, however, these boundaries are often very blurred and difficult to navigate.

Time to learn about privacy settings

Whether you realise it or not, the moment you step onto a social media platform, you start to build a reputation for yourself; your online persona becomes the precursor for potential employers to indicate who you are and what you represent. Almost all students now arrive at university with a 'baby' digital brand. The choices we make online, the items we search for and the activities we engage in not only shape the online communities that connect us but also the advertising and news feeds that we receive. Therefore, the first stage of brand development is to start controlling your digital information before others start to control it for you.

In any job, but especially one that deals with proprietary information, there has to be a level of trust that any information or documents will be kept confidential. You simply won't get hired into a firm if there is any suggestion that you don't take privacy and discretion seriously, so the first step to proving to potential employers that privacy is valuable to you can actually stem from your social media profiles. Adjusting your privacy settings creates greater safety online. There's simply no disputing it, because, if you recall, it was repeated in almost every PHSE lesson throughout your high school. Right now, it is particularly advantageous to lock down your social media from an employability standpoint.

Don't kid yourself: your potential boss will find your Facebook, Twitter and Instagram pages, and they will look at everything they think is relevant to making their decision. Taking your personal privacy seriously is the first indicator to employers that you are someone who can be trusted with sensitive information. Not only does tighter security give you an air of responsibility, but it also gives you more control over what your employer knows about you before you get into an interview. Before 2018, people weren't really wise to the power Facebook had by simply giving us a place to voice our thoughts and opinions and essentially run wild with it. We have all posted silly things online, whether it's an embarrassing picture from your teenage years or something more sinister (I'm looking at you, Trump), so creating a digital barrier between your employer and your Facebook account means that you can communicate the brand you want to perpetuate and not the image of a bad eyeliner habit.

Personally, my Facebook is like Fort Knox. Not only is there minimal information accessible to those I'm not friends with, but any post to my timeline has to be approved by yours truly. Maybe you think this is too far, but at least I can tell you exactly what has been posted on my timeline over the past few

Make sure you are sharing only what you want to share

To go to Privacy Checkup:
1 Click ▾ in the top right of Facebook.
2 Click **Settings & Privacy** > **Privacy Checkup**.

months and there is very little risk of my name being accidentally attached to something detrimental to my personal brand.

Do you REEAALLY need to post that?

Water-tight privacy settings will not save you from all evil. Even if you keep your social media accounts private, you cannot expect that nothing will get shared. CEOs, health care workers and sporting professionals have all lost their jobs because of social media remarks, inappropriate images and ill-conceived emails. University lecturers have been sacked and students have been suspended, even expelled from their courses, all because of their lack of digital discipline. So, never write anything down about someone or something that you are not prepared for that person, group or organisation to see. No matter how secure you think your social media account or your emails, someone with an axe to grind can easily take screenshots, and it may end up somewhere you never imagined it would be.

The consequences of those leaked emails and poorly thought-through posts can be unpredictable. You may be lucky and get a smack on the wrist, but companies are taking social media much more seriously than they have in previous years, and you'll likely find yourself facing disciplinary action. Get it really wrong and you may find yourself in court as the result of defamation of character action. All it takes is one person to push the issue, so don't put yourself at risk. If you have any doubt whether something is 'postable', err on the side of caution and rant to your mum instead.

Another social media snafu is oversharing. Facebook leaves us to our own devices when it comes to the content of our pages. We can post as much as we want when we want, and we can post whatever we want as long as it doesn't break any laws. This can be both a blessing and a curse. 'I love U Okay Hun?', but I don't want to be its next feature.

Sharing information about your exam results, your relationships with your tutors or your inability to get a job can have long-term consequences on how others view and interact with you. Employers don't want to run the risk of their interpersonal relationships or the reputation and qualifications of their employees being put on blast.

Sharing the good news of your sister's pregnancy or bad news such as your mother's illness or your brother's divorce may seem like a harmless way to reach out to your friendship network for support, but without express permission, sharing is almost certainly a violation of their privacy and can have negative connotations of attention-seeking if it happens too often.

The rate at which you post can also affect how others view you. Frequent posting sends signals that you are always available online and unproductive in work. You could be getting everything done, but if you're posting six times a day, people will wonder where you get the time and if professional sacrifices are being made for the sake of your Instagram following. This may increase pressure on you to manage more work, manage work-related matters outside of normal working arrangements or become overwhelmed by becoming the go-to 'shoulder-to-cry-on' person. Your time is precious, so use it wisely and put down the phone every now and again.

And it goes without saying that you should stay away from social media when you've been drinking. Your sober brain is much more effective at regulating the risks of your actions; your drunk brain is not and is probably thinking that rant is a great idea. Most lecturers will have dealt with the odd drunk student or two, and not all will respond as supportively as Mr Martin. We don't drink and dial, so we shouldn't drink and post.

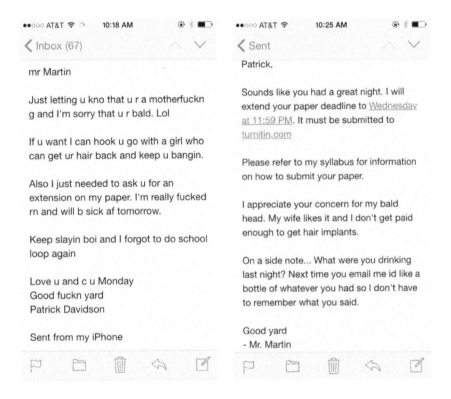

Read what you question and question what you read

Social media is a hub of information on the thoughts and opinions of others. Trump alone has an entire archive just dedicated to his Tweets. While there are those who call for such negative political or derogatory comments to be pulled down, the fact that people spread every brain spark all over the internet can be a powerful tool if you utilise it in the right way.

There is tremendous value in reading and engaging with material that we disagree with. Only by exploring material that challenges us are we better able to acquire good ideas from other people and build stronger, more evidenced and sharper responses to those we disagree with. Despite the countless range of opinions that are available to us, we are, however, becoming increasingly selective about what we are prepared to listen to, engage with and tolerate.

> There is nothing either good or bad but thinking makes it so.
>
> (*Hamlet*: Act 2 Scene 2)

Deliberately look for opposing views. Nurture friendships with people who are different from you. Being friends with someone who does not agree with your values, politics or religion can at times be hard work, but such friendships help us appreciate our own intellectual limitations and fallibility. It helps us foster intellectual humility. Pay attention in group debates and discussions with the people who say very little and encourage them to talk. Such activities may also help you identify your blind spots and erroneous beliefs. Our media providers make it very easy for us to find and watch BBC, Channel 4 or Sky News, but what is really going on across the world and how are they viewing those contentious issues? By diversifying your news outlets and seeking out sources like Reuters, Euronews and Al Jazeera, you see the other side of the coin that the big three aren't broadcasting. American news agencies such as CNN and Fox also have a completely different news broadcasting model; they mix news with entertainment and can be very politically partisan between liberal and conservative points of view. Columns and books written by the likes of Germaine Greer, Jessa Crispin, Ann Coulter, Phyllis Schlafly, Peter Hitchens, Richard Dawkins or Christopher Hitchens may never reflect your worldview, but reading their work sharpens your thinking and develops your values. Only then are you properly equipped for the task of thinking, and only then will you be better able to articulate your points, something vital in the workplace and even more vital in an interview.

By approaching the dissenting ideas and opinions of others with the intention to learn and understand their point of view, the information they rely on and the sources they cite, you strengthen your argument if you can find reasons those examples are incorrect. You can whole-heartedly disagree, but there is still always something to gain from listening, even if your mind remains unchanged.

Do not share anything on social media or any other digital communication unless you are completely certain that such information is true. No matter how amusing that material may seem, you could be spreading malicious and misleading information, even #fakenews. Everyone lies on the internet, from reading terms and conditions to full-blown catfishing, so it's become somewhat of a cliché to warn that you shouldn't believe everything you read on the internet because at this point, why would you?

However, as people become wise to the fact, they can't expect 100% trust when it comes to spreading information, they find new ways of making their point. Anything, and I mean *anything*, can be twisted to look as though it supports two very different conclusions. Lawyers do this as a sport and get paid very well to do so.

Social media, in particular, has made it enticingly effortless to share content thoughtlessly, and unprincipled people leverage idleness for political and financial advantage, from fake and hijacked accounts,[7] commercial and political manipulation[8] and the polarisation and radicalisation of society[9] to state-backed disinformation campaigns and the spreading of misinformation about ethnic minorities that have ended in genocide.[10] The realities of disinformation highlight the tension between free expression and the capacity of people to communicate in an authentic and co-ordinated way.

Statistics, in particular, can look very different when they're taken out of context, which is a common practice when spinning data for your own purpose. If there is a lack of context, whether it be geographic, populous or historical context, it might be appropriate to question why that is. Become wise to the ways in which politicians and media can spin data and information to look the way they want it, do some independent research and pay attention to that man behind the curtain.

There are a number of excellent websites to help members of the public determine the authenticity of posts, but it is critical to remember that no one source is infallible from mistakes. Useful pages include:

> Snopes began as a forum for investigating urban legends and folklore but has now developed into a key resource that enables users to search thousands of investigations and submit items for investigation. It relies on a community of readers, supporters and members to fight misinformation, spot fake images and debunk junk news. www.snopes.com/
>
> Full Fact is the UK's independent fact-checking charity, which not only checks the credibility of information but also pushes for corrections and works with government and institutions to improve the quality of information at the source (https://fullfact.org/about/). It also provides a range of links to fact-checking organisations across the world. https://fullfact.org/toolkit/#near-you
>
> NHS Choices – Behind the Headlines has a categorised page explaining the science behind the stories that make the news and an updated feed with recent news stories referencing health and well-being. This site explains the nature of the research and reports cited in headline stories to provide clarity and transparency of scientific information. www.nhs.uk/news/
>
> UK Statistics Authority is an independent body which covers three elements of the UK statistics system – the Government Statistical Service, the Office for National Statistics and the Office for Statistics Regulation – with a view to regulating and safeguarding the quality of statistics and publicly challenging the misuse of statistical data. www.statisticsauthority.gov.uk/
>
> STATS is a US research organisation which aids journalists and writers in analysing data and statistical information. It is a free service and has helpful links to other US statistical associations. https://senseaboutscienceusa.org/stats-check/

Careers in focus: media psychologists

Social media and the media more broadly hold tremendous power to change the way people think and behave. The ways in which different genders, races and sexualities are portrayed and how issues of diversity and inclusion are addressed change how we think. If psychologists can change how people think, they can change how they behave. Media psychologists apply their understanding of the ways in which people form and maintain attitudes, how bias is formed and how it is prevented. They apply their skills and knowledge in this area in a diverse range of professions, for example, designing advertising campaigns or projecting images or storylines in entertainment programmes, they work in the entertainment industry shaping our emotions through drama and humour and with politicians in the use of propaganda that shapes policies and ideological thinking.

Find out more:

Careers in media psychology: https://careersinpsychology.org/becoming-a-media-psychologist/
Postgraduate study: www.findamasters.com/masters-degrees/united-kingdom/?40w900&Keywords=digital+media+psychology

Defining and describing media psychology.
www.psychologytoday.com/gb/blog/the-media-psychology-effect/201211/defining-and-describing-media-psychology

Don't talk to me like that

As you go through university, you are already developing what will become your professional relationships with lecturers, personal tutors and even your peers. Many students make the mistake of thinking that if the quality of their work and their style of communication are not top notch at university that it really doesn't matter that much. In actual fact, you are building your brand from the minute you enter university.

A big part of your online brand is how you speak to people and how you allow yourself to be spoken to, particularly in an online forum. This could be anything from Facebook comments to email strings, but, again, the oldest rules are the ones we need to stand by: *don't talk to anyone in a way you wouldn't like to be spoken to. If you've got nothing nice to say, don't say anything at all.*

There are so many opportunities for miscommunication in digital communications, it is critical to exercise discretion about the number and types of emails you send. Think before you post or hit send, and always remember that electronic conversations and social media are not so much about your opinion; rather they tend to be stacked towards other peoples' opinions *on you*. Ru Paul once said that other people's opinions of you are none of your business, and while I think there is some truth to that, it can't be the case when you're building your brand.

Everyone has a sort of duality when it comes to their personal and professional lives. We dress differently, we talk differently and, most importantly, we communicate differently. Facebook is a great platform for self-education but also gives you the opportunity to educate others. While, personally, I wouldn't recommend getting into every Facebook argument you can find, there are benefits in being able to share your knowledge and expertise with those who lack it. As a private use platform, this is something you should feel free to do in your personal life but also something you should be conscious of keeping a lid on when you're in your professional sphere.

Do not be tempted to turn your professional communications into a public performance. If you do not have a rational need to communicate more widely, do not do it. Emails breed emails. They fill up our inboxes and reduce work productivity. If you're the source of that email thread which is unnecessarily clogging up everyone's email inbox, you're going to look unprofessional. So, only cc people on emails who have a rational reason to be copied in. Have you asked for their involvement? Do you need a direct response? Is this something they absolutely need to be made aware of? If not, then they have no business being on that email thread.

If you are ccing other people out of fear, accountability or positive reinforcement, do not do it (it is called grandstanding). Only communicate with the person that you need to communicate with. Do not be tempted to start copying in more peers or senior people than relevant to make a point or to have your voice heard. If you are in any doubt about whether they should be copied on the thread, start the email by addressing each recipient. (Dear name, name, name, name). If you cannot find a reason to speak to them in person, then what are they doing being copied in?

When crafting the email itself, clarity is essential. Always start with the point of the conversation in the first few sentences. Then explain yourself afterwards as succinctly as possible. If you have to write a long email, it should not be an email; it should be a meeting. Long emails at best take a long time to respond to and at worst do not get read at all, so do not send the recipient on an information hunt. I have lost count of how many times I have started to read a long email and been interrupted in the office, and then, because that email is marked as read, it never gets responded to. You might think you can solve that issue by perhaps marking non-urgent emails as urgent to get the attention you want or a speedy response, but you'll soon be seen as the boy who cried wolf, and people will start ignoring the emails. If it really is urgent, why are you spending the time to write an email? Make a phone call and take the time to resolve the issue or ask for help in person. Not only will the matter be resolved faster, it's much harder to deny help to someone standing in front of you than it is to say, 'Nah' to an email.

Asking for an email receipt is another way of making the non-urgent urgent. It also displays distrust in the person you are emailing. You run the risk that people will just click no, and your message may even be shunted straight into the junk folder. Even if you get a receipt, it doesn't follow that the email was read, so a polite follow-up email, if you do not get a timely response, is the more appropriate course of action.

Finally, and sometimes, more importantly, grammar and spelling matter. Do not be tempted to let shorthand and colloquialisms creep into your academic and professional communications. Learn to discern the right time and place for casual language. Text-speak isn't cute; it is risky and could be perceived as sloppy. If you struggle with the rules of English, then invest in some technology to help you. Most software packages have built-in editing tools that are helpful at correcting common errors in writing, but they do not go nearly far enough towards systematically detecting mistakes at a professional level. Programs like Grammarly are able to go deeper into the tone of communication. They not only detect and eliminate errors but provide you with a perception of how a piece of writing will come across. You can, for example, modify the intent and the tone of a piece of writing to come across the way you need it to: create a more confident or friendly tone; tailor the domain to an academic, business or more casual audience and change the intent of the piece of writing.

Check yourself before you wreck yourself

There is a useful behavioural management philosophy applied in primary schools that works just as well for adults working online. These are three steps that will buy you some time to stop and reflect before you post something or hit send on an email.

Are you ready? Are you sure you have all the facts in place? Have you verified your sources? If you do not have all the facts, STOP. How are you feeling? Is what you are about to do driven by emotions? If so, STOP.

Are you respectful? Is your message long? If so, STOP. You need a conversation. What is the underlying intention of your message? How will what you are doing potentially be received? Will your message be misinterpreted because of the way it is being delivered? If you are not sure on any of these points, STOP.

Are you safe? Can you cope/live with the outcomes of your actions? If you are not sure, STOP. You need a conversation, with the caveat that if you want to do great work, sometimes you will have to be unsafe.

'Snowflake' is not a dirty word

You cannot afford to blend in. If lecturers and potential employers cannot distinguish you (in a good way) from the herd, then no matter how good you are (or think you are), your efforts don't mean squat. Lecturers are human, and the extent to which members of an academic team remember you specifically influences the effort they will put into writing references for you, keeping up with developments in your career, inviting you to give alumni talks and even contacting you in person about those all-important job openings. So, don't be afraid to stand out and be a bit of a snowflake but only by doing things which separate you positively from your flurry.

In particular, we live in a world where Facebook is the be-all and end-all of personal and professional lives. People sharing silly things gets them in serious professional trouble and can change the course of someone's career, no matter who they are. But with a world that lives online, we forget that there is an entirely offline social network. It's called talking to people. Don't be afraid of trying it some time.

Works well under close supervision

Everyone has worked with someone who is quite happy riding on someone else's coattails. If you haven't, take a look at whom you're grabbing onto. Whilst asking for help when needed is important and learning from others who are more experienced has a distinct advantage, managing students who do lack initiative (and take it from me, they're everywhere) is exhausting. It's exhausting for academics, it's really exhausting for other students and, at some point, you will either lose your grip or they'll take the coat off.

So, what is so attractive about my coattails? you might ask. Often, it's not really about your coattails at all; at the heart of the issue is the well-known problem of lack of self-esteem. Psychological studies have demonstrated that humans often seek out others who compensate for their deficits,[11] and whilst this might be acceptable in romantic partnerships and close friendships, university students who consistently use their friendship network to self-regulate their personal performance will eventually be drawn into conflict. Left unchecked, such behaviours most likely won't improve; what tends to happen is that the behaviour becomes refined and then established; people get better at it and will eventually undermine their workplace relationships.

There is an importance in developing your reputation with your lecturers *and* your peer group. Don't forget, the people you are studying with right now are going to one day be colleagues or someone you might just need to ask a favour. If they have a bad memory of you copying their homework, they aren't going to want to work with you again, and that might mean in the next assignment, or it might mean in the workforce. Taking responsibility for your own work and education is almost entirely the point of university. Sure, it's partly to do with getting the qualifications for the right job, but what good are you to a team if you don't actually know what you're doing at the end of three years? Taking ownership of a project, or at least the part assigned to you, changes the way people see you. If you take proactive charge of making sure things get done and smoothing the bumps along the road, you become the problem solver, not the problem. Don't underestimate the power of solving someone else's issues, because you don't know who they're about to become. All of these skills are critical for that ultimate career-defining assignment (revealed Chapter 9).

The parasite diagnostics test

Psychology students, you know the drill. Think of someone you think might be a parasite. How much do you agree with the following statements?

5= strongly agree; 4 = agree; 3= I really don't care; 2= is this a validated measure?; 1= strongly disagree

This person . . .

1 They regularly turn up late for meetings.
   1   2   3   4   5
2 They complete tasks at their own convenience, not anyone else's.
   1   2   3   4   5
3 They fail to respond promptly to messages and requests, and responses are almost always at the last minute.
   1   2   3   4   5
4 They do not provide critical information before or when it's needed.
   1   2   3   4   5
5 They dump on the team at the very last minute.
   1   2   3   4   5
6 They are territorial about ideas and areas of work but do not respect the boundaries of others.
   1   2   3   4   5
7 They take credit for others' ideas and the work of others.
   1   2   3   4   5
8 They blame others when things go wrong.
   1   2   3   4   5
9 They copy the work of others.
   1   2   3   4   5
10 They restrict the circulation of ideas and information.
   1   2   3   4   5
11 They seek out opportunities for personal advancement or activities that make them look good but do not share that information or support their team to do the same.
   1   2   3   4   5
12 They try to make others look bad.
   1   2   3   4   5
13 They try to make strategic friendships or present themselves in a friendly/ close way (for example, trying to befriend the boss, lecturer etc.).
   1   2   3   4   5

Total the scores

SCOTTSMIND

"I DON'T SEE MYSELF AS A PARASITE...
I'M JUST WORKING THROUGH SOME ATTACHMENT ISSUES."

😊 If you scored between 13 and 26, you are clearly scoring your own behaviour. Hmmm. I see you!

😈 If you scored between 52 and 65, bad luck: you are clearly currently working with your peers on a university group project.

😑 If you scored anything else, you are taking this way too seriously, but good: you are the kind of person people will want to employ.

Fun fact. Parasites alter the behaviour of their hosts by tapping into their host's neuronal circuits and manipulating its cognitive functions. The parasite secretes compounds that operate on their host, encouraging them to become more aggressive (to protect the parasite's offspring) or even commit suicide in environments more favourable to reproduction. Zombie insects, *bleurgh!*

Libersat F, Kaiser M, Emanuel S. (2018) Mind control: how parasites manipulate cognitive functions in their insect hosts. *Frontiers in Psychology*, 9, 572. doi:10.3389/fpsyg.2018.00572

Further reading

A few of these of these require subscriptions, but most university libraries will have free access.

Psychology, health and well-being
The National Elf Service, making evidence-based research more accessible and usable for busy health and social care professionals. www.nationalelf service.net/

Politics
Slugger O'Toole is an award-winning news and opinion portal, which takes a critical look at various strands of political politics in Ireland and Britain. It tries to bring its readers 'open source analysis' from both the mainstream media and the blogosphere. https://sluggerotoole.com/

Huffington Post: Described as left, or left leaning, the site offers news, satire, blogs and original content and covers politics, business, entertainment, environment, technology, popular media, lifestyle, culture, comedy, healthy living, women's interests and local news featuring columnists. www.huffingtonpost.co.uk/

Guido Fawkes: Described as right, or right leaning, *Guido Fawkes* is described as an explosive website that discusses and dissects the murky goings-on in Westminster. Guido Fawkes – Parliamentary Plots & Conspiracy https://order-order.com/

Wings over Scotland: A Scottish political website which focuses particularly on the media – whether mainstream print and broadcast organisations or the online and social-network community – as well as offering its own commentary and analysis. https://wingsoverscotland.com/

Reddit: Reddit is broken up into more than a million communities known as 'subreddits', each of which covers a different topic. The homepage shows you various posts that are currently trending on the site, pulled from a variety of subreddits.

Quora.com: A platform to ask questions and connect with people who contribute unique insights and quality answers.

The *New Statesman* is a British political and cultural magazine published in London. www.newstatesman.com/uk

The Fastcompany is the world's leading progressive business media brand, with a unique editorial focus on innovation in technology, leadership, and design. www.fastcompany.com/

Forbes is a global media company, focusing on business, investing, technology, entrepreneurship, leadership, and lifestyle. www.forbes.com/

Harvard Business Review is a general management magazine https://hbr.org/

https://thefinancialdiet.com/

Notes

1 Hurlbert, J. S. (1991). Social networks, social circles, and job satisfaction. *Work and Occupations, 18*(4), 415–430. doi:10.1177/0730888491018004003
Wolff, H.-G., & Moser, K. (2009). Effects of networking on career success: A longitudinal study. *The Journal of Applied Psychology, 94*, 196–206. doi:10.1037/a0013350
Akhter, M., & Siddique, M., & Masum, A. (2011). Analysis of social network and its effect on job satisfaction and employee performance. *ASA University Review, 5*(1). Retrieved from https://ssrn.com/abstract=2568290

Bagdadli, S., & Gianecchini, M. (2019). Organizational career management practices and objective career success: A systematic review and framework. *Human Resource Management Review, 29*(3), 353–370. doi:10.1016/j.hrmr.2 018.08.001

2 Adler, P. S., & Kwon, S. (2002). Social capital: Prospects for a new concept. *The Academy of Management Review, 27*(1), 17–40.
 Denworth, L. (2019, August 12). Debate arises over teaching "growth mindsets" to motivate students. *Scientific American*. Retrieved from www.scienti ficamerican.com/article/debate-arises-over-teaching-growth-mindsets-to-motivate-students/

3 Denworth, L. (2019, August 12). Debate arises over teaching "growth mindsets" to motivate students. *Scientific American*. Retrieved from www.scientificamerican. com/article/debate-arises-over-teaching-growth-mindsets-to-motivate-students/

4 Dweck, C. S. (2006). *Mindset: The new psychology of success*. New York: Random House Inc.

5 Oliver Wyman. (2019). *Women in healthcare leadership 2019*. New York: Marsh & McLennan.

6 Wichert, I. (2011). *Where have all the senior women gone? 9 Critical job assignments for women leaders*. London: Palgrave Macmillan.

7 Williams, C. (2019, February 11). 620 million accounts stolen from 16 hacked websites now for sale on dark web, seller boasts. *The Register*. Retrieved from www. theregister.com/2019/02/11/620_million_hacked_accounts_dark_web/

8 Ghosh, D., & Scott, B. (2018, March 19). Facebook's new controversy shows how easily online political ads can manipulate you. *Time*. Retrieved from https://time. com/5197255/facebook-cambridge-analytica-donald-trump-ads-data/

9 Arthur, C. (2019, March 11). *Social media polarises and radicalises – and MPs aren't immune to its effects*. Retrieved from www.theguardian.com/commentisfree/2019/ mar/11/whatsapp-facebook-extreme-polarise-radicalise-mps-politicians

10 Mozur, P. (2018, October 15). A genocide incited on Facebook, with posts from Myanmar's military. *The New York Times*. Retrieved from www.nytimes. com/2018/10/15/technology/myanmar-facebook-genocide.html
 Isaac, M. (2019). *Facebook finds new disinformation campaigns and braces for 2020 torrent*. Retrieved from www.nytimes.com/2019/10/21/technology/facebook-disinformation-russia-iran.html

11 Shea, C. T., Davisson, E. K., & Fitzsimons, G. M. (2013). Riding other people's coattails: Individuals with low self-control value self-control in other people. *Psychological Science, 24*(6), 1031–1036. doi:10.1177/0956797612464890

Chapter 5

From applications to
interviews that win

Green-print students

Three decades ago, education practice in the United Kingdom made a systematic shift towards action-learning approaches to learning (e.g. group work, problem-solving, reflection), and students have been resentful of their peers ever since. The introduction of the work of David Kohb (1984) and others meant that experiential learning and reflective learning became front and centre of quality processes and the methods and practices of teaching that emerged from them. Kohb's work was seminal in providing an educational pipeline that would support the birth of a new profession: the knowledge worker. A knowledge worker is someone who applies theory and analysis acquired through education and training towards the development of products and services. Unlike skilled manual workers, for example, craftsmen, builders, plumbers or electricians (we might call them blueprint workers), knowledge workers think for a living. Writers, academics, computer programmers, engineers, lawyers and, of course, psychologists are all knowledge workers. As such, 20th-century psychological training has a particular focus on helping students think critically, reflect, share knowledge and ideas, apply this abstract knowledge to practical problems, work autonomously, think divergently and seek continuous improvement.

The systematic skills of science that psychology students are equipped with mean that they leave university furnished with the ingredients for growth and development. This green-print thinking has equipped psychology students for change, to challenge the status quo and the commonly accepted, to innovate and to develop new knowledge for problems that we do not even know exist yet. Green-print students are equipped to test the limits of their learning and competencies, seeking out opportunities to learn even more than they already know and to share that knowledge to create further awareness. The green-print mindset means that psychology students will thrive when the jobs they eventually obtain are intellectually challenging. Unchallenging but 'cushy' work can feel nice for a while, but longer-term students will also find themselves feeling understimulated, chronically bored, disaffected and frustrated at work. Applying for the wrong job is a common mistake that many students make. A misplaced application increases rejection rates and lowers morale, and for that reason, we have spent quite a bit of effort laying the foundations of self-knowledge before you start the application process. If you have jumped ahead, no cheating, because recruitment managers do not like having their time wasted with unsuitable applicants, and you will end up feeling bad about yourself.

Career in focus: green print career story

"Having worked in facilities management for over 10 years I felt like a change and was fortunate enough to go to university as an adult learner. I had a relatively good job, but it was never what I truly wanted to do, so I decided to do something I was actually interested in and chose to study psychology. When I started my degree, I was all in on clinical psychology. I had this idea that clinical psychology was where the big money was and so I put all my focus into that. I aspired to get a PhD, work as a clinical psychologist in a hospital or prison, seeing patients and eventually become chartered so I could work for myself. Being older, I could appreciate the mistakes I had made in the past; such as wasting time or not putting effort in when I should have (hindsight is 20/20) so this was sort of a second chance and I was going to go all in.

While on my degree I was able to study different disciplines of Psychology, in particular, positive psychology which looked at areas such as happiness, productivity, self-esteem and flow states. Psychology is one of the few subjects where you'll get to learn about yourself as much as others. It's a very person-centred subject and there'll be plenty of things that'll relate to your own experiences, good and bad.

My occupational psychology professor highlighted that it was far better to be great in a niche subject than average in a popular one. It was arguably one of the best pieces of advice I have ever received! If you are in a field where you are at the top of your academic game and you love what you do, money will be a by-product of your success anyway and what you do will feel less like a 'job' . . . it's probably why so many lawyers are miserable! When armed with this realisation I went after what interested me most and focused on things such as productivity, self-esteem, happiness and flow states. I became interested in my own happiness and productivity and worked on myself more than I ever had before. I researched goal setting, SMART goals, habits and routines. If someone achieved success in something I wanted to know how. It was an area of psychology that I was drawn too and thankfully, has paid me back in dividends.

When I left university, I was fortunate enough to get a job in Student Support Services, where what I had learned could be applied in the real world. My role was to work with students who had additional needs or disabilities and ensure they received the same experiences as other students. I worked closely with students who had Autism Spectrum Disorder, ADHD and even Schizophrenia to build positive routines, habits and goals. As well as helping them academically I also worked with them on personal goals, such as communication and confidence which would help them long after university.

While in this role I also worked as a Learning and Engagement Coordinator for a company which specialised in motivational speaking and education. My role was to help adult learners achieve a qualification in leadership and management. As well as building the online application which would track their progress through statistics, I would also provide guidance on how to build goals and become more productive. Granted, on my degree I certainly had moments where I thought "why are we doing statistics in psychology?" Later, I found that it was what set me apart from the other applicants and secured me the job!

As I look to the future, I have plans to grow my business but also further my psychology career by studying a masters in speech and language therapy which will allow me to work in an industry where I'll be making a positive impact on people of a younger age group. My aim is to work with children and families who are living with autism spectrum disorder and, through good routines and positive habits, give them a positive learning experience in and outside of school. I have no doubt that I wouldn't be where I am today (or the future) without going to university. While it gifted me with knowledge and experience, the greatest lesson I learned was not to follow the crowd to a field you think you 'should' be in, but be guided by your passion because when you're passionate about something it will feel like freedom, not 'work', and that's where you'll find happiness and be able to make the most difference".

Gary Stevens, Postgraduate Student & Learning and
Engagement Coordinator

Defining your criteria

What are the critical criteria for a job? What are the essential and desirable aspects of the role? Employers will list their essential and desirable characteristics of the person they have in mind for the role, and you should also spend a bit of time carving out your key criteria for what your ideal job is. There is no point in applying for jobs that require unsocial working hours if you value family time and weekends or jobs that you do not have the skills and abilities for. You might achieve the position but end up being miserable and leave for something else. It does neither you nor your employer any good to always have 'one eye on the door'. Remember, however, that there is no absolutely perfect job, but with the right attitude and energy, you can make the imperfect perfect enough.

Career story in focus: clinical psychology

"My PhD supervisor had moved universities and encouraged me to apply for full funding in her new Department of Psychology in Wales. I was incredibly fortunate and managed to gain a funded PhD with the option to undertake a lectureship the year following the completion of my thesis. I enjoyed research and writing thoroughly, spending three years exploring links between works of art and neurodegeneration. It still feels like such an enormous privilege to have been given the opportunity to have done this. Though I enjoyed academia, there were aspects of it (teaching!) that I felt overwhelmed by and knew that others did much better than I could. I knew that I wanted to explore career options within Clinical Psychology, so towards the end of my PhD I applied for lots of Assistant Psychology roles. Most of my applications did not receive a response and I had a few failed interviews before I was offered a position of Assistant Psychologist with an Older Adults NHS service in the South East of England.

I know that obtaining an Assistant Psychologist position can be incredibly challenging and I am aware that there may be some reading this hoping for some useful advice. Sadly, there is no magic formula. Being an Assistant Psychologist is not a mandatory prerequisite for getting a place on the Clinical Psychology Doctorate. For example, several of my cohort did not have any assistant experience but had worked as IAPT therapists, carers and heath care assistants. As such, the following advice is based on my own experiences: I checked NHS jobs on a daily basis; I tailored my application form specifically to the service and job role I applied to (taking care to mention the service within the application); I outlined my previous clinical and research experience and reflected on how it might be applicable to the service and job role; I proofread my application several times; during the interview I gave examples which demonstrated my experience but also reflected on where things had not gone to plan and what I had learned on those occasions; I prepared a couple of questions to ask at the end. I also think that I have been very, very lucky".

Tamsin Williams, Clinical Psychologist

Thinking about the kinds of organisations you would like to work for is also an excellent way to eventually land your dream job, because it helps pivot your focus towards your career story and the organisation's story and away from the nuts and bolts of 'the job'. This means that in the short term, whilst your employer gets to know you, you should spend time investing in that joint partnership. You are both aiming to give and receive in equal amounts. Good organisations spend time developing their staff. They nurture highly committed workers who do their jobs well, so it is worth taking a longer-term view of your career and considering

Table 5.1 Defining your criteria

Criteria	Find the facts	Take note
Preferred areas of work	Accountancy, banking and finance. Business, consulting and management. Charity and voluntary work. Creative arts and design. Energy and utilities. Engineering and manufacturing. Environment and agriculture. Health care.	Think about the company, not the position. If it is a great company, one that you feel passionate about, consider accepting a job below your skills, knowledge and abilities and start working your way up.
Level of responsibility	Receives on-the-job training while working under close supervision, typically working on small tasks within larger projects. Performs activities/tasks with occasional direct supervision. Performs activities/tasks with limited direct supervision and solves problems. Also makes some decisions for which they assume responsibility. Works in a complex area without direct supervision. Works from broad task objectives, is accountable for significant activity/task decisions and may train others. Holds a senior position and may act as a manager or consultant. Independently conceives programs and defines problems to be studied or objectives to be achieved. Is involved in long-term planning for the organisation. Performs a senior management role with overall responsibility for projects while supervising teams of professionals.	**Ask questions at interview:** *What opportunities and routes for career and skill development are provided at the company? What are the career advancement opportunities with your organisation?*

		How much tax will you pay?
Features and benefits	Salary Pension Company car Holiday entitlement Private medical insurance Corporate discounts Tickets to events Childcare vouchers Paternity/maternity leave Notice periods	Use this service to estimate how much income tax and national insurance you should pay: www.gov.uk/estimate-income-tax Most benefits will be taxable. You will, for example, pay tax if you or your family use a company car privately, including for commuting. You pay tax on the value to you of the company car, which depends on things like how much it would cost to buy and the type of fuel it uses.
Contract	Full-time, part-time, flexible working, consultancy	
Distance to work	Journey time and commuting costs Parking costs	
Travel as part of the role	National/international Weekly, monthly, annually	

applying for and accepting a role that is below your competence level. You are unlikely to be limited to that role in the long term, and your hard work and commitment will make you stand out and be noticed. Sheryl Sandberg, for example, was VP of global online sales and operations at Google when she went to work for the unknown Facebook.

Looking at jobs you truly aspire to in the future is also a great way of thinking about what skills and knowledge you have yet to develop. There are a few key pieces of information around the recruitment process that are worth getting really familiar with. There is, of course, the job advertisement, but behind the advert is some important documentation: the job description, the person specification and the application form.

Recruitment companies

There are a few organisations that will still advertise in the printed press and on their own webpages and sector-specific webpages (for example, jobs.NHS.uk or jobs.ac.uk for academic posts), but most organisations now place their job adverts online; as such, the majority of job openings are widely accessible on the World Wide Web. Some organisations will use specialist recruitment consultants (head-hunters), but these tend to be for highly skilled and senior positions.

www.indeed.co.uk/ provides job adverts and company reviews, and you can upload your CV for recruiters to view.

Milkround.com is a digital job resource for graduates in the early stages of their career. In addition to job adverts and internship opportunities, it offers careers advice and matching/placement services, and you can post your CV to be viewed by recruiters. www.milkround.com/

Monster offers careers advice and job adverts, and you can place your résumé with it for potential recruiters to see. www.monster.co.uk/

Receive job alerts, register your CV and more with Jobs Graduate. www. jobs-graduate.co.uk/

LinkedIn for students: https://university.linkedin.com/linkedin-for-students

---

To make your life easier, some organisations will also provide 'about us', which includes documentation such as vision and mission statements, organisational structure and general marketing material. It is very important that you study this information because there will be opportunities in those documents for you to demonstrate how you are best aligned to that organisation. Even if your perusal of the literature is only aspirational at this time and even if you are applying for a post but do not end up being successful for that position, the time is not wasted.

Each time you immerse yourself in 'about us' documentation, you are building up your knowledge of that organisation and the industry it operates in, and you never know when you might meet them at a networking event.

Use the careers services

It has been over 20 years since the Dearing report[1] placed graduate employability on the university agenda; careers services are now embedded in the strategic role of the university. Whilst these services can vary widely in both the range and quality of information they provide to students, they are still a good place to start your search. Careers services focus on providing a range of resources to students. They will have access to the most up-to-date labour market information, employer literature, occupational profiles and training and education routes, as well as hands-on support with job search strategies, CV and application letter writing, interview practice sessions, psychometric testing and graduate networking events. There is good evidence that students who visit career services are more likely to get jobs and those jobs are more fulfilling,[2] and they are particularly effective in contributing to more equal outcomes for students from lower socioeconomic backgrounds.[3] So do not wait until your final year to start using these free and impartial faculties. Make the most of it from the moment you enter university by setting up some time for a short consultation to explore your skills, interests and further ambitions and begin to explore the kinds of roles that might be good for you. Build a relationship with your careers advisor. They can become a critical ally in identifying suitable volunteer, placement and internship opportunities that may come up. Then as you progress through your degree, you will feel more confident speaking to them about your concerns and identifying areas where you need to improve.

Careers in focus: careers advisors

Careers advisors provide information and guidance to help individuals make decisions about career paths and different industries and sectors as well as giving direction and advice on additional training and education. The work is varied. You may be working to design digital and print literature, carrying out face-to-face consultations, running group sessions or giving public talks. The scope of the role is not limited to university students. Advisors also work with school children over the age of 13 or adults who are seeking a career change. There are also a number of specialist areas where careers advisors play a vital role in transforming people's lives by helping people overcome barriers to employment, such as working with adults with learning disabilities or with ex-offenders.

Find out more

National Careers Service
https://nationalcareers.service.gov.uk/

Remploy: disability employment specialist
www.remploy.co.uk/

Prospects: careers advisor role profile
www.prospects.ac.uk/job-profiles/careers-adviser

Scope: disability equality charity
www.scope.org.uk/employment-services/

Prisoner Education Trust
www.prisonerseducation.org.uk/

SAQ: interview questions

What challenges are you seeking from this position?

Understanding what challenges you in the first place will help you start to formulate and answer questions such as these and connect your answers to the job you are pursuing. (Possible motivators – think abstractly; for example, high-performing teams, innovation and creativity, partnerships and relationships, customer satisfaction, the feeling of achievement.)

How would you describe your approach to problem solving?

Psychology teaches students to be outstanding abstract thinkers, reflecting on ideas, attributes and relationships. For example, rather than focusing on human failure in the workplace as a 'person-error' problem (*What did that person do wrong?*), psychology teaches students to think more widely (e.g. What is wrong with the work system that created this problem? How could I investigate this problem?).

What did you do to remain productive during COVID-19?

Perhaps don't mention becoming a wine connoisseur. If you do get a question like this, remember to frame your answer within your subject knowledge. For example, think about the psychology behind goal setting and how you might have applied your knowledge to your own productivity, health and well-being. Also, ensure you describe how you will apply your learning and experience to the role you are interested in.

Getting to shortlist

The vast majority of positions that you will see advertised will have approached hiring in the same way. The process starts with a detailed job analysis, which is the process of examining job incumbents to determine the range of activities they perform in their role and the knowledge, skills and attributes they need to complete their responsibilities effectively. From this job analysis, decisions of pay scale are formulated in comparison with others within the organisation fulfilling similar tasks and externally with other posts in the field. Consideration is then given to how the applications will be compared against one another. The job specification derived from the job analysis was a useful device to keep the interviewers on point. They could rate and rank the candidates more objectively and transparently, thus removing the risk that unconscious bias would come into the interview process. For roles that required specific aptitudes and skills, psychometric tests of personality and cognitive ability were added to the selection process, followed by even more complex assessment centres, whereby candidates would be exposed to work-relevant tasks, interviews and problem-solving activities as a way of making more accurate predictions about their suitability.

Career in focus: the psychometrician

Students of psychology spend a substantive amount of their education on issues such as test reliability and validity and the circumstances, cultural differences or socioeconomic barriers that may influence test results, but outside of the field, it is concerning how many testing misperceptions persist. That is why many psychology graduates go on to have careers in areas such as psychometric testing and HR.

A psychometrician is a person who is skilled in the administration and interpretation of psychological tests. Psychometricians also go on to develop their skills so that they are able to devise, construct and standardise psychometric tests. The British Psychological Society offers advice and guidance in the further training of graduates.

Find out more here: https://ptc.bps.org.uk/bps-qualifications-test-use

---

The job advertisement

Adverts tend to be fairly limited in the information that they are able to convey. Most are short and snappy, with the key criteria listed in brief (contract, location, salary and whom they are looking for). If the advert is asking for a psychologist with marketing experience and you have no relevant experience, do not be tempted to spend time applying. You are wasting your time convincing yourself that they will be interested in your application; pivot your focus elsewhere.

The job description and person specification

The job description is a formal account of the main duties that come with the role, the management and reporting structures and the duties and responsibilities that come with the role. The description is useful because it gives you a picture of what the job would be like, and it has most likely been drawn up by the person making the recruiting decisions. The job description can also be critical to monitor how roles change over the course of time. The jobs that we are doing can change significantly as organisations change in line with social, environmental, political and technological advances. For human resource managers and employees, job descriptions are therefore a key resource to enable organisations to revert back to the specification to judge the degree to which any job re-evaluation in regard to training, development and payment grades has changed.

Example job description and person specification

JOB REFERENCE **AHSM/134B**: ASSISTANT HEALTH AND SAFETY MANAGER ROLE RESPONSIBILITY

- Working with health and safety manager to ensure a safe workplace without risk to health and ensuring adherence to regulatory requirements;
- Communicate to staff all health and safety policies, procedures, rules and regulations and ensure that staff are compliant with protective and preventative measures;
- Complete and review risk assessments for work, equipment and transport operations;
- Co-ordinate the development of health and safety policies and safe systems of work and procedures and ensure the completion of tasks;
- Document all accidents and support investigations as appropriate.

Qualifications	Essential	Desirable
Degree in a relevant discipline (2.2 or above)	x	
NEBOSH diploma (or prepared to train to NEBOSH)	x	

Qualifications	Essential	Desirable
Experience		
Health and safety management experience		x
Understanding of the health and safety executive and other applicable legislation		x
A confident and articulate communicator	x	
Problem-solving skills and a 'can-do' attitude	x	
An influencer who can work to change behaviour and attitudes	x	

The person specification goes into much more refined detail about what the ideal new employee will have in terms of knowledge, attitude, skills and abilities. These competencies could include formal qualifications, for example, a BPS-accredited psychology degree or chartership in psychology, but they could also include physical attributes such as good eyesight and physical fitness or social and personal qualities such as being prepared to work unsocial hours and remaining flexible. Each criterion should have been selected to appear on the person specification through a rigorous job analysis, which is the process of gathering information about the human and contextual aspects of jobs and then analysing those criteria for relevance.

The person specification provides potential applicants with the level and complexity of the jobs they will perform and with the criteria believed to be either essential or desirable. Essential criteria are considered critical for satisfactory performance, whereas desirable criteria enhance an individual's capacity to do the job but could also be picked up or developed in the post. It also makes for a smooth and transparent recruitment process. It operates as an objective standard by which to evaluate candidates against both the criteria and against one another, whilst objectively protecting the interview panel against unsound judgements that might be based on criteria that are irrelevant to the job such as gender, religion or race.

If you wish to be shortlisted, it is essential that you manage to demonstrate how you meet each of the essential and desirable criteria. Consider each aspect of the application a question to you. If the application lists team working experience, clearly demonstrate how you meet that criteria. It is not sufficient to state 'teamwork experience'. The response must be much richer and detail the explicit nature of the teams you have been involved with:

Teamwork Experience: "My most formative team working experience was membership of my university swimming team. When not competing nationally, we train together and learn from one another's performance; we would pitch up even if we were not competing and we would cheer each other on. I learned the importance of supporting my teammates' performance and also how critical learning from others is to sustaining high performance".

When you approach your letter of application in this way, you are sending a constant stream of positive messages to the recruiter. It therefore makes it incredibly easy for the person reviewing the document not only to pinpoint your suitability to the position but also to visualise the virtues that you will bring to their organisation. You can take this one step further if you take your examples and demonstrate how they would fit within the organisational culture, values and ethos.

> Teamwork Experience: "My most formative team working experience was membership of my university swimming team. When not competing nationally, we train together and learn from one another's performance; we would pitch up even if we were not competing and we would cheer each other on. I learned the importance of supporting my teammates' performance and also how critical learning from others is to sustaining high performance. One of the reasons I was attracted to your organisation is its partnership with the Youth Sport Trust. I would welcome the opportunity to become involved in supporting your organisation to meet its charitable objectives, perhaps by writing blogs or giving talks on the subject".

This response now clearly tells the recruiter that you have spent the time and energy (i) exploring the personal specification and providing relevant information, and (ii) you have spent time getting to know the organisation's values and demonstrated the added value that you would bring outside of the 'day job'. You are the kind of person prepared to go the extra mile.

CV/résumé/covering letter

A CV is more detailed and can cover the entirety of someone's career
A résumé summarises job relevant information
A covering letter demonstrates how you meet the person specification

Top tip. Build a CV. Keep it constantly updated. Then harvest the relevant information into the résumé for each job you apply for.

Beat the bots

One of the challenges with this kind of application process is that hundreds of people are quite possibly doing the exact same thing. The more qualified and specialised you become, the less the qualified and specialised competition, but as a new graduate, you will be competing with the masses. The problem is so significant that many applications are never processed by humans at all; they are fed into a CV screening software system that can process hundreds of applications efficiently. Your carefully crafted CV and application letter can end up quickly filtered out by résumé bots. Rejection rates for application screening software can be as high as 75%, so if you want to win, you need to learn to speak bot.

Bots speak one language: keywords. To beat the bots, you need to fit in before you can stand out. This means spending time on the application webpages, examining how bots handle your data. For example, LinkedIn for students has an applicant insights function. If you spot a job you are interested in or aspire to, you can scroll down to the bottom of the advert, and you will see that the bot system has already identified the extent to which you have evidence in your profile of the criteria posted by the recruiter. You can then go back into your profile and add skills that you may have overlooked to ensure a better match. This system also gives you a heads up based on your skills and qualifications of whether you are likely to be at the top of the applicant pile. So, if you are not likely to be in the top percent, then you do not need to waste your precious time applying.

Ensure you commit time to closely examining the person specification and look at the language that is used and mirror it in your application. Ensure that you pepper your work experience with relevant keywords that are the same or similar to the person specification and keep content such as job titles, attributes and abilities as clear and simple as possible; 'innovator', for example, works better than the unicorn status of 'disruptor'. You must list the relevant qualifications, skills and experience, but do not be tempted to list everything you have ever done. In particular, irrelevant content, no matter how interesting, will increase the chances that your application will be rejected. Do not use fancy formatting or tables because the bots cannot cope, so no matter how pretty your application is, it will end up in the bin, and photographs are not acceptable. Most organisations do not permit them because they increase the changes of bias in the application process. Another useful tip is to create your résumé and CV in the usual way in Word, but then remove all of the formatting and save them as text files. You can check the text file to make sure that the information is

correctly captured (and edit as needed). Upload that file. Usually what you will find is that once you have uploaded that content, there is an additional opportunity to upload a second file. This is where you can place your formatted document in the system. The bot is happy. It has its basic text and, should you get through to the shortlisting state, the recruiter can see your lovely résumé and application letter.

If you can find a way to network your way past the bot system through your contacts, you will have a better chance of selling yourself, and you are also less likely to find yourself in a limiting, generic job that you are perhaps not so well suited to. Recruitment mistakes are costly for organisations, and for that reason, they are much more tolerant of misperceiving candidates, perceiving that they are bad candidates when they are good candidates, and more tolerant of hiring people they know or are familiar with. In most cases, there are lots of good candidates, so if a few great applicants fall to the ground, it is not really a problem that organisations care about. There is nothing you can do except develop your personal connections. So, use your psychology to break into the hidden job market and get yourself hired by working your connections or making direct approaches. Very few candidates are this bold or unconventional. What is the worst that can happen? HR might just bat you back to the bots, or you might just land a conversation with one of the recruiting team, who can give you a meaningful conversation about what the job is actually like. Organisations are always in search of confident, quality people to join their teams. So seek out the company leadership team and connect. If their email address is not obviously available on the organisation's web pages, there are a number of well-practiced strategies for tracking them down. One of the most transparent and easiest ways to make a connection is to find them on LinkedIn and send a connection request. Presuming they accept (most people do; it is the beauty of LinkedIn), you have the opportunity to explore what has been going on and, through your own posts, impress and persuade.

Danger danger

Phantom job openings: Stay away from jobs that have a torturous and unusual list of person specification criteria and are advertised for a very short period of time. Those jobs are already taken. The organisation has someone in mind. Do not kid yourself, because you will not be successful.

'Super-duper' job descriptions. Super-dupers have all the criteria of previous employees in that role, with more super-duper criteria added just for kicks. Tells of super-duper job descriptions are when a post you were (are) interested in is re-advertised. They cannot fill the post because their recruitment processes are broken, and that person does not exist, so do not apply.

Contact details

Make sure you put your name and contact details at the top of the page, and do not be tempted to give over more space than is necessary. If an application form is requested, some organisations would in fact consider writing your address at the top of your CV a waste of space. By the time you have prepared your CV, supporting letter and application form, you could have provided your details three times, so consider the overall balance of your application and avoid, where possible, repeating yourself.

Formatting

CV formatting tools and templates are notorious for creating space-wasting documents (hated by bots *and* recruitment teams) that come across as overly elaborate, pretentious and pointless. Save creating your own headed paper until you have an organisation of your own and, even then, keep it simple. Keep your text constant, because there is nothing more annoying than body text changes in font or size. Make sure you do a thorough check of the overall impression of your font and text size, because sometimes differences can drift in as a result of cutting and pasting from different documents. Choose a font that is professional (Calibri, Garamond, Georgia, Arial). Do differentiate between the main text and header. Perhaps try the heading functions in Word to obtain a suitable balance. Justify your text for clean alignment. Justification gets bad press for decreasing readability, but in documents where the information is dense and someone is trying to keep track of where they have got to, it makes sense to justify. The strong verticals stop the reader from accidentally jumping to the next section. Keep indentation to a minimum. Indents waste space and make the page look uneven.

Qualifications

List qualifications with the most recent at the top. You do not need to list everything (especially poor grades). Unless your A levels are all outstanding, do not be tempted to list them on your résumé. You may be asked for them on an application form, and you should not omit that information (or lie), but your D in geography is not a great addition to your résumé.

Work experience

In Chapter 2 we demonstrated the range of skills and knowledge that psychology students have developed during their degree. The challenge ahead is to communicate that expertise in a way that others outside of the discipline can make sense of. A typical example of work experience that we often see looks like this:

Sep 2019–Jan 2020, Part-time Research Assistant
Jan 2019–May 2019, Cleaning Assistant with Gleamz Cleaning
June 2018–Nov 2019, Shop Assistant, Waitrose, Chester
May 2017–June 2018, Waitress, Starbucks, Chester

Because people sometimes see their early work experiences as menial in nature and because that work is often quite historical, that information tends to remain highly underspecified in resumes. This is a shame, because there are often excellent opportunities to demonstrate a wide range of competencies. At first look, a career history presented in this way can also give the impression that the applicant's career is drifting. They started in Starbucks and have ended up as a part-time research assistant. This is a missed opportunity because the key skills for a cleaner are:

- A reasonable level of fitness;
- Punctual, reliable and trustworthy;
- Able to manage time effectively;
- Ability to work both alone and in a team;
- Awareness of health and safety procedures;
- Math skills for measuring cleaning fluids.

> **Top tip**
> **Do not** be tempted to list your skills like this, like a 'shopping list'.
>
> **Skills need to be leveraged and applied in context.**

If the original advert and person specification were not stored, you are also unlikely to have at hand the list of competencies for that role. Fortunately, Google is at hand. Search for adverts that are similar to the role you had, or you can also use any number of career planner webpages that list innumerable job titles and descriptions in detail. Gather those key words and pepper your work experience section with them. Use the context in which they were acquired to bring them to life.

Sep 2019–Jan 2020, Research Assistant

> **Top tip**
> Be careful of repetition in your statements and descriptions. This paragraph lists "I have" three times, and it makes for a repetitive read.

This role required significant attention to detail, sensitivity to the matters being researched and strong technical skills in qualitative research analysis. I have carried out empirical studies involving a variety of methods of data collection, including experiments, observation, questionnaires, interviews and focus groups. I have evaluated data and evidence through qualitative techniques such as grounded theory and quantitative techniques such as statistical analysis. I have presented my work to peers, lecturers and the general public and am now competent in the analysis, presentation and defence of my work.

Jan 2019–May 2019, Cleaning Assistant with Gleamz Cleaning

As a cleaning assistant, I have high levels of personal fitness, and I am punctual, reliable and trustworthy. Juggling this role with my university studies has required me to develop outstanding time management skills and team-work behaviours such as trust and responsibility. I am particularly proud of my ability to daily apply mathematical skills in the handling and measurement of cleaning fluids. I ensure that I am always up to date with the most recent health and safety legislation as applies to my workplace.

June 2018–Nov 2019, Shop Assistant, Waitrose, Chester

Provided excellence in commercial awareness by developing expert product knowledge and keeping up to date with food and drink trends. Customer service aware, putting customers first and managing customer queries and complaints constructively. Took initiative to solve problems such as staff illness or staff shortages.

May 2017–June 2018, Waitress, Starbucks, Chester

Developed expertise in shift planning and teamwork under pressure by training as a barista, then training as a learning coach to support and guide new hires.

Organising your covering letter

Writing a covering letter that will stand out is possibly the most challenging part of the application process. If you keep a 'live' CV document and get in the habit of harvesting the relevant content from it, the process does become easier, but you still have to do the research and put the effort into creating a letter that pushes you to the top of the pile. Do not be tempted to send out the same letter for each position that you apply for (with or without a few minor tweaks). Organisations can spot this, and you may even leave a few mistakes in the document and, for example, name the wrong organisation.

Make sure the first paragraph is gripping. This means avoiding at all costs starting the letter with 'I am applying for the job that I saw in *blah blah blah*', which is a total waste of words and will send the recruiter to sleep. The first paragraph needs to make a statement, so be bold and enthusiastic. If you can, name drop, which immediately personalises the communication. Make it clear what has attracted you to the position and why you want this job, and, if you can, lead with a major personal accomplishment.

The main body of the letter should explicitly state how you meet the essential and desirable criteria, and it should emphasise the personal and any added value you bring to the organisation. There may be quite a few criteria, so you need to spend a bit of time blending your experience so that you can demonstrate how you hit the criteria in as brief a space as possible. Your letter has to be succinct, but don't forget it is backed up by your CV. You will want to appear up to date with industry developments, so ensure that you weave into your letter any external forces that may influence the organisation. Influences that shape organisations include the political and economic climate and social and technological (PESTs) changes. The level of understanding that applicants have on these issues and their ability to express that information in a way that an organisation needs are major factors in separating the great candidates from the mediocre. So, where you can, make reference to relevant market forces and, if possible, demonstrate how, through your experience, you have tackled such issues before.

End with a strong conclusion to your application. A clear message that draws on why you would be a good fit with their organisational mission and values is always a safe bet. It demonstrates you have studied the organisation, you are engaged and you have given some thought to how you would fit into their working practices and culture.

What my CV really says

IT skills: Microsoft Word, PowerPoint and data analysis packages such as Excel and SPSS.

(Employer reads: "*Candidate able to follow the herd and put a list of menial skills that everyone has, except perhaps my nan. And what is SPSS?*")

Tip: Ditch the shopping list in favour of specifics, goals and metrics. The key is to think of something tangible that you have worked on that reflects your IT abilities, teamworking and leadership skills.

For example,

IT skills: To create quality content and facilitate group working and collaboration, I have expanded on my competence with client software packages (such as Microsoft Office) with blogging and social media tools (for example, Canva, BuzzSumo, Wordpress) and file storage and synchronisation services such as Google Drive and the cloud. In the past 12 months, I have used these tools to write X number of assignments/blog posts/articles, which resulted in me exceeding my goals to obtain a grade point average of 65 percent across my degree. I am particularly proud of one piece of coursework which required me to create a virtual network with other interested and enthusiastic students in the creation of a psychology newsletter article which explored the critical nature of psychology students' advanced analytical skills and competence with statistical programme (for example, SPSS or JASP) in the world of the future.

(Employer reads: *"Applicant has an IT arsenal. They can build a team using technology and produce outputs of value, and I didn't know that psychology students had advanced analytical skills. Isn't that interesting?"*)

This makes it easy for the recruiter. There are checks and balances in all organisations, and they will have to demonstrate to someone higher up the food chain why they have hired you. If your application provides them with that explanation, then your path to the post could be significantly smoothed.

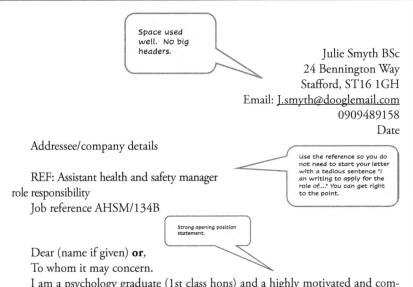

Space used well. No big headers.

Julie Smyth BSc
24 Bennington Way
Stafford, ST16 1GH
Email: J.smyth@dooglemail.com
0909489158
Date

Addressee/company details

REF: Assistant health and safety manager
role responsibility
Job reference AHSM/134B

Use the reference so you do not need to start your letter with a tedious sentence "I an writing to apply for the role of...." You can get right to the point.

Strong opening position statement.

Dear (name if given) **or**,
To whom it may concern.

I am a psychology graduate (1st class hons) and a highly motivated and committed student volunteer with the Samaritans. I am a passionate ambassador for student well-being and mental health with applied experience in the health and safety industry. This position was recommended to me by Dr Matt Flowers, who speaks of BAE as being an exceptional organisation that supports early career psychologists. I would like to take this opportunity to draw your attention to examples where I feel that I meet or exceed the criteria for this position.

Influencer, team player problem solver.

My final year psychology dissertation explored the determinants of psychology student graduate employment. Throughout my studies of this subject, I discovered that there are many competing perspectives; for example, it is widely acknowledged that students should develop a wide range of qualities and attributes that contribute to their employment, yet such attributes are impossible to develop without real-world work experience. I used my developing expertise in this area to lobby for better placement

> Clearly addressing the desirable and essential criteria by showing that she is a skilled communicator and that she has health and safety experience but also how she was able to apply these skills to solve a research problem.

> Work experience blended with attributes.

support for psychology students so that they might find effective work experience opportunities and that this knowledge might be used to help them better understand the theories and research that they were engaging with throughout their studies.

For example, although my work experience to date has been limited to the cleaning industry, I have been fortunate to work with an organisation that has supported my professional development. I have been regularly provided with training and development in areas such as health and safety. This experience helped me apply learning from my psychology degree in areas such as human judgement, decision-making and error, which resulted in the successful completion of a team project. This project focused on student risk-taking behaviour and the role that nudge theory can play in encouraging improved decision-making under pressure.

> Application of work experience to research.

Through my volunteering work, I have become much more aware of the role that health and safety play in workplace mental health. I have managed many situations where Samaritan clients have felt overwhelmed by their working conditions, leading to physical and mental health problems. I feel

> Added value.

that I could bring these insights to your organisation with the purpose of developing good working practices and training initiatives that would minimise pressure and potential workplace stressors.

Strong closing paragraph. You need a strong paragraph that sums up your strengths and details what you bring to the organisation. It should be polite and confident. For example: I am curious, I want to learn and I am ready to seize career opportunities as they emerge. Work-life balance to me means achievement, pride and enjoyment. I would be

> Strong closing paragraph that says something about them and how you are a great fit for their organisation.

thrilled to learn more about this job opportunity and show how I can help (name the organisation) in its mission to do (name something from the mission statement).

Yours faithfully,

> If you've begun your letter with the person's name, then you should end it with 'Yours sincerely,' followed by your signature, followed by your name. If you don't know the name of the person you're writing to, then you end your letter with 'Yours faithfully', followed by your signature, followed by your name.

Why do you want to work for our company?

The one thing that can be said about interviews with any certainty is that they are predictable: you will arrive, be greeted, enter the room and some gentle introductions and small talk will take place to settle you into the meeting. You may be asked to give a presentation; then questions will gradually become more difficult (or they may be divided into themes or topics). At the end, you will be asked if you have any questions, and then the interview is concluded and you are compared at the end against the performance of the standard criteria and others who were also interviewed. This predictability does not, however, do much to reduce or even manage the understandable anxiety that most people feel when they are brought to a strange place to talk to and be judged by people in a position of authority. The good news is that there are a number of steps that you can take to manage this anxiety and present the best version of yourself.

My hot tip is be yourself. That's obvious to say and incredibly hard to actually achieve given the high stakes and the feeling of pressure that creates. Just remember, the interviewer is a human being. *If you imagine you are meeting them outside of a high stakes situation, such as meeting a friend at a café, you'd speak to them in an entirely different way. You'd be yourself. Free yourself up to be you.*

Steve, Apps Recruitment Consultant

Try to arrange an informal conversation

In many circumstances, there will be a contact provided at the time of advertisement for prospective applicants to discuss the role with. If this opportunity exists, take advantage. On many occasions, that individual will also be on the recruitment panel, so it makes good sense to phone and begin to develop some rapport. This gives you the opportunity to ask questions such as: Why did this role come about? What plans does the organisation have for expansion? What are the organisation's key priorities at the moment? You can also ask questions about salary and therefore enter the final stages of the negotiation at a bit more of an advantage.

The organisation wants to know what *you* know, and they want to know what impressed you. You will want to know if this is the kind of organisation you really want to work for. Therefore, when you arrive at the interview, continue to keep this strategy front and centre. When you meet the receptionist or other welcoming committee, be polite and engaged, and ask lots of questions, because you never know who will be asked for an impression of what you were like.

Ditch the beige small talk

Interview panels are often uninspiring experiences, and by the time the interview panel has listened to the third person talk about weather and traffic, they are often in the pits of despair. Do yourself a favour and do not fall back on beige topics; find something that is going to differentiate you from everyone else. If it is beige, make sure it is linked with something more interesting: "I managed to avoid the rain by nipping into the local market and buying some amazing peppers. I am going to attempt to make some chili sauce". "I got here early and spent my time exploring the local (insert museum, monument etc)". Take a look at the LinkedIn profile of the panel, and see if you can identify a common interest, but do not present yourself as an online stalker. "I saw you playing football with your kids on Instagram; I love little kids" is not a great start. "I got here early and spent my time in the Liverpool football shop trying to pick up some memorabilia for my little brother" is better.

Might we possibly return to that question later?

If you have done your organisational and PEST research, this will greatly reduce the chances that you will be asked a question you just cannot answer. It is worth accepting up front, however, that at some point in some interview, you will be asked a question that will make you flounder. Spending a bit of time thinking about this uncomfortable scenario and imagining how you will handle it is a critical interview preparation technique. Yes, nobody wants to think about not being able to perform in a situation where you are being judged, but it will happen at some point, so being prepared means that you will be in a better position to move on quickly and nail the remainder of the interview. One bad answer doesn't mean a failed interview unless your nerves get in the way and you dwell on it.

Take your time. "Hmm . . . that's an interesting question. I will need a minute to think about that" may be sufficient to ensure that you do not blurt out the first response that comes to mind. Then, if you are still struggling, you can answer, explaining why you find that question particularly tough to answer. Or simply ask if it might be possible to return to that question later in the interview. This shows a more careful response, and it gives you time to collect your thoughts. If they say no, then you might want to question why you would ever want to work with such an inflexible organisation.

Can we return to that question in a bit?

"I was once asked to talk about something that had gone wrong. This totally threw me. I could not think of a single incident not a one. Which is ridiculous because everyone has experienced failure. I was completely functionally fixed on the question of "wrong". My brain would not let me out of the trap of what had gone "wrong" and I started blurting.

It was only later in the interview, once I had relaxed, I realised what the issue was. I tend not to dwell on what has gone wrong, rather than what the solutions had been put in place to make the process better. If they had asked me what I had done to address challenges or problems at work, I could have spoken all day. At that moment and under pressure, my thinking had narrowed to the point where all I could do was say, I cannot answer that. It was a horrible experience and I performed badly through the rest of the interview.

Towards the end I was able to pull it back around. I knew I had fluffed the interview so had relaxed so when I asked if there was something more to add, I was able to talk about being functionally fixed on the word wrong, because it did not reflect my usual thinking style or problem orientated approach".

Author

Preparing to SOAR

SOAR is an established technique for organising accomplishment stories. SOAR supports candidates by helping them to develop responses that are contextualised from direct experience. As such, candidates are buffered from blurting out unstructured general responses, and they start to speak with confidence about their accomplishments.

Why did you leave your last job?

Practice your exit statement and ensure that you have at least two objective people look at it. In most cases, candidates will be pursuing career advancement, but if your reason for applying for the post was more push than pull, be careful how you exit. It is a very risky strategy to complain about a previous employer at the interview. No matter how poorly treated you have been, your narrative will be received as complaints and excuses. Second, you would be surprised at how many people look back at their old employer with rose-tinted glasses. The future is never certain; you never know when you might need your old employer. So, keep your exit statement focused on the positive: what you have learned and your personal achievements, and focus on the next steps for your career, not what has gone in the past.

SAQ: SOAR practice questions

For each of the questions in the SAQ, write out SOAR responses and consider what skills were used in the process.

1   Tell me about a time when something went wrong.
2   What goals or objectives did you set in your last position?
3   Tell me about your experience of organisational change.
4   How do other people benefit from working with you?
5   Tell me about at time when you had to work with a difficult co-worker.

Situation: *Describe the situation*
Obstacles: *What obstacles were faced?*
Actions: *What actions did you take? And what skills did you apply?*
Results: *What were the results of your actions?*

What are your salary expectations?

This is possibly one of the most critical aspects of negotiating your contract, and because I can feel my editor (and you) twitching at how long this chapter already is, we deal with it in Chapter 8. Read it, because it will change your bank more predictably that a lottery ticket ever could.

Don't blow it

Always remember that the greatest skill that you have is communication. It really doesn't matter how much thought and preparation you put into your application, CV and interview performance; if you fail to get the interview team to listen to you, then your preparation was useless. Interview panels have notoriously short attention spans. People only ever really take in about 40% of what they hear. This is not because you are boring as heck; rather, the listener is always ahead of the person doing the talking.[4] People think roughly four to five times faster than the person doing the talking, so if you are not careful, they will quickly become preoccupied in their own world.

Remember that any interview panel will be testing your *communication skills*, and those skills are much more than the sum total of the information you want to convey or the number of boring, banal and PowerPoint-obsessed talks you delivered as an undergraduate. To be a great communicator, you need to think about how you will get your message across and what your audience will be willing to listen to, because zero attention = zero communication = zero results.

Getting people to pay attention was something that Aristotle turned into a craft. Aristotle's three appeals (tactics) were:

THE UNEXAMINED LIFE, COMBINED WITH AN MSc, IS HIGHLY MARKETABLE.

©2010 Stivers

1 Logos: *rationality, logic and facts*
2 Ethos: *creditability, authority and reliability*
3 Pathos: *emotional appeal, imagination and sympathy*

Logos: these are the words that you use; how you stop and get everyone's attention with a story that is worth telling. Ethos is how credible you appear. This is why it is important to have a story to scaffold your logos. If you cannot ground what you are saying in personal experience or a good story, then no matter how clear the facts of the message, you will appear inauthentic and dull, and your audience will quickly become disinterested. This is why some of the most memorable (and most popular) TedTalks are wrapped in a 'detective' story that brings the listener on a journey to the truth (a bit like *Pulp Fiction*) because the entire point of 1 and 2 is to get the listener to point 3 (pathos). This is the emotional appeal that gets *your story* to complement *their story*. This is why spending time researching the organisation and its interview panel gives you secret storytelling power. You become more able to speak directly to their stories and demonstrate empathy and insight into their thought processes, values and priorities. In short, if you want to keep your audience's attention, there should not be too much 'me, me, me' at the expense of 'you, you, you'.

And when you do blow it . . .

Where interviews are concerned, people do not generally fear failure; it is observation, criticism and judgement that are hard to take. There will be a lot of that before you land your dream job. In the early days of the job hunt, failure will come thick and fast, but slowly you will get better and better at interviewing, and you will eventually land that job. Anything that is worth doing attracts admiration and criticism; it is the natural consequence of success. Listening to interview feedback is unlikely to be your best experience of the week, but you risk far more by not putting yourself out there and having that conversation.

If you are rejected, it doesn't mean that you were not good enough or that you made some terrible mistake; it simply means that on that day at their interview, your story did not match their story. There can be many different reasons for the lack of story matching, many of which are entirely out of your hands. There may have been an in-house candidate behind the scenes, or there may have been a superhuman applicant, or you may have completely tanked the interview; if you always do what you always do, then you will always get what you have always gotten.[5] You may never entirely know the exact reasons why you fell short, but you can get closer to understanding by asking for feedback, and next time, you might just do something differently.

Feedback is a unique opportunity to obtain some objective information about yourself from strangers, and that opportunity has substantive value to the job hunter. Second, you are again building rapport with the recruitment team and the organisation, and you never know when another opening may come about. They may have been unable to recruit you for that job because you fell short on a particular attribute, but they may have noticed other employability characteristics of value. There have been many occasions where organisations have gone about creating a new post for an exceptional candidate who was not a good fit for a particular role. If you bury yourself in self-pity, or, worse still, start to challenge the individual giving the feedback, you may end up losing a job you never even knew you were in the running for.

It helps if you can get yourself feedback ready, and the first step to this is separating the bad news and the unhappiness that comes with this from the feedback itself. When you are telephoned and told you have not obtained the position, ask if you can have a follow-up discussion in a couple of days to explore your interview performance. This delay will help you position yourself in the best possible way to listen to and absorb the feedback.

Asking questions

Every interview will conclude with a chance for you to ask questions. Make sure you have some.

Can you tell me about how this role came about?

What career path opportunities are there for me?

What kind of management style do you try to foster?

What do you see my biggest challenges in this role as being?

Why should I want to work for you? This one takes a lot of confidence, but how people respond can tell you a lot about an organisation. If someone snaps back, "Is that not a question for you?" then you possibly do not want to work for them. The great organisations will talk enthusiastically about their organisation.

The following are 30 interview questions for you to practice. Remember that you can answer these questions from the perspective of work experience and from your university experiences.

The questions with * are traps. You need to remember to talk not only from your personal perspective but also frame the answer with reference to human resource policies and procedures. Organisations want to know that you will comply with their regulations and guidance and not fly by the seat of your pants. For example, *"How do you manage the stress of others?* I take a sincere interest in the lives of my peers and try to provide opportunities for them to raise issues that they are struggling with. Such conversations, I find, are an opportunity to provide a safe and open space for my peers to discuss their work and personal pressures. This personal touch has on occasions been beneficial in supporting my team to become more self-aware of their healthy and unhealthy working practices. In my experience, human resource departments are the best place to start to explore working policies as well as restorative opportunities such as employee assistance programmes. With the increase of absence due to stress, it is critical that staff be aware of and compliant with health and safety regulations, and I would welcome attending any organisational training on this area".

1   Tell me about yourself.
2   Why do you want to work at our company?
3   Why should we hire you?
4   What is the biggest challenge you have faced in your career?
5   What do you feel was your major accomplishment for your last employer?
6   What did you like least about your previous role?
7   What are your greatest strengths/weaknesses/blindspots?
8   Where do you see yourself five years from now?
9   How do you think your qualifications have prepared you for this role?
10 What do you think the major challenges are for our industry in the next five years?
11 How have your qualifications/experience prepared you to tackle the challenges facing our industry?
12 Who has inspired your career to date?
13 Tell me about your philosophy for dealing with failure.
14 Give me an example of a time when you had to think creatively.
15 What psychology theorists have influenced your work and why?
16 Tell me about a difficult decision you have had to make.
17 How do you 'do' boredom?
18 How do you deal with difficult people? *
19 Are you willing to relocate or travel?
20 What would your work peers say about you? How would they describe you?

21 You have had a long period of unemployment. How did you remain productive?
22 You have stayed in your current position for a very long period of time. How do you personally manage change?
23 Can you tell me about a time when you have had to face conflicts of interest or ethical dilemmas in your previous roles? *
24 Can you give me an example of a time when you had to manage competing priorities?
25 How do you manage stress? *
26 How do you manage the stress of others? *
27 What do you want to do differently in your next role?
28 What motivates you at work?
29 What are you really good at but want to stop doing?
30 How did you prepare for this interview?

Further reading

Zhang, L. 5 Ted talks to watch before your next interview. Themuse. www.themuse.com/advice/5-ted-talks-to-watch-before-your-next-interview

Notes

1 Dearing, R. (1997). *Higher education in the learning society (HMSO)*. London: Her Majesty's Stationery Office.
2 Gallup. (2016). *Great jobs. great lives. The value of career services, inclusive experiences and mentorship for college graduates*. Retrieved from www.luminafoundation.org/files/resources/great-jobs-great-livees-3-2016.pdf
3 The Bridge Group. (2017). *Social mobility and university careers services*. Retrieved from https://static1.squarespace.com/static/5c18e090b40b9d6b43b093d8/t/5cd18164f63f57000157b2aa/1557234030200/07+Research+2017+UPP.pdf
4 Thompson, A. (2009, October 15). Speed of thought-to-speech traced in brain. *Live Science*. Retrieved from www.livescience.com/5780-speed-thought-speech-traced-brain.html
5 Doyle, C. C., Mieder, W., & Shapiro, F. (2012). *The dictionary of modern proverbs* (p. 57). New Haven: Yale University Press.

Chapter 6

Starting work

Measure up and make a difference

Starting a new job is nerve wracking. The uncertainty you will feel about making a good impression and saying and doing the right things is a challenge, and you will have to introduce yourself constantly and attempt to remember everyone else's name as well. The first part of this chapter provides some tips, tricks and advice for getting work ready. It applies the old army adage "Proper Planning and Preparation Prevents Piss Poor Performance" to help ensure that both you and your career get off to a good start and you do not derail yourself before you even begin. We address everything from getting to work and time management hacks, to understanding what a work contract should do. The second part of this chapter delves a little deeper into one of the biggest challenges that new staff (and some established staff) face: that of the difficult conversation.

For most of us, difficult conversations are the stuff of everyday life. We are content to discuss disagreements in our personal lives, usually with the aim of making things better. Such conversations are inevitable, and a healthy pattern of creating lifelong friends and loving relationships is a worthwhile consequence. We work through our issues, stick at it through good times and difficult times, and as a result, our relationships are functional and successful. The next time we face a personal challenge, our personal resources are more abundant because we have the successes of the past to draw upon. Being able to handle difficult conversations at work is just as critical but often much more of a challenge. The capital that psychology students bring to an organisation is their knowledge, their communication skills and their relationship-building expertise. Knowledge is one of the most significant organisational resources, so these 'knowledge economy skills' are highly sought after. Knowledge is the key to an organisation's competitive edge and having the right knowledge in the right place dictates the speed at which organisations can respond to change. As such, organisations will seek out students with the most sophisticated levels of understanding, knowledge and cognitive and social capabilities. The negative side of all this knowledge is that people are becoming increasingly concerned about looking stupid and in addition rooting out the stupidity of others.[1] When the end game is simply to avoid mistakes, to give the appearance of not being stupid and appear educated and knowledgeable at the expense of true mastery, learning opportunities are lost. True learning comes through embracing difficulty and failure. This means that we need to be open to our failures because constructing barriers by avoiding, denying or trying to spin failure poisons learning.

It's time to be an adult

Just like the very un-British idea of the prenuptial agreement, having something in writing about your conditions and expectations at work will make everyone's life easier. Just like the prenuptial agreement, a written contract of work is not a legal requirement. In both cases, thankfully, the lack of written contract does not mean you do not have rights.

You and your employer's agreement are the 'contract', and your contract is considered broken if either you or your employer does not follow a term within that contract. All employees are entitled to have the details of their employee contract covering the main terms of their working arrangements within 2 months of starting work. Seek to obtain a written contract where possible. Verbal contracts are notoriously difficult to enforce and are sometimes invalid. Should disputes arise, a written contract is accessible and clear and will reduce the likelihood of a dispute going to court. Sign your contract and keep it safe. Your contract will contain express and implied rights. Express rights are:

- The name of your employer;
- The date you started work;
- The title of the job;
- How much you are paid and how you are paid (weekly, monthly etc);
- The hours that you work, overtime and any legal limits on the hours that you can work per week;
- Holiday pay and how much time you are entitled to, if this is available from day 1 or if it has to be accrued over time;
- How bank holidays are treated (you may be expected to work them but are given time in lieu);
- Probationary periods;
- Notice periods;
- Redundancy;
- Pensions;
- Sick entitlement.

Implied terms include matters of trust. For example, sick entitlement is not actually an 'entitlement' to be taken unless you are actually sick. Some organisations have very generous sick entitlement, anything from 3 to 6 months for people who are seriously ill, and up to 10 days for minor illnesses. These days are not something that employees are 'due'; they are in place to keep employees safe. Taking sick days when you are not sick is unethical; it burdens your teammates and costs the UK economy billions of pounds. If you need a personal day for a dental or GP appointment or because you need to care for a sick child, talk to your employer about taking a personal day. Employers face these challenges every day, and they will value your transparency. If you need to take days because you are feeling tired, burned out or depressed, you must talk to your employer and ensure that you follow the in-house protocols around reporting in sick and providing the necessary medical evidence.

Aim to get there early

Before the COVID-19 pandemic, daily commutes were incrementally increasing, at a significant cost to both our bank balances and well-being. Whilst many organisations are now much more flexible with their approach to home working, unless a unicorn comes and collects you from your bed each morning and deposits you safely at your desk, this is likely to remain an inescapable part of your day. Yes, you do have to work 8 hours, and it starts early! This can be a major shock to the system of the average undergraduate, who has rocked out of bed at lunchtime following a late night on the tiles. You need to quickly get into the habit of sorting your shit out the night before, getting up at about 6.30 a.m. and making sure that the booze breath and bed head are things of the past. Being early means you can park more easily, you do not need to worry about train or bus delays, you avoid traffic jams and you can get a coffee and sit down and plan your day. Being early also results in better impressions of you.[2] Employees who start their days early are perceived as more conscientious than those who start their day later. This morning bias can mean that some groups of individuals are potentially vulnerable to perceptions of underperformance, so if you do have to do the school run or other morning commitments, make sure you keep your boss reliably informed.

> *Trains and buses*: If you know your working hours, then book all your tickets for the month. This will save you a lot of money and is almost always a better value than booking a season ticket. It takes some work to master the art of the early purchase ticket, but apps such as Trainline make it easier. Apps often charge a small fee for ticket bookings, but they also enable a bit more flexibility about changing and cancelling your tickets. They also make it easier to spot cheap upgrades to first class and figure out where in the train you are most likely to find a seat. Put the app on your phone so that when the inspector arrives, you don't have to spend time groping in a panic in your bag.
>
> *Be clean*: Over the course of your degree, you may have stopped smelling yourself, but your colleagues will notice, and it is not just a matter of a good scrub of your teeth. Alcohol metabolises all over your body, and a component of that is saved for your breath and urine (this is why the police use breath tests to check for drunk drivers). There is nothing more revolting than your work colleagues rocking up with donner kebab, Jack Daniels and Jägerbomb seeping through their pores, so do not be that person. 'Self-cleaning' hair is also not a thing. Your hair might eventually be happy with the 'right amount of oils', but it will still get dirty and it will need washed. Nails need to be clean, and if you wear nail polish, make sure it is not chipped (and that includes your toes). Clean teeth are also a good indication to others that you are taking care of yourself, so get that descale at the dentist.
>
> *Take control of your schedule before it takes control of you:* The adrenaline of last-minute time constraints might motivate some people to push their performance to their limits; for others, the effect can be paralysing. Nobody works better under pressure for sustained periods of time, so avoid crisis mode by mastering some work-life hacks that secure high levels of productivity. Distant goals can also lead to procrastination. By nature of their place in

the future, they are often perceived as more difficult in nature, and somehow, because they require more effort and resources to achieve,[3] procrastination sets in and work-critical tasks get pushed to the last minute. Be early with your projects and build in time to revise, adjust and review your work so that you can ensure you get it right the first time. Tasks that are not completed and returned to actually take much longer to get completed. A typical task that takes 45 minutes more at the end of the day to complete will take twice as long the following day. In point of fact, it may not even get completed the following morning if another work-critical task arrives in the interim. This can mean that you end up faced with an ever-increasing pile of uncompleted tasks, something which rapidly becomes a major source of work-related stress.

Time hacks: digital

- *Save time and trees:* Learn how to create and use a digital signature. Then email it to yourself.
- *Join* the note-taking ecosystem. If you did not already start with products like Evernote during your university degree, then now is the time to get started with OneNote, Google Keep or Omni notes.
- *Digital diaries are not a CCTV focused on your whereabouts:* Paper diaries make it impossible for your teammates and boss to schedule appointments. They result in a stream of unsuccessful email threads whilst PAs and secretaries try to schedule appointments. Help everyone else do their job and ditch the paper diary and get your calendar on your phone. You can also have the calendar on multiple devices such as your phone and computers. The annoying habit of always having your phone on you means that you are less likely to miss a meeting ever again.
- *Phone security:* Set your phone to regularly back up to your cloud. Perform a security-setting review of your technology, make sure your phone is regularly updated and insure your devices. Thefts and security breaches do happen, but more likely it will be spilt coffee or water, a dropped backpack that shatters your laptop or a lost device. A backup will save your work, and insurance will save you money.

Time hacks: rucking

If you are using public transport, all kinds of disgusting particles, human and non-human, will quickly attach themselves to your bag. Forget about style and think about grime. Buy a backpack because it is easier to keep it off the ground, and do some research on your purchase before you hand over your hard-earned cash. It should have lots of different sections and two wide padded shoulder straps, and a waist strap can also be a good idea for weight distribution, and it should be as light but as strong as possible. You will want this backpack to never let you down, so if your budget is small, consider finding a well-known reliable brand (Samsonite, for example) and looking for a second-hand bag on eBay. Amazon reviews are a good place to start, but there are also plenty of great review webpages to explore features and benefits.

- *Wired for sound*: Audio book or music app: essential to make the journey bearable. As well as being a great source of literature, Audible also helps you self-develop and grow, and if you hate the books, you can return them and have your credit refunded. Don't forget the headphones and keep a spare set in your bag because they will break.
- *Personal products*: Tissues, masks, hand sanitiser, lip balm, tampons, mints, painkillers, deodorant and a toothbrush (because *you never know*).
- *Quick charge* and *phone charge*: Portable computer power chargers are now ultra-slim and competitively priced. An absolute godsend if your phone or laptop are running low on juice. Ideally, you need three phone chargers (one for home, one for your office desk and one in your backpack). Never ever be tempted to remove your backpack charger unless you are charging on your commute. If you remove it from your backpack, you will run out of phone power on your commute. Your phone now holds all your contacts, banking details and train tickets, so if you do not have your charger, you will be so stressed, Npower will be able to attach you to the national grid.
- *Work shoes/commuting shoes*: Can you *really* run for the train in those heels?
- *Food*: Lunch, collapsible coffee cup, water.
- *Stuff*: Umbrella, pens and a small notebook, makeup bag, wallet.

Now that your backpack is larger than a Navy SEAL about to invade a small principality, you are ready for rucking. 'Rucking' crushes calories. For an average man, a 30-minute walk burns 125 calories; throw a weighted backpack on, and you burn 325 calories. Carrying a weighted backpack properly (and not slung over one shoulder like a sulky teenager) can both help prevent and relieve back pain. After spending all day in the office flexed forward at a computer, the backpack holds your torso up and pulls it back into line. You do not have to work just as hard to straighten yourself up, and the pressure on the discs in your back is reduced. Over time, hip and postural stability are improved, and you become more injury proof. Carrying a rucksack as part of your commute is a convenient and free way of improving your overall fitness, but you do need to remain aware of how much weight you are carrying. It should ideally weigh no more than 15% of your overall body weight.

Thanks but no thanks for the feedback

Three things to accept before you start work: you will make mistakes; your intentions and the intentions of others are complex and you have contributed to the problem. Difficult conversations are part and parcel of any healthy relationship, and good relationships power us forward, but that doesn't make the difficult conversations easy (otherwise this section would be called easy conversations), and here we find out why.

There are roughly three types of feedback. Everyone needs all three, but generally people are very poor at understanding what type of feedback they need and asking for or giving feedback in the format that will be most useful.

1 Appreciation (*thanks, great job, well done*)
2 Evaluation (*loud and hurtful*)
3 Coaching (*what better way is there to do this?*)

Appreciation lifts people up; it makes us feel welcomed and safe, and it energises us to perform. Evaluation helps us understand how well we are performing against our goals or a benchmark, whereas coaching explores what can be learned and developed in order to improve to reach a desired goal. Becoming expert in seeking out the right kind of feedback is essential to great work performance. A boss who hands out constant praise might feel nice and safe for a while, but you are never going to know exactly what you need to address to become better. You have to seek out tough feedback and evaluation. A boss who only ever hands out evaluation will end up with a demotivated, stressed team who never learn how to regulate their performance.

At some time, everyone receives a 'shit sandwich'. It goes a little bit like this . . .

Praise: "Ryan, our management was impressed with the attendance to the sales conference. The food and drink were excellent, and the keynote speaker was outstanding, but we should discuss the timing of the breakout sessions".

Criticism: "By the way, you overspent by 35%. Next time, can you please keep a closer eye on budget?"

Praise: "I understand you worked very hard co-ordinating everything; we missed you on some key activities, so can you debrief your strategy with Jon? He will be taking over for the next conference".

Difficult conversations are difficult because they are fraught with emotions, ego and vulnerability (on all sides). Few managers enjoy criticising, and they worry just as much as their staff about potential relationship damage. Whilst there is nothing terrible about not wanting to cause hurt or upset at work, trouble will follow if being nice is always the purpose of the conversation. In organisational psychology, we call this the culture of nice, and the culture of nice is damaging because it encourages managers to artificially sweeten feedback with useless platitudes.

There is no diplomatic method by which to deliver a bag of trash. If the stinking pile of rotten vegetable matter is decorated with sweetness and appreciation, it is still going to stink to the person who has to dispose of it. 'The sandwich' is far more damaging to performance and long-term relationships because the misplaced praise completely obscures the criticism, and the misplaced criticism completely obscures the praise. Staff members may become untrusting of positive feedback or, worse still, be completely

"You can't call it minestrone - minestrone hasn't got newts in it."

Source: Printed with permission of Punch Cartoon Library/TopFoto

broadsided if the matter escalates. Ryan is now left wondering what this all means for him. His feedback is like a tin of soup with the label washed off: you do not really know for sure what was in it; it could be tomato and basil, or it could be oxtail (*bleurgh*). What Ryan needed was initial appreciation, followed up with a learning conversation with review and evaluation and then an agreement around next steps. That is not what he got, and his initial response is about to potentially escalate the problem.

Ryan's inner chatter

> *What kind of feedback was that? I did well, but I am over budget and Jon is taking over for the next conference. I have been planning this event for weeks. She signed the budget sheet, but I am to blame! What exactly am I supposed to be doing? I imagine she is just trying to make a name for herself. I have a good mind to email her and tell her what I think of her and this module!*

24 hours later: *Gosh, really tired. I cannot believe I stayed up to 2 a.m. writing and re-writing that email last night. Thank goodness I didn't send it. She was right. I knew the project was over budget and didn't draw her attention to it at the budget review meeting. I knew she was in a rush that day, and I didn't make it clear what the implications were. I feel really stupid; I wasted so much time. I cannot begin to imagine how much worse it would have been if I had emailed her. I think I need to get out a bit more often and get some fresh air. I really need to get some perspective! I will go and see her and apologise.*

The truth hurts, but information wins wars

We have all sent emails that we regret. If only there were a switch that we could press on our computer that stopped us from sending an email in anger. Dr Steve Peters, the psychiatrist to our Olympic team, called this thinking with 'the chimp' side of our brain (2014). We never really have the upper hand in our dealings with our chimp, because our chimp stops us from thinking clearly. People, companies and organisations make mistakes – big mistakes – when they do not stop, think, seek out and listen to feedback, clarify their thinking and accept reality. "Eating a bowl of Kellogg's Frosted Mini-Wheats cereal for breakfast is clinically shown to improve attentiveness by nearly 20%" cost Kellogg's $4 million dollars. "Nothing artificial" and "all natural" Kellogg's again this time $5 million on their Kashi products. Smooth Joe Camel adverts aimed at children cost the US marketing team of R.J. Reynolds $10 million dollars. The KLM Tenerife airport disaster was in part caused by the captain's failure to listen to the co-pilot's concerns regarding his interpretation of the take-off clearance. Senior members of NASA's advisory panels were 'removed' in the build-up to the Columbia space disaster:

> "I cannot speak for the others," one could speculate I was removed because I was saying things that some people found uncomfortable.
> (Richard Blomberg, former chair of NASA's watchdog, the Aerospace Safety Advisory Panel)[4]

If you have ever watched the HBO series *Chernobyl*, you get the idea. Even when half the plant had been blasted to the heavens, the operators still would not accept that something had gone wrong. Good organisations try to avoid such faulty thinking by preventing disaster by fostering a culture of openness, whereby the employees can feel free to advise, challenge and give honest, frank feedback with one another. Humans, being humans, however, are not always great at handling feedback, especially the negative kind and especially if it is handed over as an unending stream of criticism. But what does it take to give and receive feedback well? Even if your manager is skilled at providing timely feedback that is relevant and precise, more often than not, nothing really changes. Why? Because it is the receiver of the feedback who is actually in control. We are all wired to learn and develop, but we are also wired for acceptance and love. Without a way of truly seeing ourselves, we can 'get in our own way'. Changing is difficult. We are motivated to retain our existing sense of ourselves because it gives us a sense of personal identity and control.

The best crisis is one averted

Positive psychology is the scientific examination of the conditions that lead to life satisfaction, flourishing and the good life. Most significantly, positive psychology teaches us how varying our perspective can lead to significant shifts in our personal happiness and quality of life. The simple act of pivoting our focus away from what is going wrong in our lives, what needs fixing in our relationships or addressing in our careers, towards what is going well in our lives has been demonstrated as improving well-being, increasing life expectancy and improving personal performance at work. Positive psychology achieves this by helping people recognise that negativity is important in signalling to us that all is not well; however, rather than dwelling on and becoming absorbed in the negative aspects of mental illness, abnormality, trauma and pain, positive psychology refocuses our energy on concepts such as personal strengths, happiness, self-esteem, self-efficacy, confidence and well-being. These concepts are argued to be the mechanisms for enhanced life quality.

Positive psychology is distinct from *positive thinking*. In positive thinking, the focus is on the control of our thoughts. By controlling this 'self-talk' in a more positive way, we encourage ourselves to believe that the best is going to happen, not the worst. Positive thinking then prevents us from agonising over every decision or questioning every judgement that we make. Ignoring the negative, however, does not mean that the negative will ignore you. Problems ignored have a habit of just getting worse. Poor performance is an issue in and of itself, but without gripping the reasons behind failure and dealing with those reasons, the problem will quickly snowball.

Positive psychology works to help us be more aware of the seductive nature of the short-term gains that come with avoiding problems, particularly problems that promote anxiety. Our reward systems quickly identify that there are self-soothing advantages to not addressing our failings; however, students, graduates and new and old employees who succumb to such avoidance instincts may end up finding problems much more difficult in the longer term. That initial sense of relief that comes with avoidant behaviour only leads to increased anxiety in the future, and this anxiety can rapidly spiral into other areas of our life. We become unable to broaden our attention towards achieving long-term goals, which will stunt performance.

Focusing on the inevitable feelings that come from criticism, rejection and failure at the cost of critically evaluating your performance can mean that you are missing valuable opportunities to present yourself in the best possible light. This is because we *need* negative emotion. Negative emotion acts to interrupt the usual in our lives; it triggers a sense of urgency and energy and propels us into the search for alternatives. This is why greater resilience in student populations results from being able to experience and manage a full range of emotions and to manage those emotions in a way which energises and facilities high performance (Fredrickson, Tugade, Waugh & Larkin, 2003).

There are three key negative emotion triggers that prevent us from absorbing and adapting to feedback; truth, relationships and identity.[5] While these three triggers cause enough problems in isolation, the role of 'boss', 'supervisor' 'leader' or 'manager' often evokes feelings of injustice across all three. You might find yourself in a situation where your boss criticises you unfairly, appears to take credit for something you have done or gives good feedback but delivers it poorly.

When we hear the substance of feedback and feel that some sort of injustice has taken place, a 'truth' has been triggered, and emotions of anger, resentment, injustice and even hatred may be stirred up. "*That's wrong, it did not happen like that, you are not taking all the facts into consideration, how dare you!*" The feedback is rejected as incorrect, unfair, biased, bad and just plain wrong. Whilst we defend, deflect, reject and perhaps even counterattack, we engage in a negative emotional landscape that will prevent us from fully understanding our feedback. Psychology training does a terrific job of helping its students self-reflect and learn, but we are all still prone to defensiveness and blind spots in our behaviour. Working to accept (or even partially accept) critical feedback may mean that we have to let go of some truisms that we hold about ourselves but overcoming your defence mechanisms and understanding your feedback can quite literally save your organisation millions, if not in fact save lives.

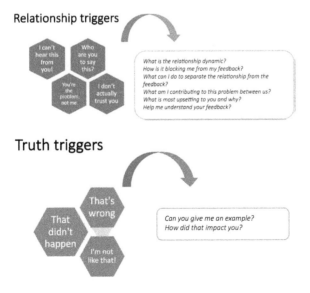

Relationship triggers are responses to the trustworthiness of the feedback source. How credible we feel the message source is, how we see the motives of the person delivering the message and perhaps how appropriately we feel the message was delivered. Even the most accurate feedback, delivered insensitively on the stairwell to your office with an audience, is never going to be received well and may well trigger suspicion about the motives of the sender. Stone and Heen describe this as switch tracking. The "what" of the feedback becomes tangled up with the who or the how and the message is diluted, and when the opportunity finally comes round to have a complete feedback conversation, rather than deal with the issue at hand, the feedback giver will have to manage the question "Have you any idea how you made me feel on the stairwell?" Everyone gets caught up in a toxic revenue exchange of finger pointing. The key to breaking this cycle is to figure out the relationship system and how that is linked to how you feel you are being treated. What is the dynamic that is contributing to this problem?

Not everyone responds to feedback in exactly the same way. Students of psychology are well educated in the role that individual differences play in our temperament and personality. We all differ in characteristics such as anxiety, ability to visualise or sociability. The introvert may want some time to process the information and carefully consider their next steps, and I also know quite a few introverts who would walk up and knock on their boss's door and demand a discussion. Personality only gives us a guide to what we would prefer to do, not what we would actually do under any given situation. However, having some understanding of your personality and temperament can be a useful tool to help you to stop and reflect before you act, particularly under pressure. If you have not had the opportunity to take a psychometrics assessment, talk to your careers service or year tutor about possible opportunities. There are a number of good open source personality tests, but such tests always work best when you are able to have a follow-up meeting to discuss what the test really means to you.

Take a personality test

Open psychometrics provides free access to some established tests in the field https://openpsychometrics.org/about/

The personality project is devoted to the academic study of personality, and it provides links to Big 5–based models. http://personality-project.org/readings-measurement.html

---

Identity triggers can take much longer to resolve. Some of us have more extreme reactions to situations than others, and it really depends on where your baseline for recovery sits. If your baseline is naturally higher, then you are more likely to respond more positively faster than someone who has a lower threshold.

Individuals at the lower end of the baseline recovery tend to be hypersensitive and deny or do the opposite of what they have been told, and they may also exaggerate the impact of the feedback on their health and well-being. Generally speaking, however, the more positive interactions that we have with others, the less exposed, at risk and fearful we become. The key is to work to regain balance by dismantling the distortions in your thinking about how others view you. Finding a trusted mentor at work or a peer is one of the most powerful ways to challenge your thinking about feedback and 'change your emotional soundtrack'. Candid conversations with a trusted person can help you separate feelings from feedback, calm your inner chatter and avoid an escalation in your thinking where the problems become about everything and everyone.

Identity triggers

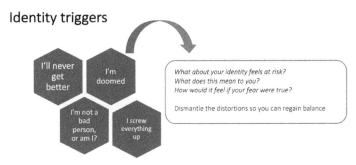

Positive Emotion, Engagement, Relationships, Meaning and Accomplishment

Positive psychology teaches us to be more attuned to maladaptive thoughts and actions and then to seek out more proactive, long-term ways to manage them. Martin Seligman, widely considered the father of positive psychology, proposes the PERMA model (Positive Emotion, Engagement, Relationships, Meaning and Accomplishment) as the five measurable elements of well-being.[6]

P – Positive Emotions	Remaining positive and optimistic. Being able to frame our past, present and future constructively and optimistically.
E – Engagement	Having activities that engage and absorb us. Activities that flood our body with positive energy, that we enjoy to the point that we do not notice time passing by.
R – Relationships	The social connections, interactions and relationships which promote trust, love, safety and flourishing help people develop healthier lifestyles, live longer and cope better with stress.

(Continued)

M – Meaning	Having purpose in our lives, feeling fulfilment and satisfaction with a life that has significance and value. Dedicating our time to something that is bigger than us and our immediate personal concerns. For example, our family, our children, the enjoyment of work, a charitable pursuit, involvement in a community pursuit or a belief system such as religion.
A – Accomplishment	The drive to identify our goals and then strive to succeed is central to well-being. Accomplishment and mastery come from personal and professional success, a human need that affirms and strengthens us to adapt to and thrive from even greater challenges.

Positive Emotions: Positive psychology focuses on what we are good at, what our strengths are, and encourages us to spend more time playing to those strengths, with the aim of becoming even better. In positive psychology, crisis reveals character. By leveraging the positive emotions associated with our past and current successes, we keep our energy levels up and remain positive by re-framing personal attributions and expectations about what is happening or what may happen in the future. This reframing is an essential component of personal and professional resilience, and it operates to keep us engaged in activities that absorb and nurture us.

Engagement: Often described as being 'in the zone', flow is the experience of being so engaged in an activity that time stands still or engaging in something so gratifying that you never want to end. This state of flow is quite different from the satisfaction that we might experience from eating in a restaurant or watching an amazing movie at the cinema. These experiences, whilst pleasurable, are transitory in nature. In flow, individuals are responsive, but consciousness is often suspended. Sporting events are classic examples of high performing athletes being 'in flow'. Their minds are totally absorbed in what they are doing to the point that often they may not be able to fully explain what took place. Similarly, when artists, painters and musicians enter flow, self-awareness fades to the point where then have been known to completely disregard their need for water, food and sleep but felt deep concentration and calm.[7]

Relationships: A successfully resilient person does more than just overcome problems as they arise. They take active steps to ensure that they have a foundation in place that increases the chance that they will actively cope during times of challenge, stress and hardship. Just as receiving support from a therapist when *not* in crisis has the most impact on helping people deal with and move on from life issues, seeking out help and support and building effective peer networks, mentors and friendships when not facing life challenges will insulate you for when the real challenges finally come. Like seasons, resilient people recognise that the resources they need to thrive during psychological difficult times are as organic as the challenges they will face across their lifespan. To meet and thrive in new challenges, they will continuously build around them the conditions for security, sensemaking, flourishing and success.

Meaning: There are many cultural and ideological answers to the purpose of our existence. What is life all about? Why are we here? The desire to understand and be understood has engendered philosophical arguments, religious contemplation and scientific investigation. These questions can promote anxiety, depression, feelings of isolation and stress to the point that individuals question their place in life (also known as an existential crisis). For that reason, many therapeutic approaches nurture thinking towards the question of "What is the meaning of my life?" Individuals who are satisfied with their lives, who experience pleasure-filled adventures and lead a life worth living are engaged in finding what they do meaningful. For many, this is about making a difference in the world, practising compassion, contributing to society, pursing a passion, making the lives of others better and nurturing the next generation.

Accomplishment: Accomplishment is harnessing internal processes towards our goals and ambitions, the pursuit of excellence through academic study, social interactions and emotional intentions towards the challenges that we have set ourselves. Accomplishment leads to personal satisfaction from the process and the journey, not necessarily the longer-term external outcome. For students, this means figuring out and then managing their emotions, persisting in the face of failure and trying out new ways of learning. Accomplishment is the process; achievement is the outcome.

A calling to counselling psychology

"I was inspired to study psychology because I was angry. I had met a young Somali boy who was sexually abused in school. He did not receive support due to stigma in society. I could not find him or his family a Somali therapist at that time and I saw how it destroyed them. I then made a decision to become a therapist and promised myself I would make a difference. studying psychology was not easy for me especially when English was not my first language. I also have dyslexia and sometimes I don't see people who look like me. I failed a couple of times and passed. Sometimes I wanted to give up, but I had amazing people around me who reminded me why I was doing this. I can see the difference it made in the last couple of years.

Before I finished my undergraduate, I did more than 500 hours of volunteering in the community raising awareness about mental health. I can see the shift in the stigma lifting little by little. Since I qualified as a psychotherapist,

I am seeing myself delivering therapy in different languages and learning more; whether it is the research side or the barrier in psychology for black people. I hope someday there are more open discussions. When I was studying, I was thinking I was just getting a degree, but I never thought my phone would be ringing non-stop from people asking for help. People call me when they are most in need. The thing I am most proud of is, during the time of Coronavirus and lock down, I was able to be there for the community delivering webinars about wellbeing and coping. Today, I work with amazing young people to end the stigma about mental health. Sometimes it surprises me when I get calls from doctors back in Africa asking me for help or advice about mental health. A lot of black young girls or parents call me and ask me "Can I become a psychologist?" Some people tell me I inspire them. My journey has not been an easy one, but it is bigger than me. I am the first woman in my family to go to university and possibly one of the firsts in my immediate community doing counselling psychology. I am glad that today I have become an advocate for mental health; helping parents and people who don't know how to get help with mental help, I was able to make a difference. The most honourable moment was when someone approached me and thanked me for being able to lead a "normal life" because they attended my workshop. Psychology for me was not just about studying, but a calling to answer".

Suad Duale, Counselling Psychologist

Being better

The first step towards being successfully resilient is recognising and reflecting on how our thoughts shape our beliefs and actions. Constant inner chatter tells us we can never be good enough and eats at our self-worth and self-confidence. It holds us back from new learning, broadening our experiences, creativity and happiness. Inner chatter plays with your emotions, changes your attitude, talks you out of and into decisions, and it goads you into arguments, keyboard battles, Instagram obsessions and Facebook guilt trips. Inner chatter convinces us to want what other people want and to want what other people have; it compels us to walk down a dark, disturbing hallway away from who we are and towards distraction, worry, procrastination, second-guessing the intensions of others, poor mental well-being and then chronic ill health.

Language teaches us how we should (or should not) label ourselves and the language, attitudes and behaviours we should use to convey ourselves. There is a powerful quote from the movie *The Iron Lady* in which Meryl Streep portrays British Prime Minister Baroness Margaret Thatcher "Watch your thoughts, for they become words. Watch your words, for they become actions. Watch your actions, for they become habits. Watch your habits, for they become your character. And watch your character, for it becomes your destiny. What we think, we become". The point is that when we place definitive or exaggerated labels on ourselves and on others, we disempower. The words 'I am stupid', 'fat', 'lazy', 'nothing special', 'inexperienced', 'loud', 'angry', 'dramatic', 'intelligent', 'expert', 'creative', 'beautiful', 'kind', 'sassy' become absorbed into a personal identity that shapes how we see our world and how we interact and build relationships with others. As we revisit our inner messages, we influence the ways in which we withdraw from or pursue challenges respond to authority, ask for or accept help, offer support to others, avoid important decisions, complete projects, follow or lead. This is the tension between our inner critic and our inner *critique*. Whereas balanced *critique* and reflection will shift us towards action, our inner critic will tell us that we do not fit or are not worthy. The key to success is to notice these thought processes, call them out into conscious awareness and change the narrative.

Everyone has this 'inner chatter', and they have to manage the complexity of emotions, feelings, behaviour and physical reactions that are all interconnected to it. What differentiates people in how they are able to manage this inner 'noise' is their capacity for good cognitive control. Exercising cognitive control over our emotions, particularly aversive emotions, is the route to improving outcomes. This is because mood affects self-regulatory signals moderating persistence and pursuit, but this relationship does not always work to our advantage. Emotional reasoning is linked to what is known as the action bias. This is the tendency to do something, even if that something achieves nothing or in fact makes matters worse (which is exactly what happened with Ryan and his post-email inner chatter). All that wasted time and energy could have been spent on the actual task. *Why?* Because people will invest in doing anything rather than stand still and reflect in the face of uncertainty. We see what is in front of our eyes as being the only possible problem, and we become so certain of the solution that we stop trying to find out what the actual problem is, and we are going to be predictably wrong. These mental enemies are particularly devious in new or unusual circumstances.

A cardinal feature of good cognitive control is that we focus on relevant information and an ability to filter out noise. It is perhaps not surprising then that cognitive control is thought to be closely related to emotional processing.[8] Understanding where our thoughts and emotions are coming from helps us accept how it is meant to be, what can be changed and what must be accepted and then act positively and proactively in ways that will enhance our self-worth in ways that are unique to us. Unsurprisingly, then, good cognitive control is a fundamental employability skill, because it supports individuals in managing the choices, conflicts and temptations that may misdirect us from our goals.

In this chapter, you have been exposed to some of the more negative aspects of work-related behaviour; however, here is the thing: it's not all doom and gloom. Every time you complete a task and look back in a critical but positive way, you are developing and improving. Future tasks become easier because you are constantly training your brain to operate in a responsible manner. Each time you accept and take ownership of your shortcomings, you move on and improve. It becomes easier the next time. Also, as you are learning and continually improving, the frequency of those awkward feedback sessions diminishes. Speaking of which, what about those relationships at work. . .

SAQ: build your tolerance for difficult conversations

A difficult conversation is anything we find it hard to talk about. At work, these might be issues of personal hygiene, race or gender discrimination, staff complaints, customer complaints, timekeeping or generally poor performance and discipline.

Discuss the following with a partner or peer but take the opposite side of the argument from what you would normally be comfortable with.

Arguments have been made in light of the Black Lives Matter movement that landmarks and statues with links to slavery and plantation ownership should be removed. To what extent would such a removal be compatible with the history and values of cities such as Liverpool, Bristol and London?

Further reading

Tobin, L & Poole, K. (2018). *Being an adult: The ultimate guide to moving out, getting a job and getting your act together*, London: Scribe.

A practical and fun book that covers everything about every life skill you might want to develop. From shopping to losing your job, this useful guide will help you get a grip on what is going on or not going on in your life.

Stone, D. & Heen, S. (2014). *Thanks for the feedback, the science and art of receiving feedback well*, Portfolio Penguin, USA.

Based around work from the Harvard Negotiation project, Stone and Heen delve deep into the essential nature of feedback and its role in healthy professional and personal relationships. A must-read for its simple framework and powerful tools for giving better feedback and receiving feedback effectively.

Notes

1 Alvesson, M., & Spicer, A. (2016). *The stupidity paradox*. London: Profile Books.

2 Yam, K. C., Fehr, R., & Barnes, C. M. (2014). Morning employees are perceived as better employees: Employees' start times influence supervisor performance ratings. *Journal of Applied Psychology, 99*(6), 1288–1299. doi:10.1037/a0037109

3 Zhu, M., Bagchi, R., & Hock, S. J. (2019). Mere deadline effect: Why more time might sabotage goal pursuit. *Journal of Consumer Research, 45*(5), 1068–1084. doi:10.1093/jcr/ucy030

4 Rose, D. (2003). *How warning signs were ignored before disaster shuttle's launch*. Retrieved July 23, 2020, from www.theguardian.com/science/2003/jun/22/space-exploration.columbia

5 Stone, D., & Heen, S. (2014). *Thanks for the feedback, the science and art of receiving feedback well*. Portfolio Penguin.

6 Seligman, M. (2018). PERMA and the building blocks of well-being. *The Journal of Positive Psychology, 13*(4), 333–335. doi:10.1080/17439760.2018.1437466

7 Csikszentmihalyi, M. (1990). Flow: The psychology of optimal experience. *Journal of Leisure Research, 24*(1), 93–94.
Csikszentmihalyi, M. (1997). *The mastermind's series. Finding flow: The psychology of engagement with everyday life*. New York: Basic Books.

8 Saunders, B., Milyavskaya, M., & Inzlicht, M. (2015). Variation in cognitive control as emotion regulation. *Psychological Inquiry, 26*(1), 108–115. doi:10.1080/1047840X.2015.962396

Chapter 7

Good relationships
at work

What is a good relationship at work?

In 1995, 19% of people found their life partners at work, a figure which dropped to 11% in 2017 with the growth in favour of online dating apps,[1] but just because it might not find you a boyfriend or girlfriend doesn't mean work isn't still an important part of our social and personal relationships. We spend some 82,000 hours at work over our lifetime, and the COVID-19 pandemic has necessitated even longer hours of working. We now find ourselves more distant from the personal contact of our peers. For many of us, impromptu coffees, lunchtime walks, chats in the corridor or doorstep meetings are replaced with phone calls and text messages, with relentless video chat and conferencing. In their seminal paper, "Bad Is Stronger Than Good", Baumeister, Bratslavsky and Finkenauer[2] demonstrated the extent that bad impressions and stereotypes are very quick to form and problematic to shift, if not, in fact, impossible to reverse. Good interactions must outnumber bad by a ratio of 5 to 1, and if it slips below that ratio, then relationship breakdown will follow.

But what does it mean to have a good relationship at work, and how can we actively work to nurture those relationships? Shared understandings and reciprocal contributions are the core of productive organisations and individual career progression and good relationships at work.[3] Your first priority is to learn your job and your obligations to your employer, do a good job, understand what your boss needs and develop trust and respect, and the relationships will follow. This chapter provides insights into how to develop personal credibility and manage yourself and your relationships at work. But we'd be kidding ourselves if we thought work was all sunshine and rainbows, so just in case you find your boss is akin to one certain queen bitch in the fashion industry, we explore how to work well with bosses that you find . . . challenging (although, to be clear, we still think Meryl Streep can do no wrong).

Choose your attitude

> Scrooge: Let us deal with the eviction notices for tomorrow, Mr Cratchit.
>
> Kermit the Frog as Bob Cratchit: Tomorrow is Christmas, sir.
>
> Scrooge: Very well. You may gift wrap them.
>
> The Muppet Christmas Carol, 1992

There will always be times at work when you will have to do things that you would rather not in a way that you least prefer. There will be hateful, difficult or dreary jobs that need to be done, and if you are new to a job and in a very junior role, chances are you are going to be first in a line you didn't realise you'd joined. These kinds of tasks are particularly effective at leaving us feeling drained and demotivated. You can be internally screaming No! so loudly that Edvard Munch will recreate his masterpiece with you at the centre, but your pay is steady, your rent is due and you can't always trust your roommate to pay their half of the bills on time. You need this job. There may not be a choice about *whether* you can do the job, but there is always a choice about *how* you do it. Apparently, JFK once asked a cleaner at the NASA Space Centre what he did, and the cleaner replied, "I am helping to put a man on the moon". For that cleaner, the actual purpose of his role was not to pick up human detritus; rather he was a critical component of the moon mission. You might hate your job, but you might also be helping to make some kind of history.

We choose the attitude we bring to work. It's all well and good to rock up to the office thinking *everyone sucks but me*, but thoughts like that just get in your own way and make tasks more difficult to perform. If you want to actually do a good job and develop a better reputation for yourself, you need to take control of your negative attitude and banish the thoughts that aren't task relevant[4] (that also includes thinking about Zac Efron's new Netflix show, *which we love, too, by the way*). You spend a lot of time at work, so why make it worse for yourself? You may as well set yourself up for at least the possibility of a good day. Since you're there, you may as well have some fun. Being upbeat and positive doesn't necessarily mean that you are going to enjoy what you are doing any better, but it does impact the way people see you. We all know that one person who just radiates sunshine, and whilst we can't all be that bright and shiny, why not at least try?[5] You may not quite get there, but you can get pretty close, and your co-workers will absolutely appreciate you for it.

Being happy and a good problem solver does not, however, mean that you must say yes to everything asked of you or seek to solve every problem. Being positive and being a people please are two very different things, and whilst the latter might feel good in the short term, it will burn you out. Figuring out where the boundaries of your job sit in the early days is not straightforward, but you will do better to ask lots of questions and seek permission, advice and validation. You're in your role to add value, not to waste time.

You really only have four choices when someone asks you to take on a task. Do it, schedule it, learn from it or say no. Most critically, if you are not the best person for the job (and you know you're not the best person for the job) and especially if there are time pressures at play, there are very good reasons for you not to involve yourself. While there is never one best way to do things, and even the best people make mistakes, you greatly increase the probability something will go drastically wrong when you are inexperienced and crunched by time. Lack of experience means ill-developed problem-solving and error-detection skills, and time pressures will only act as a barrier to good solution-based thinking, making you prone to biased thinking. Yet without those time pressures, being aware of your own weaknesses means that project may be an opportunity for personal growth and professional development. Being good at your job doesn't have to mean being the best at everything, it just means you need to know when to step back and let the pros handle it (time crunched) and when you can step up and develop yourself to be a pro for the future (non-time crunched).

If you do have to say no because of concerns around your competencies, ensure that you do (where possible) point the person making the request in the direction of someone who is better placed to help. More often than not, what the person making the request actually needs is someone to help them on the path to a solution, rather than for you to actually pick up the task at hand. Similarly, if you would like to take on the task, and you feel you have time, you should make it clear that you are not competent but would like to learn.

Not dropping what you are doing for a non-urgent, role-relevant activity is also an important skill to develop. If you drop what you are doing for every request or pretty distraction that comes your way, you'll quickly end up with a backlog of half-finished talks and loads of messy to-do lists. Half-finished tasks make your brain cross. Yes, really cross! It's known as the Zeigarnik effect, and whilst the Zeigarnik effect might allow unfinished and interrupted tasks to be recalled more easily, that cognitive tension will keep those unfinished tasks playing over and over in your mind. It creates an unnecessary stress response, using up valuable resources, just because we know something's not done.[6] The more unfinished jobs you have, the more unbearable the tension. The brain also seems to be programmed to become much more self involved and worry more about unfinished tasks than taking pleasure from completed work. Our tendency to worry about the incomplete can cause stress and anxiety and keep you up at night, but it is not entirely devoid of benefits. If used correctly, you can boost your memory and longer-term performance by building in interruptions during learning activities, periods of study or task activity.[7] This technique is particularly effective if the task you are attempting to master is of high personal value; the more motivated you are to complete the task, the more effective interruptions are to recall.[8]

Three questions to ask yourself before you say yes:

1 **Does this request fit into my goals and ambitions?** Specifically, will this nurture my professional development? This opportunity might sound really interesting, but if you cannot specifically articulate how it will enhance your personal development and career progression, it might be better to postpone taking part until you have a clearer picture of the direction it will take you in.

2 **Do you have the personal reserves to spend on this activity right now?** If you are developing new knowledge of skills, do not underestimate the cognitive reserves and personal commitment involved. What other activities at work will compete for your time and attention? Is there anything on the horizon that is coming your way? Can you give this activity justice right now or do you need to create more space in your life before you finally give a definitive yes?

3 **Will this lead to new opportunities?** The path to success is rarely predictable and simply planned. So, even if you are possibly low on personal
reserves or not entirely sure where this opportunity will take you, you need
to weigh the potential that this opportunity has in furthering the unexpected. For example, the development of new networks and new avenues
that you may not be able to currently anticipate but also the chances that
this opportunity may or may not come around again.

Fitting in

While it would be very nice indeed if everyone got along all the time, they're just
not going to, but that's okay. Sometimes people are just going to push your buttons
and you are going to push theirs, and sometimes you'll do it because it's fun 😺.
It is not your job to make your colleagues like you, make friends with them
or even seek their approval. That's what your actual friends are for. What you
want is respect and support, which you'll get in spades if you behave responsibly;
act dependably; stay away from gossip, moaning and the 'oversharing'; roll your
sleeves up and get on with the job.

Having positive relationships at work is directly related to increased well-being
and productivity, purpose and commitment,[9] but don't kid yourself into thinking that these relationships are simple. When it comes to friends at work, think
quality over quantity. People at work have a problematic tendency to prefer people who are just like them because familiarity creates a sense of reassurance and
warmth and acts as a social magnet, which for some ethnic and other minority
groups means getting the sharp end of the stick. Similar-to-me bias at its worst
can infiltrate hiring decisions, with highly qualified but more diverse candidates
overlooked. This can create a significant risk to organisations. High-achieving
teams need people with different experiences, interests and personality types to
function. If everyone is an extrovert, high on openness to experience and agree-
ableness, then the organisation is at significant risk in high-risk endeavours.
Sometimes you are going to need someone to bring you down and stay calm and
calculating (and for that, we love a good introvert).

Diversity increases creativity and productivity because multiple perspectives bring better ideas and more agile thinking. Unsurprisingly, organisations
with a diverse workforce have a return on investment 53% higher than companies with a homogeneous workforce.[10] If you feel very comfortable in the
environment you work in, make sure you spend some time seeking out the
company and counsel of people who are not like you. Conversely, if you have
trouble fitting in at work, then it could be that you are working in a homog-
enous culture and you are the different person. Make sure you speak to your
boss and make them aware, because your organisation needs lots of different
people to be successful.

If diversity increases organisational performance, then you can be sure as hell that it is enriching to your life individually. We all need a different perspective, someone to honestly tell us how it really is and also shine a light on the social privileges, taken-for-granted assumptions and other biases that 'similar / different' to me attitudes cause.

Even people who seem very similar to one another can differ quite dramatically in the ways that they are prepared to seek personal support and help. When those personal thresholds are crossed, even with the best intentions, the results are often very negative.[11] The opportunity for such boundary crossing has increased incrementally with advances in technology, to the point where boundary crossing is only one click away. You might feel that having the odd cheeky snoop through your work colleagues' Facebook photographs and Instagram is okay. Having a cheeky Facebook stalk isn't exactly out of the ordinary, but you might want to question your motivation for being nosey. What's actually driving you to stalk Susan in the next office over? Is it emotional, and what emotions might be the trigger for that? What if Susan stalked you back? At the end of the day, we're fine doing the stalking, but I bet you still get a little creeped out knowing you've been stalked. Ultimately, the lesson here is that if you do get a friend request from a co-worker, or even your boss, the costs of saying yes are much higher than those of saying no. If you don't want to be so rude as to straight up reject them, ignore it. If they ask, say you never saw it (because no one can prove you wrong).

When you talk at work, be aware who it is you're talking to. No matter how close you feel, or how important those relationships are to you, spilling your guts in the office over every drama in your life will change how your colleagues see you. You might think you are being perceived as funny, socially attractive, outgoing and vivacious when in fact your work mates are rolling their eyes and wishing you'd stop. If you are moaning about your boss or threatening to apply for a new job, not only will you pull the morale of your work mates down, but you are also inviting trouble. Describing yourself constantly as 'stressed', 'overwhelmed' or 'furious' will result in your capabilities being questioned and you being overlooked for promotions and interesting projects. This warning extends outside the office also; you have no idea how many people have been fired from their jobs for complaining on Twitter or clearly posting during working hours. Until you have built up some understanding and experience of workplace dynamics and the balance between sharing enough information so that you look like a balanced

---

SAQ: Think like a stalker. Trawl through your historical Facebook photos and posts. Is there anything you would rather your work mates did not see? Consider how professional your profile pic makes you look. You might be at your skinniest on that drunken weekend in Benidorm, but you're not 18 anymore and it might be time for a change.

human being and oversharing, you will make some mistakes. So, until you are assured and safe, save your sharing for drinks with friends who absolutely do not work with you. Extra points if they don't even live in the same country.

Managing up

Everyone, at least once, should work for someone who is well and truly awful. Horrible managers and bosses can have a devastating impact on productivity, staff morale, health and general well-being. It might seem counterintuitive, but it is not all bad working for a bad boss. Ricky Gervais shaped a career around channelling cringeworthy behaviours through his middle management character David Brent. Seth Gordon[12] (cowriter of *Horrible Bosses* with Mark Markowitz) is quoted as saying that he is grateful that Markowitz suffered, because he wrote a great script. Michael Caine argued that he learned something from every director and boss, good bad or ugly that he ever worked with, and for however long you are stuck with them, you have to do your best to make it work:

> Although it is much more difficult to do a good job under a bad director it can be a valuable experience. I think of it as the actor's equivalent of an athlete training at altitude and running on sand. It's bloody hard work and you're not going to achieve your personal best, but it means that when you get to work with a good director, or run on a hard track, you're able to perform better than before.
>
> Sir Michael Caine, p. 148, CBE[13]

Believe it or not, there can often be good reasons behind your boss's behaviour. Most organisations are facing considerable COVID-19 upheaval, and all organisations are struggling to get back on their feet, if not in fact survive. Your boss may have zero bandwidth to pick up slack in a team to cover illness, redo poorly presented work or even, for that matter, bid for new contracts. Most managers are also trapped in the vacuum that is middle management. They will be constantly trying to navigate power dynamics both horizontally and vertically across organisations while attempting to motivate and shape the performance of those further down the hierarchy. These constant transitions produce role conflict, particularly when middle managers have to shift quickly from a situation where they are in deference (receiving bad news from a superior) towards a situation in which they must be assertive (instructing the team that expectations have changed). The middle manager is also much closer to their direct reports and will have first-hand knowledge of the stressors and barriers to their performance and what additional demands are likely to impact staff morale and working relationships. This means that in all likelihood, your boss is navigating not only a complex system of power relations but also the psychological response of their direct superiors. On the ground, they can be switching between sympathy and celebration, between commiserations and congratulations or performance management to promotions; emotional baby-sitting, whiplash and labour. It is not surprising that high numbers of middle managers end up with conditions such as hypertension and anxiety.[14]

Bad bosses

Winston Churchill, Nelson Mandela, George Washington and MK Gandhi; by trying to identify and understand the qualities of these great leaders, we can then try to develop those qualities in ourselves. However, most of the leaders that we see every day are operating well within their comfort zones. They decide what projects to pursue, set performance targets, organise tasks and decides who does what and how it is done, the majority of which is fairly pedestrian, if not in fact outright dull or robotic. But, interestingly, it is this boring trait that makes some leaders really great; they are predictable, constant, apolitical and unselfish. They do what's safe and what makes others feel safe around them (if just a little bit bored). This is a bit of a concern when we consider that many leaders, particularly corporate CEOs, are known to have psychopathic tendencies.[15] One explanation for a Bates in the board room is that elevating others is a tough job, and their charisma and bright ideals give the impression of a social hero who will break down barriers, battle rules and regulations and win hearts and minds, because ultimately, *they must have faces you just can't help believing*.

It is possible to lead transformationally without an unhealthy dose of narcissism or a side order of Machiavellianism? This is what Robert E Quinn describes as the fundamental state of leadership,[16] and it starts with the question, 'What purpose do I serve and how can I achieve the results that I aim for?' Unfortunately, it is often only a crisis that will trigger a leadership shift from the internally focused predictable and competent state to the fundamental state of leadership. For example, Boris Johnson was widely criticised for being missing in action at the start of the COVID-19 pandemic. With the death toll climbing and the country grappling with the reality of PPE shortages, Johnson missed as many as five key emergency meetings. Finally, as the country began to nudge towards the Italian trajectory, Johnson began his daily briefings, and the country entered lockdown. Here we see external focus and results-oriented leadership, where the needs of others become more important than self-focus. Johnson is not copying anyone (except it is hard not to see a bit of Churchill in his call to arms to "stay at home, protect the NHS, save lives"). When great leaders are managing crisis, they are not usually emulating anyone; rather, what drives great leaders is their personal values and interpretation of morals. The point is that you can learn a lot from your bosses' behaviour.[17] Even the worst bosses can teach you not to do things. These are some of the worst bad boss behaviours and some of the reasons that can lie behind their behaviour.

Micromanagement

Everyone can expect a little bit of micromanagement in the early days of starting work, but if you start to see patterns in which your boss refuses to take on board new ideas, can only see one way to complete a task or continually pays attention to tiny details of what people are doing, then you can be sure you are working for a micromanager. Micromanagers will often start to control other minute details of individual and group behaviour, and this is a sure-fire way to demotivate a team and cause conflict. The strategy is doomed to failure because the whole point of being a manager is to delegate tasks and not take control of minutiae. There are quite simply not enough hours in the day for a micromanager to micro-manage the whole team.

Why do they do this? Sometimes it is a personality trait, people who are super high in perfectionism and striving for flawless performance. The foundations of perfectionism are dug early in life through a lack of reassurance and encourage-ment, perhaps even through a large dose of blame and punishment. As a result, perfectionist bosses will often be tortured by high levels of self-criticism and wor-ries about the capacity of others to live up to their high standards.[18] The challenge is that being a perfectionist is a bit like filling a leaky bucket. No matter how much you pour into it, the bucket is never full, and they are never satisfied. If trait perfectionism is driving your bad-boss behaviour, then there is nothing that you can do about it. They need a therapist, and you need to start thinking about a new job. In the meantime, you can still learn something from the perfectionist boss, including developing sharp, clear and precise communication skills and flawless time-keeping skills that optimise your project management performance. Possibly the most important thing you can learn from the perfectionist boss is the power of 'good enough'. There are a handful of activities that we perform each week that have the most significant impact on our successes. If you spend 80% of your time getting only a marginal gain in performance, then you are in fact wasting your time. Aiming for perfection is exhausting and paralysing, whereas knowing when 'good' is good enough and stopping is both liberating and prof-itable because it forces teams and organisations to pivot away from myopic tasks towards activities that produce the best overall outcome.

Micromanagement can also be the result of the loss of control. The bigger the job, the higher up the corporate level, the smaller the levels of personal control. As a boss, you want to be seen as an expert, but if something goes wrong, you are probably one of the last to find out, and you cannot just go about directly fixing it yourself. So, what ends up happening is that they hover about and become impatient for the end product. They start to ask to see work at different stages of development and become hypercritical when they should be nurturing the performance of their team. If this is your boss, then avoid playing the game. Yes, it's unfair that you're not trusted, but it doesn't mean you're untrustworthy. To be successful, you need to get out of the way of your own ego and start thinking about increasing the trust between you and your boss. To make them 'go away', you need to first pull them close. If they are a good boss who just happens to be micromanaging, eventually they will be pulled onto another work-critical task. At this point, they will have to make some decisions about who or what gets micromanaged, and those decisions will be largely emotional in nature. If they like and trust you, they will leave you alone much faster. Build that relationship by making sure you are always seen to be engaged and present, that you nurture a relationship with them by seeking out their wisdom. Remember that they want to be admired and seen to be 'the expert'. A bit of ego massage will go a long way, and you might learn something. At all costs avoid pitching up "Ta-daa" with the completed flawless task. Seek their input and provide them with regular updates.

The Peter principle

It's always the way that an employee will be promoted to their level of incompetence. People do well, and they are promoted. They do well again and become promoted. This continues until they reach a level where their talents are poorly matched to the demands of the job. When Laurence J Peter[19] originally conceived the idea in the 1960s, it was intended as satire, but the concept took hold because of its capacity to make a serious point. Promotion decisions tend to focus on current job performance, and often the characteristics of that role have little or nothing in common with the requirements of the new more senior role. The Peter principle is, for example, alive and well in academia. Professors who are outstanding researchers in their field, generating millions of pounds of funding and publications with more stars than a military general, often come under incredible pressure to take on department leadership. Managing people, however, requires a completely different skill set to the systematic and detailed skill set of scientific pursuit. Managing the feeding times of some nicotine-starved rhesus monkeys is a completely different skill to running the psychology department at a major university (although the cohort at times can feel remarkably similar).

The signs of an incompetent boss are the failure to make decisions and/or an overreliance on subordinates to achieve tasks. However, it is critical to remember that the most important successes are team successes. It's not about one person's individual performance; it's about the projects that you work on and the success of your organisation. The best teams are made up of people with different strengths,

competencies, talents and interests, so start figuring out where the most problematic boss lets deficiencies exist and then work with your team to compensate. Ensure that your team can cover a crisis. If your incompetent boss is unavailable and you can make a decision and feel comfortable doing so, then get on with it. If you start asking the opinion of your boss's boss, that can make him look bad, and nobody will thank you for it. You should never ever, complain or gossip about your incompetent boss to anyone or do anything that will make their incompetence obvious. Not to your peers and not to your boss's boss. If asked for an opinion, you must walk a difficult line, giving the whisper of an impression of knowing what the issues are but never being drawn into a *coup d'état*. That means no backstabbing, no secret conversations and no mutiny under any circumstance. Even if you ever succeed in having your boss retrained, reprimanded or removed, you will be trusted less by your peers and your boss's boss. So, at all costs, unless your boss is involved in illegal or unethical behaviour, do not turn yourself into 'Mutiny Mel', because you may well end up dancing in San Quentin with everyone else that joined you. Likewise, do not be tempted to draw on the behaviour you see around you as a road map to personal and professional success. You will end up making matters worse both for yourself and your peers, and before you know it, your environment will be more toxic than a wet market. Don't get drawn into the benefits that come from being a suck up. Sooner or later, your bad boss will be exposed, and if you have turned yourself into a sycophant, again say hello to San Quentin.

Your role is to make your boss's life easier by being both dependable and competent, so volunteer to take on some responsibility, unburden your boss from a pending assignment, keep an eye out for the mundane or uninspiring and offer to help so they can spend a bit more time on work-critical tasks or tasks that they really enjoy. When your boss is overworked, give them what they need – less work. This is what it takes to become an excellent follower, and if you do not master the art of following, you will never become a great leader. Then, as your relationship strengthens, become gradually more assertive. Great followers do not just do a good job; they also keep their leaders on their toes.

Do not expect a constant stream of praise and positive feedback. You are expected to turn up and do a good job. Nobody should be congratulated for doing a great job; you supposed to do a great job. If your boss says nothing about your performance, then you can comfortably assume that they're happy. If your inner angst is calling, 'validate me, validate me', then it is fundamentally important that you have a word with your inner (and possibly outer) narcissist. We all need meaningful praise as part of a rounded feedback process, but if you find yourself preoccupied with the lack of external reinforcement, then that's a problem, and that problem can lead to manipulative behaviours. Start cultivating experiences outside of your work environment that will bring a sense of achievement and praise, feel good about yourself and begin to reduce your reliance on others as the arbiters of your actions. Learn to feel good on your own. Additionally, if your performance is poor, you can actually end up making your boss's bad behaviour worse.[20] If this speaks to you, do not just sit back and wait for something to change. If you are having a tough time and things are not coming together in the way that you would have hoped, then do something before matters escalate and you start making mistakes and missing targets. These conversations are painfully difficult, but without taking matters into your own hands, you are setting yourself up to fail. At best, you could end up on capability management; at worst, you could end up out of a job.

While it's natural to become discouraged by your boss's behaviour, do not simply give up. If you find yourself in such thought patterns, it's critical that you find a way to crawl out of your hole. You might feel set up to fail, but you're the one doing the setting, and if it carries on, your boss will start developing lower and lower expectations of your performance.

This is a recipe for disaster. No matter what you do, your boss will eventually see you through the lens of failure, and these dynamics are notoriously difficult to repair. Get hold of yourself and stop blaming the world around you.

Psychological abuse

Nearly everyone at some point will act like a certified asshole at work. None of us are immune from a bad day at work, and at some point or another, we will engage in regrettable behaviour. It is not the single offender that we concern ourselves with but rather the serial offender. The person whose persistent oppressive behaviour creates an environment that leaves others de-energised, humiliated, disrespected and oppressed. Researchers have been amassing a body of knowledge on who does what to whom; when, where, why and with what consequences[21] for at least 30 years, and whilst much of that work has been of variable quality, what we can say for sure is that zero tolerance for workplace bullying should be front and centre of all organisational policies. Organisations must do everything that they can to recruit the right people and expel the wrong people. If your employer is not, and as a consequence people treat you badly, then you should run for the door as fast as you possibly can.

Presuming you are experiencing or witnessing bullying and/or harassment (rather than working through personal grievances) and your organisation has policies and procedures to deal with assholes, then it is your duty to ensure that you work in partnership with your boss and/or HR department to expose such wrongdoing. Not only are there significant financial costs involved in toxic workplace behaviours, the human costs are cataclysmic. One of the challenges, however, is that such behaviour is that it is often gradual and insidious. Bullying creeps up on you, wearing you down, so it may take a while for you to be fully aware and accepting of what is taking place. The situation is particularly challenging when it is your boss that is doing the damage. Not only can your boss become toxic, but because such behaviour becomes normalised, and your teammates (and even you) may quickly follow suit.

These are some useful tactics to address the problem:

1 Talk to people: there is often a fine line to be walked between constructive criticism and being critical and destructive confrontation. Even if your boss is not the greatest at giving feedback, it does not necessarily follow that he is bullying you. However, if he is bullying and/or harassing you, this may be a pattern that others have witnessed or have been on the receiving end of. Test your thinking and experiences with trusted people, and test and reflect on your thinking.

2 Keep a diary of events. Be specific and corroborate your diary where you can (copies of emails or the names of witnesses, times, dates and what people were doing at the time). Then use that information to compile a factual email to the boss of your boss, HR and your trade union if you have one.

3 Talk to your boss: Does the person know what they are doing? The eminent psychologist George Kelly was a straight up and down bully but by all accounts had no clue that what he was doing was having the impact that it was. When he realised, he mended his ways.

4 If talking doesn't improve matters, be assertive and stick up for yourself. It is really important that you do not present yourself as insecure, nervous or defeated. Publicly stating that you find their behaviour towards you demeaning and that they should change their tone and attitude towards you should help you gain back some psychological ground. When working conditions deteriorate to this stage, however, you need to be prepared that the asshole in question may well retaliate. That being said, "assholes suffer too".[22] They are frequently overlooked for promotions, sacked and sidelined as a result of their unreasonable actions. Therefore, if you can remain calm and specific, take the higher ground and not be pulled into a destructive confrontation, there is good reason to believe that matters will improve. Again, we can see this in the George Kelly example. He gave up his position as director.

5 If things continue to deteriorate, then take up outside help. The national bullying helpline provides a confidential helpline. ACAS is also a great source of information and advice.

George Kelly, the slot-rattling boss

Slot-rattling is a psychological term that explains someone who will suddenly switch from cold to warm, excited to aloof, to the point that nobody really knows where they stand. Slot-rattling comes from the personal construct theory of George Kelly, who was himself an expert slot-rattler.

Excited and creative, he would welcome people into his world, cancelling all appointments and giving them his devoted attention, but then he would suddenly switch back to a more rule-bound rigidity and aloofness. He would be sweet, then salty, or merely polite. He was no supporter of psychoanalytical theory but would draw shrewdly on Freud in ways that would undermine and humiliate his students. He would also use non-verbal tactics to get his message across. One student described the awful silence that would indicate that you had done something wrong. If he were delighted, he would blow air from his mouth and grin. If you said something he disagreed with in some way, with some theatre, he would remove his glasses and drop his head to the ground.

Kelly had control over the fates of his students and would quickly dispatch them from clinical training if they did not make the grade. To carry out this unfortunate task, he would arrive at work dressed in farming clothes, remarking to the students that 'when you have to clean the manure out of the barn, you must be dressed for the occasion'.

So high were the levels of anxiety around Kelly that in one unfortunate situation, a student was rendered silent in fear. Kelly seemed to have had no idea of the impact he was having on his students and was appalled by the student's response. He went home and promptly re-wrote his role as director. At the top of the list was 'resign as director', followed by 'move out of the office', followed by always having his office door open and coffee for students who happened to pop by.

Forsythe, A. (2019). *Key thinkers in individual differences; ideas on personality and intelligence*, Routledge.

Don't become an asshole

When you become a boss yourself, ensure that you create a workplace that has zero tolerance for this kind of activity. Power often breeds nastiness between people, and whilst we must accept that there are always organisational pecking orders, as a boss, you can do much to downplay the differences in status that can encourage destructive behaviour. Most organisations will have written policies dealing with issues of mutual respect, discrimination, bullying, victimisation and harassment, but that doesn't go far enough. These issues must be given meaning by giving them a voice. Talking with staff about issues of organisational citizenship, giving your staff a sense of purpose and a feeling of control and ensuring policies are directly tied to virtuous acts that are rewarded will create a community that will insulate your staff from toxic behaviour. When altruism, courtesy, sportsmanship, conscientiousness and civic virtue become everyone's business, bullying and other toxic behaviours are quickly robbed of oxygen.

Fun fact: mirror neurons and accountability

Research that explores the role that mirror neurons play in our emotional regulation and development suggests that when children perform a negative act, they are aware of what they have done and feel bad. Initially, they do have empathy for the person they have injured, and that empathy reduces the likelihood they will perform the task again. However, the consequences of their actions can in fact override the mirror neuron processes that are linked to empathy and thus increase the likelihood that they will become a repeat offender.

Further reading

Kalman, I. (2010). Mirror neurons, conscience and the fallacy of accountability. *Psychology Today*, Jan 24th. www.psychologytoday.com/gb/blog/resilience-bullying/201001/mirror-neurons-conscience-and-the-fallacy-accountability

---

Good communication

Oprah once said that the foundation for a good relationship rests on communication, and your workplace relationships are absolutely no different. Every administrative function in an organisation relies on good communication, and without it, work efficiency, effectiveness and staff well-being all suffer. Poor communication is a significant block to personal development, effective leadership and our overall effectiveness at work.[23]

Teams need good communication to align their goals, avoid confusion, coordinate workflow, track progress, allocate budgets and meet deadlines, give feedback, revise, move forward and continually define purpose. But just because lots of communication takes place, it does not automatically follow that any of that communication is useful or good. The constant chatter of organisational life and the growing pressure for constant connectivity are killing productivity. Described as the availability-expectation-pressure pattern[24] whereby staff are bombarded with emails (often hundreds per day), Tweets, organisational communications, 'all staff' emails, phone calls, Zooms, MSTeams and Skype meetings that in turn spawn more meetings, more emails, more phone calls, organisational communications, Tweets, MSTeams, and Skype meetings that turn into more meetings, emails, phone calls, Zooms . . . You get the idea. 'More-faster-better' is distracting; it saps time, leaving staff feeling overwhelmed and techno-stressed, and results in coping behaviours such as avoiding and withdrawing from potentially useful information (because there is just too much to deal with); adopting a wait-and-see strategy (known as queuing) or 'satisficing', which is to focus on what is just good enough for purpose (avoiding the finer details).[25] But communication overload doesn't happen because of technology, it happens because of people.

Top 10 communication tips

1 *Kill the on-screen notifications.* Not only are they likely to trip you up as they pop up during a critical conversation, they are also a complete black hole for your attention, pulling you right into something when you ought to be doing something else. Even the briefest of mental shifts can cost enormous amounts of productivity time, so practice being 'one eyed' and get the job in hand finished. Leave virtual groups that no longer serve you and turn off notifications from social media, Amazon, YouTube, MyFitnessPal or anything else that has found its way onto your phone. Set aside time for these activities so you are still connected but not interrupted when you ought to be doing something else.

2 *Who's that?* Be careful who you give your contact details to. Do not use your work email for promotional subscriptions, purchases or other activities that are likely to increase the amount of spam you receive in your inbox. Do not automatically accept every LinkedIn request that pops into your email box, because lots of people are trying to sell you stuff you really don't want.

3 *Your inbox is your nemesis*
   • Exercise some self-control and set aside a time to deal with your emails. Do not leave your emails open all day.
   • Do it once, don't do it twice. If you open an email, see it through. Otherwise it will get lost in more emails, and it will take you longer to sort the problem out. If you are waiting on something or need to follow a trail, triage your emails into folders using labels, folders and categories. A 'waiting folder' is useful for things that you are waiting for someone to respond on. This will save you enormous time trying to locate and find emails. Try to use the same approach to other tasks, not just your inbox. Completing a task to its full conclusion and

moving on to the next is generally more productive than flitting from one task to another and more satisfying and motivating. A couple of completed tasks on your to-do list is more satisfying than a bit done of everything on the list.

- Do not be afraid to delete emails, especially if they are held separately on an organisational server. Anything work critical can be recovered. Once a month, empty your junk mail and your deleted folder.
- If you send an email, only send it to the people who need to know. Do not grandstand emails or copy in people just in case. ccing everyone can also be dangerous, as it is habit forming and can lead to embarrassing consequences if you are not careful. A colleague of mine once sent a sensitive email meant only for her superior to an entire department by mistake, then had to claim that her email had been hacked by the Russians.
- Avoid having push email notifications on your phone, or you will struggle to switch off.

4   *Decide when to email and when to talk:* Only email on what is important but brief. If you find that the email you are writing is taking longer than expected, chances are it is a difficult conversation and it requires a face-to-face conversation instead. Sending an email rather than talking makes us feel a bit safer. We are spared the awkwardness of personal contact under painful conditions, but this comes with a high cost. Emails escalate conflict because people have a nasty habit of not giving each other the benefit of the doubt. Communication is a complex thing, and there is a lot of nonverbal communication that goes on in a face-to-face conversation that cannot be conveyed in an email. The tone can be very difficult to get across in an email, and while you may think you are saving time sending an email rather than getting off your rump to go and speak to Bob in accounting, it is a lot more painful having to later apologise to Bob as he has misinterpreted your email.

5   *Fight as if you are right, but always listen as if you are wrong.* There is nothing wrong with confrontation. If everyone is terribly agreeable and nobody challenges anything, nothing will ever get done and nothing will ever change. Learn how and when to fight, how to completely absorb the other person's position and when to let your position drop and commit.

6   *Learn how to get your point across by being authentic and specific.* Listen to what others are saying and what they are also not saying. Disagree without being disagreeable. Embrace transparency and straight talking but never personalise (even if it is person). Never say "you are a ___". Never say "you're wrong". Always say "that piece of information seems wrong" and say why: "how you are explaining this isn't clear". We can all read between the lines, and even though they can't accuse you of calling them names, they'll get the idea.

7   *Meetings*. At some point in your career, you will be in charge of organising a meeting. Make sure that meeting has a clear purpose and an agenda, and everyone who attends should have a reason for being there. There is no more wisdom in 'all hands' meetings than there is than having a few very carefully chosen individuals. If people want to be involved or kept in the loop, then question them. They may be trying to micromanage.

8   *Text over voice mail*. Voice mails are a pain. Two main reasons to avoid them are: people get charged for picking up their voice mails, and second, they are easily hacked (a crime that eventually closed the UK newspaper *News of the World*). As a consequence, collecting voice mails it is a laborious process and all anyone wants to do is hit delete as quickly as possible. If someone doesn't pick up their phone, hang up and follow up with a text message asking for a call back and perhaps highlighting the reason for the call. Encourage others not to leave you voice messages (but don't ignore them), and if you can, completely disable the function on your phone.

9   *Take a break and learn to disengage*. In a bid to manage what is considered excessive interference in the personal lives of employees, many countries are now trying to move towards enshrining the 'right to disconnect' into law.[26] Just like elite athletes, we all need rest periods and breaks to stay healthy and avoid burn out. Taking a break that involves moving about is particularly important if you have a sedentary job that involves long periods of desk work. A micro break, for example, a short walk, has a significant impact on increasing general well-being, increasing creativity, perspective taking and overall work performance.[27] Turn off your emails at the end of the working day and learn to disengage.

10 *Be respectful* because time is everyone's most precious asset. Lead by example and encourage your colleagues to do the same.

Old farts and young slackers

Over the past decade, there has been increased interest in the ways in which generations communicate (or do not communicate) effectively and how those differences can cause conflict.[28] Changes in career trajectory and retirement expectations mean that there are now some five generations working together at any one time, all of whom will be at different stages of their careers and thus have varying needs and expectations. The argument goes that those born post-1980 (millennials) were the first to grow up in a complex digital environment, with mobile phones, email and messaging systems. They are comfortable with digital technology both at work and in their personal lives and have a preference for computer-mediated communication (CMC). Generation Z (born between 1995 and 2015) is the true technology generation, but, perhaps because of concerns about screen time and socialisation, are comfortable both with CMC and face-to-face communication. The Baby Boomer generation, however (those born between 1946 and 1964), value personal communication. They prefer to meet in person, pick up the telephone and have a conversation and will seldom engage with instant messaging tools or other computer-mediated technology.[29] Generation X (circa 1965 to 1980) were the original latchkey kids. The first generation of children to have both parents working, they value independence and entrepreneurship.

A few researchers have put quite a bit of energy into establishing patterns of behaviour and recommendations for improving communication flows between generations. The problem is that looking for patterns between different generations made up of millions of very individual people and then coming up with broad generalisations about their preferences is frankly bad science that increases stereotypical ideas about what people 'are like'. There is no doubt that the meaning of non-verbal messages is compromised. We are social beings who rely on multiple clues, verbal and non-verbal, to interpret a message, but those are problems that transcend age-related differences.

Intergenerational conflict is likely to occur through inadequacies in the ways in which respect is demonstrated and interpreted.[30] Everyone one wants to be respected, to *feel* respected, but the ways in which respect is demonstrated are different. Three categories seem to be critical: (1) listen to me and pay attention to what I say, (2) give my opinions the weight they deserve or (3) do what I tell you to do. The latter two are predominately important to older generations, whereas being listened to and given attention are more strongly associated with feeling respected in younger generations. Such mismatches in the ways that respect is demonstrated are a strong predictor of the extent of employee satisfaction, whether employees are likely to stay with an organisation and (unsurprisingly) the extent to which conflict is likely to occur. Therefore, it is vitally important to figure out how respect applies to you so that you can clearly articulate to others your wants and needs (perhaps revisit the values exercises in Chapter 1) but also so that you can develop a sensitive approach to the needs and wants of others. These actions are critical for developing trust and loyalty and navigating organisational politics and organisational change.

Fundamentally, people want the same things, no matter what age group or generation they are from. Our values are similar, but we might express them differently, or we might behave differently, but in principle what binds us together is stronger than what pushes us apart. Responsibly for world events, the workplace and the home weigh heavy for both the baby boomers and Generation X. There is a real sense that something urgently has to change and improve, and Generations Y and Z feel they have been charged with making that change.[31] The pandemic that has upended our lives requires that we nurture such dynamics. An entire generation, already in financial deficit, will now enter a workforce defined by economic and social insecurity. The path ahead is broken, and the vanguard must be social change.

Positive working relationships

Good-quality relationships at work increase commitment; lower job stress[32] and are associated with better-quality sleep, improved socialising and more energy.[33] But is not necessarily the extent to which we treat each other well and are compassionate to one another that matters; rather, it is giving something good, something of great value, that is important. This can be compassion, forgiveness and encouragement, but most significantly, playing to your strengths, connecting with your work colleagues and helping them play to their strengths is a guaranteed formula to help everyone experience more positive emotions at work.[34] If we imagine an environment where everyone behaved in this way, it would be easy to see how organisational culture would change for the better. People would believe in their own capacity to develop and overcome obstacles. This self-belief would encourage others to think and behave in a complementary way; as a result, there would be an abundance of collective resourcefulness and discretionary effort, psychological well-being, resilience, self-efficacy and optimism.

Organisations need to create the right antecedents for these things to thrive. That means hiring the right people with the right characteristics and strengths, creating a culture that supports the development of psychological capital and making sure that the right people with the right values and beliefs are in the right jobs.[35]

Further reading

Kalish, A. *8 psychology-backed TED talks that will help you understand why you do what you do.* Themuse. www.themuse.com/advice/8-psychologybacked-ted-talks-thatll-help-you-understand-why-you-do-what-you-do

Leal, B, C. (2017). *4 essential keys to effective communication in love, life, work – anywhere!* Creative space publishing, Amazon.

Sutton, R. (2014). *The no asshole rule, building a civilized workplace and surviving one that isn't.* Piatkus, UK.

Notes

1 Buchholz, K. (2020, February 13). How couples met. *Statista*. Retrieved from www.statista.com/chart/20822/way-of-meeting-partner-heterosexual-us-couples/

2 Baumeister, R. F., Bratslavsky, E., Finkenauer, C., & Vohs, K. D. (2001). Bad is stronger than good. *Review of General Psychology, 5*(4), 323–370. doi:10.1037/1089-2680.5.4.323

3 Schalk, R. (2019). *Mutuality and reciprocity in the psychological contract: A critical review and analysis* (pp. 35–62). doi:10.4337/9781788115681.00010

4 Abele-Brehm, A. (1992). Positive versus negative mood influences on problem solving: A review. *Polish Psychological Bulletin, 23*.

5 Geue, P. E. (2018). Positive practices in the workplace: Impact on team climate, work engagement, and task performance. *The Journal of Applied Behavioral Science, 54*(3), 272–301. doi:10.1177/0021886318773459

6 Zeigarnik, B. (1975). Uber das Behalten von Erledigten und Unerledigten Handlungen. *Psychologische Forschung, 9*, 1–85; research summarized in Goldenson, R. M. (1927). *The encyclopedia of human behavior*. New York: Dell Publishing.

7 Baddeley, A. D. (1963). A Zeigarnik-like effect in the recall of anagram solutions. *Quarterly Journal of Experimental Psychology, 15*(1), 63–64.

8 Atkinson, J. W. (1953). The achievement motive and recall of interrupted and completed tasks. *Journal of Experimental Psychology, 46*(6), 381–390.

9 Weziak-Bialowolska, D., Bialowolski, P., Sacco, P. L., Vanderweele, T. J., & McNeely, E. (2020). Well-being in life and well-being at work: Which comes first? Evidence from a longitudinal study. *Frontiers in Public Health*. doi:10.3389/fpubh.2020.00103

10 Barta, T., Kleiner, M., & Neumann, T. (2012). *Is there payoff from top-team diversity?* McKinsey & Company. Retrieved from www.mckinsey.com/business-functions/organization/our-insights/is-there-a-payoff-from-top-team-diversity

11 Ehrhardt, K., & Ragins, B. R. (2019). Relational attachment at work: A complementary fit perspective on the role of relationships in organizational life. *The Academy of Management Journal*. doi:10.5465/amj.2016.0245

12 Gordon. (2011, July 8). Director Seth Gordon on 'Horrible Bosses', here and now. *The World*. Retrieved from www.pri.org/stories/2011-07-08/director-seth-gordon-horrible-bosses

13 Caine, M. (2018). *Blowing the bloody doors off and other lessons in life*. London: Hodder & Stoughton.

14 Anicich, E. M., & Hirsh, J. B. (2017). The psychology of middle power: Vertical code-switching, role conflict, and behavioral inhibition. *The Academy of Management Review, 42*(4), 659–682. doi:10.5465/amr.2016.0002

15 Landay, K., Harms, P. D., & Credé, M. (2019). Shall we serve the dark lords? A meta-analytic review of psychopathy and leadership. *Journal of Applied Psychology, 104*(1), 183–196. doi:10.1037/apl0000357

16 Quinn, R. E., & Spreitzer, G. M. (2006). Entering the fundamental state of leadership: A framework for the positive transformation of self and others. In R. Burke & C. Cooper (Eds.), *Inspiring leaders* (pp. 67–83). Oxford: Routledge.

17 Taylor, S. G., Griffith, M. D., Vadera, A. K., Folger, R., & Letwin, C. R. (2018). Breaking the cycle of abusive supervision: How disidentification and moral identity help the trickle-down change course. *Journal of Applied Psychology*. doi:10.1037/apl0000360

18 Ocampo, A. C. G., Wang, L., Kiazad, K., Restubog, S. L. D., & Ashkanasy, N. M. (2020). The relentless pursuit of perfectionism: A review of perfectionism in the workplace and an agenda for future research. *Journal of Organizational Behavior.* doi:10.1002/job.2400

19 Peter, L. J., & Hull, R. (1969). *The Peter principle.* New York: Morrow.

20 Braun, S., Kark, R., & Wisse, B. (2018). Editorial: Fifty shades of grey: Exploring the dark sides of leadership and followership. *Frontiers in Psychology, 9.* doi:10.3389/fpsyg.2018.01877

21 Einarsen, S., Hoel, H., Zapf, D., & Cooper, C. L. (2011). The concept of bullying and harassment at work: The European tradition. In S. Einarsen, H. Hoel, D. Zapf, & C. L. Cooper (Eds.), *Bullying and harassment in the workplace: Developments in theory, research, and practice* (2nd ed., pp. 3–39). Boca Raton, FL: CRC Press.

22 Sutton, R. (2014). *The no asshole rule, building a civilised workplace and surviving one that isn't.* London: Piatkus.

23 Adu-Oppong, A. A., & Agyin-Birikorang, E. (2014). Communication in the workplace: Guidelines for improving effectiveness. *Global Journal of Commerce & Management Perspective, 208–213.*

24 Stephens, K. K., Mandhana, D. M., Kim, J. J., Li, X., Glowacki, E. M., & Cruz, I. (2017). Reconceptualizing communication overload and building a theoretical foundation. *Communication Theory.* doi:10.1111/comt.12116

25 Bawden, D., & Robinson, L. (2020). Information overload: An overview. In *Oxford encyclopedia of political decision making.* Oxford: Oxford University Press.

26 *"Petition 1057".* Chambre des députés du Grand Duché du Luxembourg.

27 Kim, S., Park, Y., & Headrick, L. (2018). Daily micro-breaks and job performance: General work engagement as a cross-level moderator. *Journal of Applied Psychology, 103*(7), 772–786. doi:10.1037/apl0000308

28 Glass, A. (2007). Understanding generational differences for competitive success. *Industrial and Commercial Training, 39,* 98–103. doi:10.1108/00197850710732424

29 Venter, E. (2017). Bridging the communication gap between generation Y and the baby boomer generation. *International Journal of Adolescence and Youth.* doi:10.1080/02673843.2016.1267022

30 Deal, J. J. (2007). *Retiring the generation gap: How employees young and old can find common ground.* San Francisco: John Wiley & Sons.

31 Sobrino-De Toro, I., Labrador-Fernández, J., & De Nicolás, V. L. (2019). Generational diversity in the workplace: Psychological empowerment and flexibility in Spanish companies. *Frontiers in Psychology.* doi:10.3389/fpsyg.2019.01953

32 Tran, K. T., Nguyen, P. V., Dang, T., & Ton, T. (2018). The impacts of the high-quality workplace relationships on job performance: A perspective on staff nurses in Vietnam. *Behavioral sciences (Basel, Switzerland), 8*(12), 109. doi:10.3390/bs8120109

33 Mastroianni, K., & Storberg-Walker, J. (2014). Do work relationships matter? Characteristics of workplace interactions that enhance or detract from employee perceptions of well-being and health behaviors. *Health Psychology and Behavioral Medicine, 2*(1), 798–819. doi:10.1080/21642850.2014.933343

34 Lewis, S. (2011). *Positive psychology at work.* Malden: Wiley Blackwell.

35 Driver, M. (2011). *Coaching positively, lessons for coaches from positive psychology.* Open University Press.

Chapter 8

Influence and persuasion

Influence is relational and centres on trust and your reputation. Persuasion does not rely on who you are or the relationships you have forged; rather, it focuses on your capacity to spur people into changing their thoughts, behaviour or actions towards your goals. The ancient Greeks considered the relationship between influence and persuasion through the art of rhetoric (the art of effective or persuasive speaking and writing) an essential component of effective leadership, placing Aristotle's three appeals at the centre of their education system. *Pathos* was the use of rhetoric to trigger emotional seduction in persuasion. For example, the idea that a product can make you more beautiful or that your help and involvement in a charity will help a child escape pain. *Logos* uses logic and reason to be pursued: facts and statistics. *Ethos* is an appeal to credibility and trust, for example, adverts that quote science or medical evidence. Today, political figures and movements, lobby groups, charities and advertising agencies all use rhetoric through examples of logic and reason, credibility and trust with the use of emotional appeals to persuade us that something is true. Of course, attitudes do not always change in the face of persuasion, particularly if individuals have been told that they are vulnerable to manipulation or that a persuasion attempt is about to occur. For that reason, building influence also means being understood effectively, using language that others will listen to, being respectful to our own needs and the needs of others, striving first to understand and then to be understood and recognising that communication begins some time before any personal interaction with others.

Every step in your career is directly related to your capacity to influence and persuade. During the early parts of your career, you will be presenting yourself to interview panels in an attempt to persuade them into favouring you as their idea candidate. Later in your career, your reputation and influence may precede you and you may get headhunted, but it may also mean that people put higher expectations on you. The good news is that the art of rhetoric (persuasion and influence) can be learned. This chapter examines how you can build on your knowledge and skills, your sense of self and your values to build your influence and persuasion at work.

Personality and influence, or much ado about nothing

There is much in psychological literature about personality and how that influences the way we work, the relationships that we develop and nurture and how we go about influencing and persuading people. Do personality traits really influence our behaviour at work and our capacity to get things done? Well, yes and no. You need to have an awful lot of a particular trait to actually have something that is directly linked to some aspect of behaviour or another, and very few of us do. The situational factors also need to be highly specific for a reasonable personality-behavioural interaction to occur, and the world just doesn't operate that way. All personality tests can do is give us a sense of how people might prefer to act; they cannot tell us what we are likely to do in any given situation. So, if you would describe yourself as an introvert (or someone has measured you so), do not worry: personality is a little more complex than the results of a scale. We don't all fit into the neat little boxes, no matter how much we'd like to.

For persuasion, emotional intelligence wins through.[1] Those with higher levels of emotional recognition ability (ERA) are consistently found to be more consistently likeable and cooperative, over and above measures such as cognitive ability. This is because attitude change comes about through a process of learning, cognitive processes, message elaboration, culture and dissonance reduction. From this perspective, the external environment seems to play a prominent role in attitude and attitude change, but that persuasion can also be conceptualised as self-persuasion, the thoughts we engage in or the behaviours that we practice. In other words, if you want to persuade and influence, you need to improve your capacity to understand, communicate effectively, empathise with others, overcome challenges and defuse conflict. Simple!

We have two ears and one mouth for a reason

Another Greek philosopher, Zeno of Citium, was described as a gloomy man who did not like much company. He hated chit chat and particularly disliked speeches. Not surprisingly, he tried to encourage people to speak much less and listen more. Fun fact: Zeno died from suicide after he tripped and broke his toe. As he lay on the ground, writhing in toe agony, he rather dramatically decided to hold his breath until he died. A man of the all-round measured response.[2]

Although I wouldn't go to him for help with a splinter, Zeno had a point. There is tremendous strength in signalling to others that you value their point of view. Listening creates an atmosphere of warmth and understanding, value and encouragement. Most critically, listening suggests to others that you are strong. That you are comfortable and relaxed in not having all the answers. When you listen, you buy yourself time. Listening enables you to remain neutral while you 'dig up' the problem and see what is there. Listening enables you to unpick what people actually know or don't know and what misunderstandings or concerns people have and take your time to come up with good plans or clear alternatives. Conversely, bad listeners are generally considered persona non grata. They're too much bark and far too much bite; they also rarely find out about their piranha-like ways. Do you think Darla (*Finding Nemo*) knew she was a nightmare? No, she thought it was funny to be a piranha, and fish literally faked their own deaths to get away from her. Character assassination takes place around the scuttlebutt, so don't be that bad listener or you might find yourself on the wrong side of the tank. Open up your ears, close your mouth, start relationship building and then bring people along with your thinking.

Fun fact: Greek foot

You may have gathered by now that we love a good foot story.

Some people think your foot shape indicates something about your personality and ancestry. But we psychologists know that the only thing your foot shape is truly likely to predict is the extent to which you end up with bunions.

Morton's toe is where the second toe is larger than the big toe, and you can see this phenomenon across practically every form of art in ancient Greece. Greek statues, including Zeno, are all depicted as having 'Greek foot'. Greek foot increases the likelihood of all sorts of problems, including bunions, nerve pain and stubbed and broken toes.

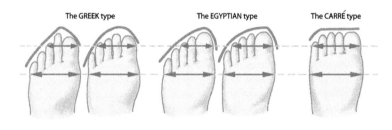

The GREEK type   The EGYPTIAN type   The CARRÉ type

How to listen and be listened to

Learning to listen is not rocket science, but it does take focus and practice. As you recall from Chapter 2, thoughts formulate very quickly, much faster than the person who is talking. In just 600 milliseconds, we can think of a word, then apply the rules of grammar to it and send it to the mouth to be spoken.[3] If we do not need to speak those words, the process is much faster (about 300 milliseconds). This means that when we are listening, our brains are actually accelerating at break-neck speed. The poor person we're talking to is earnestly trying to convey to us information, and we're busy formulating our own ideas, jumping ahead and imagining where the conversation is going. Our brain is screaming to interrupt. But by cutting the poor guy short, we never really get a full sense of the journey they wanted to take us on, and even worse, you might have just royally pissed him off.

Much the same as experimenting and discarding solutions that don't work, listening can be applied like the scientific method; hearing and discarding what is not useful and deciding what is useful is part of the process. Don't get bogged down with someone wasting your time. Keep listening, and the solution will eventually reveal itself. You don't have to understand the journey to get to the destination, so hush up because it will be an important part of yours. Taking the time to listen will build trust and respect; as you go up the ladder and move into managerial positions, information that might not be relevant to the problem at hand helps you build a picture of the people under your command. It adds to your knowledge of their competencies and their week spots, which in turn helps you to help them with relevant CPD and also what questions and tasks you ask of them.

Step 1: learn to remember

Psychology students are expert in memory. All those hours listening to Baddeley's model of working memory or how we can use Miller's five plus or minus two, with chunking to measure what people can recall. It's a bit ironic then that we don't dedicate some focused time to enhancing our own recall. Recalling facts, information and dates is the difference between prevailing and making your mark and fumbling around in the dark. In particular, the simple act of remembering someone's name is critical in helping people feel valued and respected. Remembering people's names pays them a compliment because it signals to them that they have made an impression on you, so you should make it a priority. When someone tells you their name, say it over and over (clearly inside your head) and then try to think of someone else you know who has the same name as them. People with difficult-sounding names take a bit more practice, but generally speaking, they will be used to people struggling to pronounce their names. If you can find a way of writing down their name, it will make things a little easier and break it into recognisable words that link to the sounds. Let's try the legend that is Mihaly Csikszentmihalyi (Me-high Cheek-sent-me-high) or dishy *Game of Thrones* actor Nikolaj Coster-Waldau (Neek-o-ly Cos-ter Wall-dow). There are also some smart apps that can help and YouTube videos for most complex names (see, for example, "NameShouts", which helps you search for, locate, listen to and pronounce difficult names).

Step 2: do not interrupt

Interrupting comes in many forms: blurting out an idea that you are bursting to share, constantly nodding and smiling sweetly or salty, frowning and sighing. It might even come from something external, phones ringing, people walking into you unexpectedly, fire engines and thunderstorms. If you are the one being interrupted, then the responsibility is with you to do something to reclaim attention. Judge the room, and if you have lost someone's attention on more than one occasion, then the current situation is unrecoverable; stop and offer to reschedule at another time. If the meeting is important, try not to be so obvious that you've lost the room. Make a joke or subtly wrap up. You also don't want to look like you're rage quitting a meeting because there were one too many distractions to keep everyone's attention.

Sometimes interruptions come from a bad place (see, for example, the slot-rattling boss in Chapter 7), but more often, the person doing the interrupting is trying to connect in some way. The problem is that interruptions have the opposite impact; they annoy the speaker and will just fizzle out the conversation. Even if you are very excited about what the person is trying to convey, bite your lip until they've had time to complete their thoughts. Don't be concerned that the conversation will somehow shift off topic before you have an opportunity to contribute. Wait, because you can always circle round and raise your points, and in so doing so, you buy yourself some time to formulate your thinking. Jumping in because you have had a 'great idea' and you want to get your point across before someone else has come up with it is also a pretty poor reason for interrupting. If someone else is going to come up with that idea, then it was never unique to begin with, and even if it were unique, the extra time gives you the potential to better refine the idea in the context of the values and priorities of the individual or organisation you were working for.

Men, particularly men who have been socialised to be assertive, are more likely to be chronic interrupters.[4] They are also more likely to interrupt women than men. So if you are that man, . . . *oh right he's not listening*. Well, for all you listening men out there, the good news is that if you a good listener, you are also likely to be better in bed.[5]

Step 3: you do not need to be a good listener, just a practiced one

Calmly let conversations take their course; then, when you have an opportunity, reflect back on what you have just heard: "if I am correct in understanding, you are saying . . . *x, y, z*" and avoid putting your own spin on what you have just heard. Such paraphrasing is a powerful technique that indicates to the speaker that they have conveyed their message to you and that you have received it in the way they wanted to be heard. This clarification is both flattering and reassuring to the speaker, but it also has the added advantage of sending a subtle message to everyone else in the room that you are in control and have the clearest perspective of the exchange that has just taken place. Paraphrasing takes some practice, so find some time to try it out. Use your own words and encapsulate the essence of the message. Your aim is to restate and improve the quality of the message so that the quality of the communication keeps moving forward, perhaps ending the statement with a curiosity-based question: "Where do you think we should go next?" It might not be a good idea to take your practice straight to the boardroom, though. Take a gander at some news broadcasts or politician's speeches. We recommend Obama. He's a good speaker, always saying good things, and we all need a bit more of that kind of positivity.

Take notes so that you can adequately remember points raised and what points you wish to raise if you can't remember. Those notebooks provided at board meetings are there for a reason (and if you write in it, you get to take it home!).

Step 4: learn to keep the attention of others

There are some ways that you can increase the likelihood that you will hold people's attention; getting them away from their usual workspace is a good strategy. Ask them for a coffee, or better still, a lunchtime walk. Try to avoid any unnecessary breaks in attention; anything that comes between you and a decision is death to that decision. If a discussion, negotiation or other critical activity is going well, you have got to keep that emotional high *high*. Think of breaks as like commercials. *Who doesn't hate commercials?* There you are on a Friday night, in the middle of *A Clockwork Orange*. Alex's eyes are stretched to capacity and you have your glass of pinot grigio, movie snacks and a blanket. You make a silent promise to yourself that you will never go for laser eye surgery and reach tentatively for another chunk of Cadbury's. Tension is high, and then *bam!* Sergei, Aleksandr Orlov and Oleg are irritating you with their fluffy meerkat marketing schemes. The moment is lost. Damn you, Channel 4; you knew you shouldn't have cancelled your Netflix subscription.

In the real world of work, if you are the person on the receiving end of interruptions, it is your job to reclaim the attention of the audience. Being annoyed doesn't aid persuasion; it has the complete opposite effect, because you are now interrupting yourself. You are interrupting your own train of thought and moving your eye from the prize.

Holding eye contact can help. Gazing will help keep their focus on you and prevent them from straying from your message, but don't do this in a weird *Clockwork Orange* Pavlovian mind experiment kind of a way. Or in a Jedi warrior/*Men Who Stare at Goats* kind of a way, either. You want to get a point across, not stop hearts. That being said, there is something incredibly powerful about holding a gaze. We can quite literally catch feels and fall in love from just staring into someone's eyes,[6] but if you get it wrong, you can make other people feel very, *very* uncomfortable, so remember to blink.

Step 5: the minute we think we have all the answers, we forget the questions

Once you have learned to listen, then learning when and the right way to ask questions – questions that draw out the best answers – is a skill worth mastering. The one question you should avoid asking is 'why'. 'Why' is laden with judgement and the request for an explanation to be judged. The word is synonymous with criticism, and you will never get a good answer with a 'why' question. Instead of asking why, ask "what". *What made you choose that course of action? What is important to you here?* People are not always acutely aware of the 'whys' behind their action, so a gentle reframe to 'what' empowers people to be a bit less defensive and more reflective in their answers without the fear that they are going to be on the receiving end of accusatory or hostile judgement. It also helps to build in a scaffold so you can reflect back, to show you are listening, and paraphrase what they are saying whilst building in time for just a little bit more information. *What's on your mind?/What are you thinking here?* (reflect: *so you are saying x, y, z?*) *Is there anything else on your mind?* (this question gives the person an additional chance to add further information). *What is the real challenge here for you?* (checking again for facts). *And what else?* (People always have something more).

Burgay Stanier[7] provides a useful guide for developing powerful questioning habits (see Table 8.1). The questions are organised here depending on the stage of a process and the purpose of that conversation. These are in effect all questions that relate to the leadership coaching processes. Good coaching helps improve performance by preventing people from becoming overwhelmed by enhancing focus on the present, the 'here and now', rather than on the distant past or future concerns. Good coaching reduces dependency because people are encouraged to think through their maladaptive thought processes and behaviours towards taking ownership of their problems and find their own solutions, with the ultimate aim that they will do more work that has meaning and impact. Coaching has significant impact at both an individual and organisational level,[8] so it's a habit worth developing, but you *have* to be prepared to respect other people's solutions. You are travelling from Nuneaton to London, and after a discussion, a number of routes are discarded, and you take a route. You seem to get there in a timely manner, so the assumption is that the other routes would have taken longer and the one you took was the 'right one'. But here's the problem: you didn't split into four, take the other routes and have a race. So how can you assume that the route you took was the 'right one'? Solutions are like opinions: everyone's got one. So long as they arrive at the destination and you succeed in your goals, they are all the 'right one'.

Table 8.1 Superpower your questioning

Stage	Sample questions	Purpose
Agreeing aims	What are you trying to achieve?	Clear objectives
	When are you going to do it?	Agreed-upon dates
	How will you know if you have succeeded?	Measurement
Awareness	What is happening now?	Clear picture of current actions
	What have you done so far?	Review of relevant achievements, however slight

Stage	Sample questions	Purpose
	What are the consequences?	Effect of current actions
	What do you want to be different?	
Analysis	*What can you change?*	Identify possibilities
	What are the options?	Broaden vision
	How can you change it?	Seek solutions
	What are the barriers?	Evaluate choices
Assessment	*What actually happened?*	Clarify outcomes
	Was this what you wanted?	Evaluate degree of success
	What have you gained from this experience?	Discoveries made
	How can you improve?	Establish further potential

Step 6: the courage to be disliked

Warm people are compelling. They reassure us, giving us a place to go for nurturing, respect, caring, trust and bonding. Warm people stand out in a crowd; they shine and sparkle and are gracious and kind. They do not spend lots of time talking about themselves; rather, they listen intently, looking for the best in others whilst smiling and nodding reassuringly.

The fragility of our niceness and civility has been severely tested in recent years. There has been a global breakdown in niceness that has caused considerable pain to public individuals such as Caroline Flack, Prince Harry and Megan Markle, and to private individuals and children who find themselves in toxic cyber-environments that they are ill equipped to understand or manage. We have increasing political polarisation, with individuals refusing to consider opposing viewpoints, no matter how politely those views are communicated. The end result is lower levels of civic engagement, lower levels of compromise and higher levels of public unrest.

When we want or need something from someone, they get a special halo if they are nice. It's when that halo slips that problems start, and we begin to size up our grievances in a completely different way. In short, we hold onto the bad stuff and revisit it, and then sometimes we do something with it.[9] For example, doctors and dentists who are abrupt, who spend less time listening and talking to their patients and generally demonstrate a lack of compassion are more likely to find themselves at the centre of a malpractice suit,[10] and lawyers, who know a thing or two about getting sued, have an entire code of practice around 'be nice or get sued'.

Civility and niceness are doubtless the foundation for influence and persuasion, but ironically, people who are seen as 'nice' are also often seen as weak. For women, this is a particularly irritating issue. Not only must women be confident and competent, they also have to be sugar, spice,[11] and a non-exhaustive list of all things nice. In a classic study by Frank Flynn of the Columbia Business School,[12] half his class were given a case study about Heidi Roizen, a successful Silicon Valley venture capitalist. The other half of the class were given the same case details, but Heidi's name was changed to Howard. Both Howard and Heidi were judged as equally competent, but Howard got higher approval ratings than Heidi. Heidi was not liked; students did not want to work with her or hire her. The ultimate social punishment for being a competent woman, but not necessarily likeable, was arguably demonstrated through responses to Hilary Clinton's bid for the US presidency. Problems began early in her husband's political career when she was berated for refusing to adopt her husband's name; by the time she was running for the presidency, opponents were not even bothering to disguise their misogyny, claiming she was everything from a closet lesbian to an agent of the devil and a mass murderer.[13] 'I mean business' might be fine for a man, but when a woman does it, her authenticity is questioned. *What 'business' is she referring to, exactly? Does she know what 'business' even refers to? How bossy to say you mean business? She must be lonely if she's got so much time for business.* These subtle biases invisibly influence the behaviour of women through cultural assumptions which women go on to internalise, which means that women are not only not considered to the same extent as men as potential candidates for top managing positions, but they also fail to push themselves forward.[14] A study of 25,000 Harvard Business School graduates showed that even though women spend more time on household work and childcare compared to their partners, it is not the children who are holding women back from pursuing top managing positions; rather, it's their male partners who expect that the couple will prioritise his career over hers[15] (ugh).

The powerful and influential seem to renounce warmth, inspire fear and care less about us, and we all seem to be okay with that. In reality, if you want to influence and persuade, then you have to serve two masters. So, start practicing rubbing your tummy and patting your head all at the same time if you want to develop some charisma. Charismatic people bring presence; they have an acute awareness of what is going on. When someone speaks, nothing else matters to them (think Tom Hanks as Mr Rogers). They have the competence, confidence and authority to influence their environment, whereas warmth really just increases the chances that they will use their charisma and power to help you.

Developing your charisma starts with developing your expertise and competence. Inability equates with lack of power, and you will never truly develop the social effectiveness to influence and persuade those around you without ability. With the development of ability comes insights into how things are done, how they should be done and how they might be done. The development of expertise increases our subjective well-being[16] and reduces our sense of lack of control or poor self-image.[17] With ability, our confidence grows, we feel more centred and stabilised in ourselves and we are less likely to be controlled by our past or rely on others (or the responses of others) for our sense of happiness. In the early stage of your career, that charisma blossoms from the language of your skill set (see Chapter 2) and the narrative that you build around it. This expertise, however, rapidly becomes outdated, superseded by newer, more relevant knowledge, and eventually even obsolete. For that reason, expertise is a life-long journey, and we address this in more detail in Chapter 9.

Signalling to others that you are smart or have some information that they do not have, in a way that still keeps them connected to you, is a bit of a dark art. If you don't learn how to manage this tension, then you risk sabotaging your success by being both smart and unlikeable. Exercising this skill effectively is further hindered by the increase in anti-intellectual campaigns against established knowledge, science and experts; Michael Gove and his Brexit comment that people have had enough of experts; Donald Trump and his preference for advisors with no experience whatsoever or Dominic Cummings's calls for weirdos and misfits to come work at Number 10 (and some would also say Dominic Cummings's existence in the first place). Fortunately, COVID-19 reminded us all that we do actually need clever people with abilities and knowledge, and the trend for expert bashing has somewhat begun to diminish.

Step 7: be appropriately ambitious

Developing a wholehearted belief in the value of what you are offering goes some way to helping you navigate the tightrope of being smart, being warm and projecting power. A winning mindset helps in the adoption of positive communication style and positive body language and reassures others that you have developed the knowledge and expertise to tackle challenges. This awareness is what differentiates successful people from the status quo: their ambition, commitment, hard work and capacity to push beyond the boundaries of our comfort zones. Moving out of the comfort zone (it is called comfort for a reason) only happens when you have created the mental space and emotional security to let it happen. This 'win zone' is essential in providing insulation from stagnation and settling, because as soon as you decide to settle for less than you deserve, you will end up with even less than you thought.

Possibly the most critical component of influence and persuasion is the art of negotiation. We are perpetually negotiating and renegotiating throughout our lives, first with our parents and siblings, our loved ones and our friends, and negotiating really starts with your first job offer. With those close to us, negotiation often involves discussion, emotion, flared tempers or impasse and agreement; with your employer, you are entering into a partnership of significance, a relationship whereby both parties wish to create an environment of mutual trust and respect: they need something from you, and you need something from them.

Good negotiation does not mean 'winning' where everybody wants some pie and one party gets what they want and the other ends up compromising, or, worse still, the pie gets cut in half. The Judgment of Solomon is a story from the Hebrew Bible in which King Solomon of Israel tried to resolve a squabble between two women. One mother's baby had died, and both were now arguing that a remaining baby was their child. In what appears to have been an unreasonable decision to flush out the truth, Solomon offered to cut the baby in half and give them both a chunk, and the phrase 'never split the baby' was born. This is where Solomon could have done with the advice of former FBI hostage negotiator Chris Voss. He makes a critical point: never, ever split the difference, because you always want 100% of your hostage back.

One of the most critical negotiations you will ever have is with your employer over salary. Many individuals walk into salary negotiations feeling as if all the power is in the hands of the employer; they accept the first offer put to them and the relationship imbalance continues from there. This is to be avoided. If you do not ask, you signal to an employer that you do not value your own worth, and you are also sending a subtle message that you are not prepared to push against boundaries. If you cannot ask your employer for an enhanced salary offer, then how are you going to be effective in negotiating partnerships and other types of business contracts?

Even if your employer rejects outright any counteroffer pitched by you, not to negotiate leaves you in a position of less power than an outright rejection. Jobs are fluid, working relationships; conditions and responsibilities will change over time, but it could be a very long time before you get another opportunity to renegotiate your salary. Asking for more money will also provide you with valuable insights into the ways in which budgets are set, priorities around talent management are determined and what key performance indicators are of importance. A rejection could be linked to lack of funds, it could be that they had not adequately assessed your value relative to the organisation, it might be that they are testing your competence or it could be that salaries are all locked to a scale system.

So, it is smart to ask for more money and grossly naïve to believe that the first offer you are given is fair and that somehow if you graciously accept what is offered that this organisation will take care of you. Particularly if you are a woman, you are far more likely to be facing a pay discrepancy. Male graduates entering the workforce earn 10% more than women with similar qualifications,[18] and it just gets worse. Men are four times more likely to initiate negotiations than women, and when comparisons are made between men and women in the same jobs, the cost of not asking can reach over £600,000 across a lifetime.[19]

It would be much better if interview panels waited until they had time to consider the merits of all the candidates before triggering salary discussions, but the world is unfair, and you may need to address this problem in an interview, so make sure you have done your research in advance. Many organisations will have advertised the salary in advance of the interview, and places like LinkedIn are also a good source of research for you to find out what other similar roles are paying. This is important information because it helps you ground your pitch relative to other similar organisations and you can formulate your most objective high and low position.

If you are lucky, the interview will not spend very much time on this topic, so where possible, hold back your arsenal back until full salary negotiations begin. At the interview, try to give the interviewer only what they want to hear without giving up too much bargaining power. Organisations like a story of commitment, so indicate that you have researched the data for similar positions, that you are aware that salaries command between (do not name your *actual* low position; make it marginally higher) and (your high position). Where you might sit on that range would depend on the opportunities that existed (1) within the organisation for your personal growth and development and (2) opportunities for you to increase your salary through, for example, performance-related pay.

If the recruiter comes back with a low offer or flags that your expectations are not within the remit of what they can offer, pause and think. The tension will be unbearable for them as well as for you, but there is nothing to be gained by jumping quickly back from your position. This may be a signal that the organisation does not like you that much. They have to believe that you are worth the offer, so there is nothing much to be gained by retreating from your position just yet. Alternatively, it may be that they are in a difficult financial position at the moment. If it is the former, you are not getting the post anyway; if it is the latter, you may be out of a job in a year. It may also be that the HR department has ironclad restrictions around salaries, and they will not budge without precedent. If this is the case, you can be sure that they will pick this up during formal salary negotiations, so be patient.

In your pause, weigh up how you think the interview has gone thus far. If it was a trial by fire, then politely state that you look forward to having further discussions on what they feel is appropriate once they have made their decisions. If it was a wonderful experience, then give them your elevator pitch. In 60 seconds, explain the added value that you will bring to the organisation, that you are very serious about working with them and that you would welcome having further discussions about salary post-interview. This puts you back in the driving seat.

Presuming you get through to negotiations, this is where you need a strong elevator pitch. In other words, an ambitious opener in which you must distil in 60 seconds the most important information about the value that you bring and why you should command the salary you are asking for. Reinforce again the market rate and any precedents that you might feel warrant a higher salary. Do not *ever* mention personal needs; your pitch should be entirely focused on the added value that you bring. Then practice this pitch over and over until it is seamless.

If there are a number of issues that you are uncomfortable with in the offer (salary, working conditions, contract, annual leave), make sure that you identify these simultaneously. Do not be tempted to negotiate your salary and then drop in "and there are some other things I wish to discuss". Be transparent about the entire package and do not nit-pick, or you will risk losing everything. If there are multiple areas that you wish to negotiate, do not rank order them or attach any specific importance to one area over another. If there are four areas and you say two are more important, you might end up being offered the two areas that are least important, and it looks like you have been met halfway.

Finally, take your time. Graduate students feel under a particular pressure to accept the first position that is offered to them. This is understandable, but if you can maintain a sense of perspective in the process, you will be in a stronger position to secure both the job and the salary that you want. Ideally, you would want a couple of offers on the table at the same time so that you can both consider multiple opportunities and negotiate for the best salary. That may mean slowing the process down a little so the offers arrive at the same time. So, do not jump in quickly; take your time.

Finally, if you do get what you want, avoid saying thank you. Your employer is not doing you a favour by giving you more money, they are giving you something that reflects (or is close to reflecting) your value. This is a transaction, and how you leave that transaction sets you up for the next transaction. If you get what you want, then remind them of your commitment and that you will ensure you exceed their expectations for you. If you do not get what you want, then use language such as, 'When are we able to revisit my salary?' and 'What kind of targets would be associated with the higher salary?' End the discussions with 'I am looking forward to working with you'.

Exercise: how to ask for more money

1 Practice. You need to get used to hearing the word no and being okay with that.
2 Prepare, prepare, prepare. Where have you overachieved? What have your successes been?
3 Opener: "Considering my experience and the skills I bring; I thought your offer was a little low".
4 Put your number out first and make sure you ask for more than you want. Be specific; do not talk about ranges. Give an actual number.
5 Then say why. Focus on evidence and your value. Do not talk about personal needs, travel commitments or anything else.
6 When you have a push back, try to keep the conversation going. For example, "We just have no budget at the moment to offer anything additional"; "Well do you know when there will be a budget released?"

7 If you are not happy, do not say yes on the spot. Give it a night to sleep on it and consider your options.

8 If you get something close to what you would like or even if you do get what you would like, never say thank you.

Further reading

Babcock, L. & Laschever, S. (2008). *Ask for it, how women can use the power of negotiation to get what they really want*, London: Piatkus.

Borg, J. *Persuasion, the art of influencing people*, 4th Edition, London: Pearson.

Neffinger, J. & Kohut, M. (2014). *Compelling people, the hidden qualities that make us influential*, London: Piatkus.

Notes

1 Schlegel, K., Mehu, M., Van Peer, J. M., & Scherer, K. R. (2018). Sense and sensibility: The role of cognitive and emotional intelligence in negotiation. *Journal of Research in Personality*. doi:10.1016/j.jrp.2017.12.003

2 Laërtius, D. (1925). The stoics: Zeno. *Lives of the Eminent Philosophers*, 2(7). Translated by Hicks, Robert Drew (Two volume ed.). Loeb Classical Library (pp 1–160).

3 Thompson, A. (2009, October 15). Speed of thought-to-speech traced in brain. *Live Science*. Retrieved from www.livescience.com/5780-speed-thought-speech-traced-brain.html

4 Hancock, A. B., & Rubin, B. A. (2015). Influence of communication partner's gender on language. *Journal of Language and Social Psychology*, 34(1), 46–64. doi:10.1177/0261927X14533197

5 Galinsky, A. M., & Sonenstein, F. L. (2011). The association between developmental assets and sexual enjoyment among emerging adults. *The Journal of Adolescent Health: Official Publication of the Society for Adolescent Medicine*, 48(6), 610–615. doi:10.1016/j.jadohealth.2010.09.008

6 Lefebvre, L. E., & Carmack, H. J. (2020). Catching feelings: Exploring commitment (un)readiness in emerging adulthood. *Journal of Social and Personal Relationships*. doi:10.1177/0265407519857472

7 Bungay Stanier, M. (2016). *The coaching habit: Say less, ask more and change the way you lead forever*. Toronto: Box of Crayons.

8 Page, N., & de Hann, E. (2014). Does executive coaching work? *The Psychologist*, 27(8), 582–586.

9 Kensinger, E. A. (2011, October). What we remember (and forget) about positive and negative experiences. *American Psychological Association*. Retrieved from www.expertwitnessjournal.co.uk/special-reports/892-selecting-an-expert-witness-in-dentistry-the-pitfalls

10 Physician bedside manner linked to malpractice suit. (1997). *Patient Focus Care, 5*(5), 58–59.

Talbot, T. (2017, October 17). *Selecting an expert witness in dentistry: The pitfalls.* Retrieved from www.expertwitnessjournal.co.uk/special-reports/892-selecting-an-expert-witness-in-dentistry-the-pitfalls

11 Guillén, L., Mayo, M., & Karelaia, N. (2018). Appearing self-confident and getting credit for it: Why it may be easier for men than women to gain influence at work. *Human Resource Management.* doi:10.1002/hrm.21857

12 Symons, L., & Ibarra, H. (2014, April 28). What the scarcity of women in business case studies really looks like. *Harvard Business Review.* Retrieved from https://hbr.org/2014/04/what-the-scarcity-of-women-in-business-case-studies-really-looks-like

13 Carpentier, M. (2016, October 18). *Why do people dislike Hilary Clinton, the story goes far back.* Retrieved from www.theguardian.com/us-news/2016/oct/18/hillary-clinton-why-hate-unlikeable-us-election

14 Ashcraft, K. L. (2013). The glass slipper: Incorporating occupational identity in management studies. *Academy of Management Review, 38*(1), 6–31.

15 Ely, R. J., Stone, P., & Ammerman, C. (2014, December 1). Rethink what you "know" about high-achieving women. *Harvard Business Review.*

16 Valickas, A., & Pilkauskaite-Valickiene, R. (2014). The role of career competencies on subjective well-being. *Procedia – Social and Behavioral Sciences.* doi:10.1016/j.sbspro.2014.01.646

17 Rama, S., & Sarada, S. (2017). Role of self-esteem and self-efficacy on competence-A conceptual framework. *Journal of Humanities and Social Science, 22*(2), 33–39.

18 Adams, R. (2020, June 18). Gender pay gap begins for students straight after university-report. *The Guardian.* Retrieved from www.theguardian.com/society/2020/jun/18/gender-pay-gap-begins-students-straight-after-university-graduate-data-report-uk

19 Babcock, L., & Laschever, S. (2008). *Ask for it, how women can use the power of negotiation to get what they really want.* London: Piatkus.

Chapter 9

Chart your own course and set sail!

Don't look back; you are not travelling in that direction

Dragons were featured heavily at the start of this book, where we first posed the question, do you want to be *better*, or do you want to be *safer*? *Safer* means more of the same (and absolutely nobody thinks that more of the same is going to be safe); *better* means more dragons. Before COVID-19, the world was already changing at a rapid pace. Change that was happening from year to year, if not in fact month to month, has now sped up to weekly and daily changes that are impossible to keep pace with. Financial markets are volatile and global relations strained. After nearly two decades of prosperity, we are facing abrupt and radical changes to our economy, in our social order and to our labour markets.[1] The dragon of profound and systemic change is upon us, but that does not mean that we are powerless to fight back.

We humans have a disproportionate tendency to focus only on what is happening today, at the expense of what will happen tomorrow. It is amazing how many of us do not notice the extent to which old ways of looking at things influence how we see these problems/challenges/opportunities. The ways in which we frame our lives and our careers make us feel certain and comfortable about problems and how to resolve them. Whilst there will always be good reasons and excuses to stick with what we know and to continue to do what has served us in the past, are those good enough reasons, especially now? This chapter aims to help you set a firm course, avoid being battered about in the waves and design for yourself the sacred text of the career business plan.

Reframe job security

Job security is no longer about contracts, tenure and unions. These gold watches were on the decline before the pandemic, and now they will become more elusive than ever. There is a lot you can do, however, to reframe your mindset, help you feel more secure and ensure you remain employable and climb the career ladder. What is critical is to create a plan that helps you recognise very quickly when things no longer serve you.

One of the best pieces of advice that I ever had was to become a quitter. Yes, a quitter! Not quite the standard advice of *work hard, study hard, do not give up, keep going*, because if that advice *actually* worked, then how come people who are less talented end up farther up the career ladder? I was told to work at as many different institutions (particularly early in my career) as I could and not just to focus on the 'Russell group' elite. Academia was entirely designed to make people feel bad about themselves, and therefore, at all costs, I was to avoid dwelling on job titles or seniority, obsessing over what university I was working at or where and how often I was publishing and the length of the temporary contract that

I was getting. Rather I was to take a developmental view of my career. Study and reflect on myself and continually evaluate how my interests were developing, where my skills were needed most and if they were actually being utilised in the organisation I was working for. If I was using and expanding my skills, I would never be mediocre, I would make good decisions, I would be happy and I would feel empowered to design my own life.

This piece of advice was for me revolutionary because it meant I could overcome the leaky bucket that is UK higher education. I could avoid becoming obsessed (and distressed) at my short-term contracts, the extent to which my research was being considered 'good enough' (it is never good enough), distracted about how many research hours I was getting compared to my peers (there are never enough), how much income I was generating (more, more, more), how much students loved/hated me (you are a fickle bunch), how much teaching I was expected to do (you will always be judged as having too little). Instead I was able to keep focus on the extent to which my knowledge, skills and abilities were being utilised and how much I was being stretched. I spent my career developing a sixth sense for signals of my own 'underemployment' (underuse of a worker because a job does not use the worker's skills), and when I could see the early signs, I would start 'stretching' out of the box I had found myself in. Stretching often worked, but when it didn't, I felt empowered enough to punch a hole out of the box and move on to something else, to the point that in a very well-paid and senior role at a well-known Russell group, I could see my skills and knowledge were not being used properly, and I couldn't see a career path either. I sacrificed my very comfortable existence and resigned. I worked for myself for almost a year before joining a university that I felt actually needed me and where I knew I could make a real difference. I now work in what is, for me, the best university in the world, where all of my punches only seem to reshape the box instead of breaking it.

I do not understand why this advice is still not commonplace in the academic community. We can be a myopic bunch. For career development, it is critical to work in new contexts and cultures, with different expectations and priorities. The genius that is Seth Goldin has now written an exceptional book on just this subject. Becoming a quitter is actually the smarter way to manage your life and your career so long as your quitting is not reactionary or serial or, conversely, you stay when things are painful because you are not motivated enough to quit.

The art of quitting with flair is best encapsulated in a book by Ines Wichert (although I am not sure she intended it to be so). Wichert[2] has documented a series of critical role assignments that women need in order to navigate their journey to senior leadership. Wichert has focused on women in leadership because women have fewer role models and are almost always the ones who pick up the major responsibilities of home and family. However, with the changing balance in working relationships and family responsibilities, the dynamics of intersectionality and the current crisis in men's mental health,[3] those journeys are signposted and explained here and reframed to support career journeys for everyone.

Critical job assignments

1 Become a quitter

Work for as many different organisations as you can. Working for a variety of companies gives you more opportunities to learn different skills, and you will be exposed to a variety of different people, cultures and ways of working. You will gain experience and perspective and are much more likely to gain the business acumen and commercial, technical and operational experience that you need for effective teamwork, leadership and entrepreneurial endeavours. However, quitting will come at the cost of planning your personal life and perhaps also how you are seen as dependable and trustworthy. What is key is to know when and why to quit. It is easy to quit when things are tough. If it is particularly tough, you could be on a stretch project (see section 2) and you should never quit. The mature thing is to quit when you need to quit to do the next thing. Alternatively, ask yourself are you *too* comfortable? Do you need to broaden out, work in different sectors, challenge yourself and get comfortable being uncomfortable, even if that means staying with the same company?

Always ask yourself:

- What current major trends are affecting my industry? What might the future trends be? What are the major trends currently affecting my profession? How has my profession changed? How might it change in the future?
- How are these changes affecting the competencies required for success now and in the future? What are some of the new career opportunities created by the changes in my industry and profession?
- What are the hot topics in my field that I should be able to address to remain competitive? What do I find most interesting?
- Is it time for a move? Do not be afraid to follow Sheryl Sandberg's example and take what appears to be a demotion or a sideways step so that you are useful and challenged (Sandberg dipped from a high-profile career with Google to work for the little-known Facebook).

2 Stretch early, stretch often

At the start of your new role, you will have been working through the competing demands of your role, getting to know your team and your boss and the requirements of your role, and you will begin to settle in. All of this new learning is critical to being able to do what you are paid to do; you are, after all, paid to be excellent in your role. However, to truly excel, finding a stretch project early on is crucial. If you have a bolder vision for your career, you need to become involved in a project that will build your confidence, increase your visibility and enhance your credibility.

Nathan Rothschild, the famous 19th-century banker, businessman and financier, argued that great fortunes are made when cannonballs fall in the harbour, not when violins play in the ballroom. In other words, the more unpredictable the environment, the greater the opportunity to develop, grow and achieve. The stretch project is described as being out of one's depth technically but being able to build creditability by taking on significant responsibility. This is achieved by developing close relationships with established experts and senior leaders. Particularly when 'dropped in at the deep end' with little support but high levels of responsibility, individuals have to learn very fast, often in very unfamiliar environments, in roles they know very little about. Those who are able to navigate these uncertain circumstances, to overcome personal and professional barriers and to manage their concerns about their own inadequacies whilst experimenting with new ways of working, learning quickly about the organisation and the priorities of the senior management have their careers supercharged. They have learned critical lessons about themselves and their world of work that enhance feelings of confidence and self-worth, and they have demonstrated to others what they are capable.

Training courses are all very well to develop your understanding, but for true advancement to occur, what you need is experience. The 70–20–10 rule[4] apportions how best to create the ideal corporate learning and staff development opportunities. Seventy percent of your development should be experiential – in other words, you develop while on the job – 20% should be informal, for example, through mentoring programs and 10% should be conducted through formal training sessions. The stretch project is an ideal way make some serious headway into your personal 70%. Stretch projects are more effective than action learning, mentoring, relationships, 360-degree assessments, exposure to more senior leaders and formal classroom training[5] in enabling career progression. Those who stretch are able to skip a number of steps and progress faster than their peers for two reasons: those who execute effectively on a stretch project seen to have higher levels of competency, and those perceptions influence the extent to which they are likely to be given further responsibility, and the individual feels more confident and will seek out further advancement. In other words, success breeds further success.

The questions you ought to be asking yourself and what you should be doing early in your career

Stretch assignments should develop you in three key areas: strategic effectiveness, interpersonal skills and personal effectiveness.

Strategic skills relate to your capacity to plan for the future. Success in strategic leadership requires anticipatory skills, such as being able to scan the environment for emergent trends, changes in government policy or technological advances.

- **Build your tribe**. Networking again! Your social context shapes the likelihood that you will develop new ideas, products and services. Surrounding yourself with creative-thinking people is critical, moving organisations to experience lots of different ways of thinking.[6] Your networks are also critical in providing resources. Early in your career, your networks will help you uncover and capitalise on new opportunities by signalling to you changing legislation, market trends or technological developments. They will reflect back to you when you are moving in the best possible direction and be a good source of critical feedback. Later in your career, they may provide you with much-needed financial support and potential aircover when you are managing the daily challenges of new ventures. There are always people willing to help. You need to go out and find them.

- **Learn how to write 'the sacred text'.** In the entrepreneurial world, the business plan is a sacred text because 'a problem well stated is half resolved'. Business plans help you focus and teach patience whilst you convince others to get on board with your ideas and to give you support. They help you work out what makes you unique and then chart your direction for the first few years, identifying challenges and opportunities and plan for contingencies along the way. Critically, business plans give you visibility to senior management and important external networks. You can learn a lot from the business plans of others, but the plans you learn the most from are the ones that failed. The bad ones, however, can be a challenge to get a hold of. Like the bad art by famous artists, things that did not work out tell us a lot about vision and execution, but they are frequently painted over for something much better.

- **This cannot be done.** *Oh yes, it can; oh no, it cannot.* We have all been there. Strategic skills also require that you be competent in challenging others. This means pushing against the usual or the commonly accepted, but it also means careful reflection and examination of a problem, taking many different perspectives in an attempt to get to the root cause of a problem before taking decisive action. Develop your capacity to engage others towards collective actions. Peoples' resistance to personal and organisational change will always be your most significant challenge, so you need to become comfortable dealing with resistance, bureaucracy and infrastructure constraints. That is not to say that all bureaucracy is bad (it is remarkably efficient at managing scale), but rather it does not need to be an eventual result of creating something successful. Familiarise yourself with alternatives to bureaucracy (for example, practices such as *rendanheyi*)[7] and educate yourself in concept of the entrepreneurial bureaucrat and partnership working.[8]

 Strategic experience is nothing without top-notch **interpersonal skills**. Again, this is where psychology students have a significant advantage in the workplace: being self-aware, a cognate listener and 'room reader'; being respectful and showing empathy and understanding. When highly developed, these skills enable us to respond flexibly to the demands of a situation by drawing on a range of emotions. We become aware that whilst feelings are important, they are not an objective measure of reality. We become better able to gain perspective by calming ourselves when we are upset. To be able to focus on values, rather than feelings, and, importantly for others, we can be spontaneous and authentic in our responses. Through this emotional awareness, we are able to accurately self-assess our personal states, and the states of others. These skills are key to relationship management and communication.

There has been quite a bit said already in this book about how to develop your interpersonal skills, but it is probably worth reminding you that all psychology students have studied the theories and research relating to emotional intelligence. If there is one significant piece of advice, it is to adopt a positive frame of mind. This is not just an important work skill; it is possibly the most important life skill as well. Poignantly captured by the actress Demi Moore: "When you decide who someone is, you take away the opportunity for them to be anything else" (2019). The actress is talking about her difficult relationship with her mother and how her characterisation of how her mother 'was' got in the way of her mother's capacity to be anything else. We are all capable of reducing someone's behaviours down to a few stereotypical explanations and thus limiting their capacity to be seen in any other light. Adopting a positive outlook, taking a sincere interest in people and finding positive traits to focus on is paramount to developing your interpersonal skills and relationships both at work and in your personal life.

Personal effectiveness is another area we have spent quite a bit of time probing your thinking on. Self-awareness, goal setting, being organised, setting deadlines, being prepared and continually learning. In other words, getting your shit in order so you are dependable and capable of delivering.

The following are a list of assignments that will help you develop competencies in organisational strategy:

- **Managing up:** Shadow your strategic leadership team. Use your psychological thinking and expertise to explore the values of senior leadership and identify how those values drive their thinking and behaviour and in turn how those values shape organisational policy. Use that understanding to spot something in the organisation that needs improving. Develop a plan for continuous improvement and write a policy statement.

- **Cross-functional leadership:** Join a project that requires different people from different functions and different levels of seniority to work together towards a common goal.
- **Customer management:** Performa a deep dive into your customer base. Spend some quality time with your customers and clients. Conduct a customer-needs/gap analysis exploring the competitors to your client base. Consider what your organisation could do to ensure the competitiveness of your clients. Then report back to your team.
- **People management:** Pull your team together and carry out a stakeholder analysis. Who are your internal and external stakeholders, and what are their opinions of your organisation? Whom do you need to closely manage, keep informed and keep satisfied? Develop a plan and policy statement about how to best involve, communicate and develop strategic relationships with those groups.
- **Competitor management:** Analyse and evaluate your competitors: what products and services are they currently offering? Draw on your psychological research skills to objectively analyse how those products and services compare with your organisation's.
- **Developing people:** Explore opportunities for the cognitive, emotional, intellectual and social development of your peers. What can you do to enhance their capabilities? Discuss their development needs and lobby for and design a training programme.
- **Managing failure:** Find a project that has been unsuccessful or a problem that has been difficult to solve. Organise a 'hack week' where a taskforce works closely on this problem in an attempt to find a new solution, focus or direction.

Exercise: bagging a stretch assignment

Ask your mentor

1 Were there any key events that charged your career quickly forward?
2 Is there something you struggle with or a habit you have never managed to overcome?
3 What are your priorities right now?
4 Am I in the right place now for my career?

Ask your boss

1 What are your priorities?
2 What do I need to be doing more of/less of?

3 I would like a stretch assignment, something that really pushes me. What projects are on the horizon that I could take a lead on? I am happy to work in areas that I have not previously been exposed to.

On your stretch project, ask yourself: "Does this feel hard? Does it feel as if nobody is supporting you?" This is a stretch project; start looking about to see who the experts are who can help you (make sure you consider options outside of your organisation). Is the blockage your blockage or someone else's? Once you have done some soul searching, then stop and ask for help if you need to. Do not let the project derail because you are feeling overwhelmed. Talk to your boss. Asking for help and regrouping is all part of the stretch project. ***You got this!*** Psychology graduates already have the bedrock for strategic thinking. You can cope with ambiguous situations and gain a strategic perspective by listening to the perspectives of others, working with a range of people from different professions in influencing and problem solving.

3 The international assignment

There is a reason gap year travel, micro gapping or short-term study abroad periods are such great opportunities for students. Travel is preparation for life; it enhances growth and maturity, it builds networks and relationships and it teaches you how to get things done in a culturally different environment and broadens your career horizons.[9] These skills and experiences are critical preparation for roles that require the management of complex organisations; global talent and international legislation, customs and practices. International assignments are possibly the most formative of career experiences. Success demands the management of people and processes on a superordinate scale in an environment where your support network and trusted allies are not readily available. There are undoubtedly issues around loneliness, feeling like an outsider and realising that the methods and approaches that you have always trusted no longer hold true. However, the career and progression benefits of a foreign assignment outweigh the negatives. They include enhanced access to high levels of senior organisational teams, enhanced international expertise and knowledge, linguistic and cultural capabilities,[10] expertise in running virtual teams and distance leadership[11] and all-round flexibility and adaptability.

Barmy true story: Sir Francis Galton's international assignment

The eminent (and controversial) psychologist Sir Francis Galton was well placed within an affluent social circle and could have enjoyed a sedentary

Victorian existence, but for the advice of a phrenologist. At that time, phrenologists were using the now-discredited practice of estimating the relative strengths of a person's mental faculties and their suitability to different careers by calculating the size of bumps on different parts of their cranium. In what sounds like a double entendre, Galton's phrenologist concluded that Galton had one of the 'largest organs of causality' that he had ever seen. So, Galton promptly joined the Royal Geographical Society on a noble two-year trip to South West Africa applying his 'organ of causality' to the mapping of previously unexplored territories. Galton, however, found himself trapped between warring tribes. The Orlam were brutal, hacking off the feet of women and gouging out the eyes of infants. Galton's pressing issue, however, was not the well-being of the local women but more to do with the Orlam chief, Jonker Afrikaner, preventing his travel through Damaraland.

With all the usual Victorian formalities, Galton penned an indignant letter demanding that Jonker gave passage. Jonker, however, remained indifferent, and so Galton constructed a flamboyant response. Resplendent in a scarlet coat and a hunting cap, he mounted an ox. An ox? Yes, Galton had previously released all horses into a field to graze, where they were promptly eaten by lions. Cutting a dash with is red coat, hunting cap and ox, he charged to Jonker's hut. At the last moment, the confused animal bolted, then somehow managed to jump the moat in front of Jonker's hut, propelling itself through the air with Galton clinging to its back. The beast and Galton landed headfirst through the door, startling the living daylights out of Jonker, who had been quietly smoking a pipe. The sheer madness continued as Galton proceeded to give the astonished Jonker a 'piece of his mind'.

This ham-fisted intervention was a success. Jonker agreed to cooperate and behave in a more peaceful way, and Galton, energised by his success in peace negotiation, self-appointed himself ambassador and began travelling around all the other local villages, forewarning chiefs and setting up a common moral code of conduct. Concluding that he had solved peace in Africa, Galton continued his journey, murdering the odd giraffe as he went. On his return to England, Galton was awarded The Royal Geographical Society's gold medal for the encouragement and promotion of geographical science. Galton promptly penned his book *Hints to Travellers*, which included such gems of advice as 'the best way to roll up shirt sleeves so they remain in place for hours' and 'the burying of valuables in your arm'. Apparently, all you need to do is make an incision into your arm and pop a jewel into the open flesh; once it heals over, you will always have a pot of ready dosh for an emergency.

Unless you are Francis Galton, landing an international assignment is, however, not that straightforward. Global projects are major risk for organisations, so there is a heapin' heck of a lot of groundwork that needs to be achieved in advance. Apart from the fact that there needs to be a sound business case, you need to give some careful consideration to where you sit within your organisation. What is important or specific about you? What skills and experiences do you have that your peers do not? Why should your employer be willing to invest in your worth to the detriment of others who may be just as suitably qualified? In other words, laying the groundwork and creating the right environment for your international assignment starts some time before you start booking your flights.

The questions you ought to be asking yourself and things you should be doing early in your career

- **Online working:** Pandemic conditions have given us an opportunity to experience the greatest international assignment of our lives. You can work from home but be delivering your services to anywhere on the globe. Develop your cultural competencies as you would for that physical international assignment and start building your international networks. What do I know about the values and priorities of other countries? (suggested reading *Cultural DNA* by Gurnek Bains and *The Values Compass* by Mandeep Rai).
- **Communication**: What language skills do I have and how can I develop them?
- **Where am I** in the scheme of things? Is my performance consistent? Am I tasked with meaty, challenging targets? Do I deliver? Where can I improve?
- **Visibility:** Am I highly visible/a strong public image for my organisation? What can I do to become more visible?

In all areas, it is important to focus on rising about your peers. That way, you position yourself in the strongest possible position to secure your manager's support.

4 Building a high-performance team

At my university hometown of Wolverhampton, Nuno Herlander Simões Espírito Santo (known as Nuno) has shifted Wolverhampton Wanderers FC up to 37th in the world. That shift represents a jump of some 305 places (according to the FIFA world team rankings). Training

is tough for the players, but he balances this by placing an emphasis on team involvement, organising team paintballing, zip wiring and deep dive match debriefs. Nuno has created a small group of unified players. Everyone is involved, and nobody sits on the bench for long.

The competencies involved in getting the right people with the right talents in position and creating the right environment for focus, understanding how the strengths and talents of your team manifest for better and worse and getting the best out of everyone is the backbone of career success. Great team leaders are outstanding at relinquishing control by identifying their personal strengths (see Chapter 2) and then building a team that balances and complements those strengths. Few organisations, however, have the luxury of recruiting people who carefully balance and complement each other. Most teams come about more through circumstances than design, which can mean that team leadership is as much about sorting out people problems as engaging, driving and progressing projects. Without the necessary people skills to ensure you can manage people problems effectively, you can quickly find yourself constantly peace-keeping and troubleshooting, which will ultimately reduce your capacity to deliver much-needed results.

The questions you ought to be asking yourself and things you should be doing early in your career

There are four key domains for team performance. These are project execution, influencing, relationship building and strategic thinking.[12] The best ways to develop insight and expertise in those areas are early exposure and self-development. By doing this, you can better incrementally manage your developing competencies in preparation for larger projects that you may land later in your career. These are some of the questions that you can use to guide your development.

- **Small steps:** Start by managing small teams, then, as you move up the career ladder, seek out more complex opportunities. Push yourself to do something that is out of your comfort zone by keeping an eye out for taking initiative such as volunteering to head up a small project, but where possible, avoid large-scale management too early. Whilst developing your exposure, explore the following:
- **My natural style:** Where are my strengths? (suggested reading: Chapter 2 and *Strengthsfinder* by Tom Rath). What can I do to strengthen my strengths?
- **Trust and conflict management:** How can I build trust in others? Do I often find myself in conflict with others? (suggested reading: *Racial Candor*, Kim Scott). Am I often called upon to peacekeep conflict in others? How do I manage that? What interpersonal development would help me to be viewed as a trusted confidant?

- **Control:** How do I really feel about the success of others on my team? Do I work to ensure others are successful, or do I secretly feel resentful? Am I good at identifying strengths in my peers and encouraging them to take on more responsibility or new challenges?
- **Challenges:** How can I relinquish control and feel comfortable when mistakes happen? Do I dwell on mistakes or focus on making things better?

5 An avalanche of accountability

Without experience of how all the parts of an organisation come together to deliver the correct quantity and quality of a final product, progressing up the career ladder to the top jobs is highly unlikely. Operational experience involves overseeing everything that organisations do: manufacturing, purchasing, supply change management, distribution, marketing, HR and finance are just some examples; there are many more. Managing large numbers of people, crisis management, managing competing priorities and demands, the gathering of time-sensitive information and coping with and managing the undesirable outputs that goods and services often create (for example, waste or slave labour) make operational experience not only critical to organisations but also to career development. Operational experience requires you to be highly visible and accountable, and it also require high levels of credibility drawn from a broad base of skills and knowledge. Most individuals will have built up credibility in one specific area, and, as such, this breadth of knowledge can be a challenge in building up cross-functional credibility.

The questions you ought to be asking yourself and things you should be doing early in your career

- **Timing:** Life is busy, and operational management makes life busier because it requires a commitment to long and unpredictable hours. Start building in health routines now that will carry you through in the future. There are also times in your life when you are going to be more available for those kinds of demands. For example, building up some experience early in your career might make it easier to scale back when other parts of your life have to take priority.
- **Decision-making:** Learning to make far-reaching decisions by yourself is an important life skill. Testing out your thinking is key to building up confidence in your own judgements. This is where your network and peers are essential in building up a trusted resource of people who will test your thinking and not just agree with everything you say.
- **Cost saving is everyone's business:** Pay attention to resource allocation and care about it.
- **Finance:** Develop profit and loss (for profit) and surplus and deficit (charities) experience. Find some training courses (there are lots online for free);

perhaps join the finance committee at work or as part of another external organisation. One of the best ways to obtain meaningful commercial experience is to set up and run your own business. This gives you profit and loss experience, but it also means that you learn the meaning of true accountability.

- **Risk:** Develop your hazard perception by joining a health and safety committee at work. Brush up on your occupational psychology, in particular ergonomic and psychosocial risks at work.

- **Engagement:** Consider ways of engaging employees across your organisation.

Career in focus: business development

"When I graduated there was a shortage of roles for those with psychology degrees unless you wanted to do PG study or go down clinical route or become a teacher – none of which appealed to me. I was at the peak of psychology undergrads, there were over 300 in my graduating class alone! So, I worked in sales and then as a chalet host to keep myself busy but when I returned to the UK, there was a shortage of graduate roles in general. I sent out a bunch of cover letter and CVs to any company that had anything to do with stats and data analysis which was something I'd enjoyed as part of my degree. Luckily, a consultant (specialising in medical statistics) in Glasgow picked it up and I ended up setting up my own business as a stats consultant for a few years. I was able to work with career consultants on designing psychometrics, pure research projects with social workers and clinical psychologists, DFID on the Millennium Development Goals and supported PhD students with their data analysis and research designs before becoming an assistant statistician with the Scottish Government as I felt I should get a proper job! I hated it and ended up taking a big back step to go back to working in Higher Education and executive Ed. A step I wouldn't have been able to take if not for still running the business on the side lines. It's been a very wonky career path, but I love my career and current role – I use my psychology degree pretty much every day in some form or another".

Christina Blakey, Strategic Business Development Manager

---

6 Get on board

Every public company is required by law to have a board, and many private and charitable organisations have boards as well. The board is tasked with management and oversight, to drive forward the organisation or business but also keep it under prudent fiscal control; to be sensitive to short-term needs and pressures but also be long term focused; to be sensitive to the needs of its employees whilst also balancing the commercial needs of the organisation, its business partners and society as a whole. To meet what can often seem like competing priorities, the board is made up from people who work for an organisation (the executives) and also external directors, known as non-executive directors, sometimes also called trustees or governors, and executive directors. The external directors are considered to provide an additional level of scrutiny and objectivity and often enhance the board, providing skills and knowledge from other professions and industries. This balance of expertise is essential because the board must have a sufficient level of knowledge about the organisation because it is answerable for the actions of the organisation and expected to present a fair, balanced and understandable assessment of the organisation's position and prospects.

Being on a board is good for your career; it helps you build up market and industry knowledge. You will learn about the inner workings of an organisation, and you will be engaged in leadership at a corporate level. All of this gives you opportunities to gain knowledge and skills outside of your professional area; you will grow and sharpen your professional network and gain visibility and exposure, all of which will make your CV stand out from the posse. However, a word of caution. One of the signs of a bad board is people on it who are fairly obsessed with what the board is doing for them. Boards take up a significant amount of time and personal resources, and often you are not paid for your time. This is because being on a board should not be too comfortable. They want people who are dedicated, will make time, and are prepared to scrutinise properly and rock the boat. Boards need good governance, vigilance and people who are unflappable under pressure.

The questions you ought to be asking yourself and things you should be doing early in your career

- **Get used to governance**: Become a student representative. You will learn how to connect with internal and external university stakeholders, become confident in having your voice heard and learn from listening to others.
- **Ethics**: Board members must be trustworthy; therefore, they are scrutinised for having high levels of self-awareness, integrity and high ethical standards. One of the easiest ways for students to develop themselves in this area is to join an ethics committee. Ethics is a substantive component of every psychology programme and understanding, engaging with and ensuring that others conduct themselves appropriately demonstrates to others that you do not see ethics as a mere source of burden and that you can be trusted to know the difference between right and wrong.
- **Commitment**: Being voted onto a board often means joining an organisation as a volunteer and taking on a project for another board member. This kind of commitment and dedication are invaluable in demonstrating to other board members that you are a committed and safe pair of hands.

- **Board room skills**: What relevant experience can you bring to a board? There are a number of easily available board skills matrixes on the web which span skill sets across industry knowledge, technical skills and experience, governance competencies and behavioural competencies.

Career in focus: the consultant

"I think the realization of the impact of studying psychology dawned on me the more I had to collaborate with other people. I had undervalued the extent to which having studied psychology gave me a whole lot of insight into not only the motivations of others but also the way context impacts so differently for individuals. Following my first degree I trained through a 2-year post grad diploma to be a speech and language therapist: quite a usual route.

However, about 4 years in to working with people who mainly used alternatives to speech to communicate, I realized the biggest difference I could make was to help create authentic opportunities for choice and control. This is where my interest switched to creating enabling environments more generally and at the same time, I was offered a place on the NHS General Management Training Scheme. There followed many different leadership roles across a diverse range of settings.

Initially managing clinicians operationally linking with General Practice, then working regionally with a focus on implementing health and social care policy and ultimately working strategically directing health systems with a focus on integrated working to enhance the care people with complex needs receive. Interestingly when I decided that NHS policy took me to one restructure too many I went back to my roots and completed an MSc in Occupational Psychology part time as an element of a negotiated voluntary redundancy package, whilst I built up my consultancy skills.

In my mid 40s the fundamentals of psychology had provided a key pivot point for my career reinforcing the breadth of application and the transferability of my knowledge and skills. Next up I found myself leading an international faculty delivering online Master programmes world-wide on behalf two UK universities working inside a multinational education delivery organisation: totally different context and a real stretch but just what I needed! I felt that drawing on my experience combined with the knowledge gained from the further degrees really made the most of what I had to offer and again I realized the power I was able to share as a psychologist first and foremost. Quite a few years on I run my own consultancy business offering development support to individuals, teams and organisations".

Sue Jones, Director, JG Consults

Your career business plan

Being fully strategic about your career is more than just having an ambition to become a professor, premier football manager or CEO of a major corporation. Those kinds of vague, distant career ambitions regularly lead to professional drift because the components of how exactly you will get there are lost to you. Setting aside time and bandwidth to properly think through your long-term plans and how to develop and best deploy your talents means that you are in control in what happens next. You will have a vision for yourself when things get rocky. This has never been more urgent, and a career business plan is your road map to success.

The business plan is considered the most critical document in the business world because it identifies, describes and analyses what an organisation is going to do and how it is going to do it. Business plans help businesses, their partners and their financiers make better decisions by setting out their goals and tracking the progress of those goals. Therefore, to conclude this book, we refer to the sacred text that is the business pan and suggest that you should leverage its plan-tastic capabilities for your personal career journey. The primary reason is that it will help you make critical decisions, iron out the kinks in your strategy, avoid making big mistakes, nurture your curiosity, drive your entrepreneurial passions and articulate clearly who and what you stand for. It takes practice to write your business case, so take your time and do not be afraid to rewrite it multiple times, if not in fact scrap it entirely and start again, before you have your master document in place.

My mission

The first step in any business plan is to set out your mission statement. This is a concise description of what you see as your purpose with a clear statement of your core values and goals. The mission statement is where you start articulating your values. To do that, you might also consider what you think of as 'success' and how that forms your values. (The epilogue in this book is written to give you a bit of insight and inspiration.) This part of the statement is often a challenge to get just right, so take your time; it may need several recrafts. When you feel you have a draft of your mission statement ready, the next step is to map the ways in which your long-term goals are aligned with that vision. Where do you want to be ten years from now? Circle back to your values. Why do you want to achieve this goal in the first place? Then break back and visualise what the mid-point of the journey will look like; again, does this vision fit with your values?

When you think you are ready, reverse-write your résumé. Document the roles and responsibilities that someone of that level would have achieved. Be specific with job titles and the kinds of organisations at which such experience would have been garnered. Think about your external reputation. Who are your networks, inside and outside of your organisation?

When you are ready, start thinking about setting some action-focused, short- to mid-term goals that can firmly set the direction of travel to the bigger accomplishments of the future. For example, how can your current skill set be leveraged to reach those short-term goals, and what gaps in knowledge and competence can you identify? Where are there opportunities for you to address those gaps, and what are the key challenges that you can see? This section is key to helping you figure out what you have, what you need and where to find what you need. It will include details of the networks you may need to develop, the training courses you may need to attend, the attitudes and soft skills you will want to craft and the experiences you will need to, well . . . *experience*.

Operationalisation

Ordinarily in a business plan, the operational section is where the ins and outs of what will take place will be detailed. Whilst you may not be able to add the detail to this section that an organisation might, you can still consider what career expectations you have for yourself and think about the roles and responsibilities where you want to grow; the teams you want to work with and when, where and how you want to lead. Check and challenge your plans through trusted friends, your peer network and mentors. Ask them to keep you accountable, and do the same for them. Just like going to the gym with a buddy, you are far more likely to try different things, think creatively, go the extra mile and take on additional challenges that you did not think you were capable of.

Conclusion

When I started this work, the two biggest challenges facing us were the Brexit debacle and the challenges and opportunities that the 4th Industrial Revolution brings to the world of work. I wanted this book to be a revolution for students, providing them with a template that would help them through one of the most challenging phases of their life: the transition into adulthood. However, revolutions rarely go to plan, and by March, we were all stockpiling toilet paper and ordering 'bum guns' on Amazon (*or was that just me?*).

If you were hoping to go back to the way that things were, we will not, because we cannot. The COVID-19 pandemic crisis has triggered an acute sense of urgency for issues of health, environmental and social responsibility. As we sail into our new normal, individuals and companies can continue in the pursuit of unbridled financial profit. Those that continue to do so will pay a heavy price from activist groups, political parties and consumers. The future is in sustainable wealth creation, equality of opportunity, the fair treatment of workers and sound governance from both corporations and governments working together. Besides, having stared COVID-19 in the face and survived, why would we wish to continue to spend time doing something just because we get paid?

To bring this journey to an end, I want to leave you with these questions. What is success really about? In a bid to answer this question and to give you all something to think about, I asked some very important people (my friends and peers) and some bigwigs and top-notch folks to define success. I also asked some cool cats and kitties (yes, the legend that is Carol Baskin did reply), and because success is a lifetime endeavour, I also asked some kiddies for their opinions as well.

And, in a bid to find out what everyone's 'Bestometer' was reading (love that image; I just wanted to put it in one more time, and, weirdly, he looks a bit like husband number one), I also asked 'What does it mean to be the best in the world?', the best in your world?

What does success mean to you?
What are you arguably the best at in the whole world?

"When you walk out of the office/ward/workplace do not dwell one second longer on it (as much as they may want you to). Don't. This is your time. Not theirs. Learn time management that is as sharp as a knife. Every bit of faff on work is a minute taken away from time that belongs to you and you alone. Develop hobbies and passions outside of what is naturally perceived as 'success'. Spend your down time fully and richly. Run away from cleaning the windows and towards a mountain".

Lyndon Adams
Staff Nurse

(arguably the best in the world at reflecting and learning from my mistake . . .
eventually)

"We are all ONE. Everything is happening exactly as it should and for the betterment of us all. Be grateful for every challenge because that's when you remember we are all in this together to reach a higher level of enlightenment".

Carol Baskin
CEO of Big Cat Rescue, BigCatRescue.org/smile
(arguably the best in the world at making lemons into lemonade)
"Success is getting whatever you set out to do done. Like Yoda said: 'Do or do not. There is no try'".

Prof Maria Uther
(arguably the most productive procrastinator in the world)
"An underappreciated aspect of success is whether it is just for you, or for a wider circle. I value individuals and groups that not only accomplish what they want to (the usual definition of success) but who also take into account how what they do (or don't do) affects others".

Prof Howard Gardner
Harvard Graduate School
(arguably the most distinguished developmental psychologist in the world)
"Be sceptical, question authority. Don't conform and never be ordinary. Shun the mob, think for yourself. Be your own special creation".

Peter Tatchell
(arguably the most arrested human rights protester in the UK)
"Failure isn't falling, it's failing to rise after a fall".

Flight Lieutenant Paul Fowler
(arguably the best in the world at seeing the best of a person before the hindrances of personal concepts and perceptions take over)
"Success is learning and growing from every experience in life".

Natalie Sumner-Cole
(arguably at least the third best executive officer in the world;
if you want to know who the top two are, you need to consult the league tables for EOs)
"There are two types of moans in life; one that you can do nothing about, so accept it and shut the hell up, and one that you can do something about, so shut the hell up and do something about it'.

Michelle Owen
PhD student
(arguably the least moaning person in the world)
"Success for me means understanding the power of not yet".

Dr Mark Jellicoe
(arguably the best in the world at continuing to try)
". . . is the repeated search for and achievement of, ever more stretching goals".

John Amaechi OBE
(arguably the best storytelling Jedi in the world)
"What is success? The outcome to a great deal of striving, from learning from defeat, and by focusing on the process".

Prof Andy Lane
(arguably the best boxer ever to become a professor in the world!)
"In our society, success (and happiness) is often equated with economic capital – Success (and happiness) = £££££. In contrast, I define success as something more intrinsic and personal. Success is a process of proactively working towards your goals in a way that is aligned with your core values. Hard work, discomfort and risk are simply part of the deal when we pursue meaningful goals and should be treated as indictors that we are on the right path. Each step we take towards our goals, however small a step it might be, is a marker of success in its own right".

Dr Kathryn Leflay
(arguably the best gardener since Monty Dom)
"Whatever the dream career you follow, work hard, but don't let that become your sole identity. Or all other things in life are lost".

Prof Peter Saville
(arguably the most highly acclaimed psychologist within the business psychology profession)
"The secret of success is the ability to manage failure".

Gerald Ratner
Jeweller and Motivational Speaker
(arguably the person who has taught us the most about branding)
"Success is achieving your full potential, in your terms and at your own pace".

Prof Geoff Layer
Vice-Chancellor of the University of Wolverhampton
(arguably the best vice chancellor in the world)
"Life evaporates in microscopic units. Stop worrying about things that don't matter. So much energy is wasted in trying to be perfect . . . forget not your purpose or your dreams".

61-Year-Old Theatre Nurse Still on Top of the Job
(arguably the best theatre nurse still on top of her job at 61)
"Success is the evidence of making a difference, despite the feeling of screwing up".

Garrett Kennedy
Counselling Psychologist
(arguably the best maker of chocolate-swirl-meringues in this solar system)
"Success for me is to be able to look at myself reflectively and be happy with what I see, to know that I tried my best regardless of the outcome, whether this is as a researcher, husband, father or friend. It doesn't matter how, or what, others see when they see me beyond my integrity and faithfulness".

Prof Matthew Wyon
Professor in Dance Science
(arguably the best in the world at striving to do a good job at helping dancers
perform better and for longer)
"Liverpool retaining the title this year".

Reds Fan
(arguably the most partisan in the world)
"Learning, not winning".

Mark Stivers
Cartoonist
(arguably the best at writing Christmas cards in the world)
"Having lots of bad ideas".

Prof Alex Forsythe
(arguably the best in the world at having lots of bad ideas)
"Sh** not dying"

Avid Allotmenteer
(arguably the best in the allotment at shoveling sh**)
*"Success is walking your path. Overcoming your doubt, turning challenges into
successes, and making a positive impact in people's lives"*.

Dan Aktins
Founder of Buses4 Homeless
(arguably the best in the world at changing homeless people's lives)
"To create a role that is as unique as you are".

Nikita Mikhailov
(arguably the best psychology at work blog in the world, https://psychologyat-
work.blog/)
*"Success is any accomplished task, being genuinely pleased with the outcome and
learning something from every experience"*.

Hayley Carruthers
International Marathon Runner
(arguably the best in the world at underestimating my ability to suffer)
*"Success is truly realising that you are valued by others, and have made a positive
impact, whether that be in your personal life, career, or both"*.

Professor Luke Dawson
Vice Dean
(arguably the best in the world at challenging traditional educational practice)
"The only place where success comes before work is in the dictionary".

Dr. Laura Nicklin
Research Fellow
(arguably the best at fancy dress in the world)
"Success is not the outcome but what you make of the journey along the way".

Dr Roz Collings
(arguably the best in the world at turning roadblocks into steppingstones)
"To earn loyalty from friends and love from family".

Dr Niall Galbraith
(arguably the best in the world at ensuring my children clean their teeth twice a day)
"Tomorrow . . . I'll run tomorrow. . . . Running is all about the mental build up, people need to take more time to think about it before doing it".

Paul Smith
Relationship Manger with England Hockey
(arguably the world's best at running procrastination)
"You're never too old to try. A degree is a very small percentage of your overall work life. Use the degree as a springboard to try lots of different things".

Alison Attrill-Smith
Senior Lecturer in Cyberpsychology
(arguably the world's best at trying)
"It means you got it right".

Daisy, 7
(arguably the best in the world at being strong when people are mean to my friends)
"Dancing like a poo poo pants".

Brie, 3
(arguably the best in the world at drawing)
"Success is loving the life you've got".

Aisha, 13
(arguably the best in the world at ballet)
"Being happy is success".

Lawrence, 12
(arguably the best in the world at painting)
"Becoming a doctor and being the best at that is success".

Jake, 13
(arguably the best in the world at biology)
"When my band becomes successful in the future, I will be happy".

William, 13
(arguably the best rock star in the world)
"Success is having a family who loves me, and I love them".

Aisha, 12
(arguably the best in the world at baking in my family)
"People think that success is a state of being, some perfect set of circumstances that will eventually be achieved. It's not. Success is a continual process of improvement, not only of one's circumstances, but of one's self".

Dr Danny Hinton
Chartered Psychologist
(arguably the best at cuddles in the world, according to his daughter)
"Success is not the key to happiness. Happiness is the key to success. If you love what you are doing, you will be successful".

Ánitá Køšnik
(arguably the best police officer in the world)
"Success is not final, failure is not fatal, it is the courage to continue that counts".

Gillian Nicholl
(arguably the best mum in the world)
"Success is whatever the hell you want it to be, from finishing a whole cake to marrying the person of your dreams".

Harvey Virdi
Academic Coach
(arguably the best "dad joke" maker for someone that isn't actually a dad yet in the world)
"What is success?
To laugh often and much; to win the respect of intelligent people and the affection of children; to earn the appreciation of honest critics and endure the betrayal of false friends; to appreciate the beauty; to find the best in others; to leave the world a bit better, whether by a healthy child, a garden patch or a redeemed social condition; to know even one life has breathed easier because you have lived. This is to have succeeded!"

Professor Orla Muldoon
(arguably the best at receiving rejections and turning them into resubmissions)

Further reading

Bains, G. (2015) *Cultural DNA: The psychology of globalization*. Wiley, UK.

Ohemeng F.L.K. (2017) The entrepreneurial bureaucrat. In: Farazmand A. (eds) *Global Encyclopedia of Public Administration, Public Policy, and Governance*. Cham: Springer. doi:10.1007/978-3-319-31816-5_666-1

Rai, M. (2020). *The values compass, what 101 countries teach us about purpose, life and leadership*, London: Nicholas Brealey.

Wichert, I. (2011). *Where have all the senior women gone? 9 critical job assignments for women leaders*, Palgrave Macmillan, UK.

Notes

1 Schwab, K., & Malleret, T. (2020). *COVID-19, the great reset*. Geneva: Forum Publishing.

2 Wichert, I. (2011). *Where have all the senior women gone? 9 critical job assignments for women leaders.* Basingstoke: Palgrave Macmillan.

3 Porsche, D., & Giorgianni, S. J. (2020). The crisis in male mental health: A call to action. *American Journal of Men's Health.* doi:10.1177/1557988320936504

4 Lombardo, M. M., & Eichinger, R. W. (1996). *The career architect development planner* (1st ed., p. iv). Minneapolis: Lominger.

5 McKinsey and Company. (2019, October). *Women in the workplace.* Retrieved from www.mckinsey.com/~/media/McKinsey/Featured%20Insights/Gender%20 Equality/Women%20in%20the%20Workplace%202019/Women-in-the-work- place-2019.pdf

6 Sørensen, J. (2007). Bureaucracy and entrepreneurship: Workplace effects on entrepreneurial entry. *Administrative Science Quarterly, 52*(3), 387–412. Retrieved September 23, 2020, from www.jstor.org/stable/20109930

7 Hamel, G., & Zanini, M. (2018, December). The end of bureaucracy. *Harvard Business Review.* Retrieved from https://hbr.org/2018/11/the-end-of-bureaucracy.

8 Ohemeng, F. L. K. (2017). The entrepreneurial bureaucrat. In A. Farazmand (Eds.), *Global encyclopedia of public administration, public policy, and governance.* Cham: Springer. doi:10.1007/978-3-319-31816-5_666-1

9 Witkowsky, P., & Mendez, S. L. (2018). Influence of a short-term study abroad experience on professional competencies and career aspirations of graduate stu- dents in student affairs. *Journal of College Student Development, 59*(6), 769–775. doi:10.1353/csd.2018.0073

10 Suutari, V., Brewster, C., Mäkelä, L., Dickmann, M., & Tornikoski, C. (2018). The effect of international work experience on the career success of expatriates: A comparison of assigned and self-initiated expatriates. *Human Resource Manage- ment.* doi:10.1002/hrm.21827

11 Poser, N. (2017). Distance leadership in international corporations. In *Why orga- nizations struggle when distances grow.* Wiesbaden: Springer Gabler.

12 Rath, T., & Conchie, B. (2008). *Strengths based leadership. Great leaders, teams and why people follow.* New York: Gallup Press.

Index

For Product Safety Concerns and Information please contact our EU
representative GPSR@taylorandfrancis.com
Taylor & Francis Verlag GmbH, Kaufingerstraße 24, 80331 München, Germany